Lexical Works by
Paul Dickson

Words

Names

Jokes

Slang

War Slang

Family Words

The Congress Dictionary (with Paul Clancy)

The New Dickson Baseball Dictionary

LABELS

FOR

LOCALS

What to Call

People from Abilene

to Zimbabwe

Paul Dickson

Collins

An Imprint of HarperCollins*Publishers*

An earlier edition of this book was published in 1997
by Merriam-Webster.

HarperCollins books may be purchased for educational, business,
or sales promotional use. For information, please write:
Special Markets Department, HarperCollins Publishers,
10 East 53rd Street, New York, NY 10022.

FIRST COLLINS EDITION PUBLISHED 2006.

Designed by Mia Risberg

Library of Congress Cataloging-in-Publication Data has been applied for.

ISBN-10: 0-06-088164-X
ISBN-13: 978-0-06-088164-1

06 07 08 09 10   WBC/QW   10 9 8 7 6 5 4 3 2 1

Contents

demonym. *n.* **1.** [from Greek *demos* "the people" or "populace" + *-nym* "name"] A name commonly given to the residents of a place or a people. The names *Briton, Midwesterner, Liverpudlian, Arkansawyer,* and *Parisienne* are all demonyms.

    2. An adjective of residence. It may be the same as the noun (*Haitian*) or it may be different (*Swede* for the noun, *Swedish* for the adjective).

Introduction

When the state of Israel was founded in the late 1940s, the rest of the world wasn't sure what to call the citizens of the new country. Some began using the biblical name *Israelite*. It was then officially suggested by the foreign secretary of the new Jewish state that the name should be *Israeli*. It was pointed out that this construction fit in with the style of the area that made a citizen of Iraq an *Iraqi* and a person from Baghdad a *Baghdadi*. *Israelite* was relegated to the status of a historic, biblical name.

Israeli worked, but there were many other choices that would have fit in with the broad rules for naming citizens. Commenting on the choice at the time, the National Geographic Society issued a press release stating that the Israeli could just as well have been called "an Israelian, in the manner of the Brazilian, Egyptian, or Babylonian." It added, "He could be an Israelese, following the form for the man from China, Japan, Siam, or Portugal. Taking a leaf from the book of the New Yorker, the Asiatic, the Frenchman, or the Nazarene, he could be, respectively, an Israeler, an Israelic, Israelman or Israelene." The society went on to say that even *Disraeli* was a plausible alternative.

What this points out is that the rules are so broad and the exceptions so varied that such "citizen names" offer a field day for name collectors. Everyone knows what to call someone from Boston, but what do you call the person from Little Rock, or, for that matter, from Arkansas? Some of these questions never seem to be resolved. The author grew up in Yonkers, New York, where most of us called ourselves *Yonkersites* but a few held out for the higher tone of *Yonkersonian*. H. L. Mencken noted in *The American Language* that the *Atlanta Constitution* used *Atlantan* while the *Atlanta Journal* used *Atlantian*. This particular conflict is now resolved, however. The *Atlanta Journal*, which is under the same ownership as the *Constitution* and uses the same style book (news stories even regularly appear in both papers), refers to city residents as *Atlantans* as well. (On weekends and holidays a single paper is published, the *Atlanta Journal-Constitution*.)

Over time I have learned that people are concerned about what others call them. Call a person from Indiana an *Indianan* or *Indianian* and you will be told in no uncertain terms that the proper form of address is *Hoosier*. *North Carolinian* is acceptable but not to those who prefer to be called *Tar Heels*, and when it comes to Utah the folks there prefer *Utahn* over *Utaan* or *Utahan*. *Phoenicians* lived and live in antiquity—and Arizona—while *Colombians* are from South America, *not* the District of Columbia, where *Washingtonians* reside. These *Washingtonians* are not to be mistaken for those *Washingtonians* who live around Puget Sound.

If this seems confusing, there is a modicum—but no more than a modicum—of order in this realm. Some years ago historian, onomastician, and novelist George R. Stewart Jr. outlined a set of principles for such names that boiled down to this: If the name of the place ends in *-a* or *-ia*, an *-n* should be added; if it ends in *-on*, add *-ian;* if it ends in *-i*, add *-an;* if it ends in *-o*, add *-an;* and if it ends in *-y*, change the *-y* to an *-i* and add *-an*. If, however, the place ends in a sounded *-e*, *-an* is added; if it ends in *-olis*, it becomes *-olitan;* and if it ends with a consonant or a silent *-e*, either *-ite* or *-er* is added.

These rules work for many names—like *Philadelphian, Baltimorean, New Yorker, Tacoman, Floridian, Kansas Citian, Annapolitan*—but they also make *San Franciscoan* (not *San Franciscan*) and *Arkansan* (not *Arkansawyer*). Paris (France or Texas) yields either *Pariser* or, worse, *Parisite*. The people of Guam long ago decided that they wanted to be called *Guamanians,* which, if Stewart's rules had been followed, should mean that the island is called *Guamania.* A person who hails from Richmond can be a *Richmonder* if he or she is from the Richmond in Virginia, or a *Richmondite* if he is from the Richmond in California or Indiana.

H. L. Mencken was so fascinated with these rules—which he immediately dubbed "Stewart's Laws of Municipal Onomastics"—that he sat down and wrote an article for *The New Yorker* in which he heaped a list of "disconcerting exceptions" onto each of Stewart's laws. He also added a law of his own, which was "that the cosmic forces powerfully tend toward *-ite.*" Mencken found that places with perfectly serviceable names of residence (for instance, *Akronian* for a resident of that Ohio city) drifted into suffix changes (*Akronite,* officially, since 1930).

Since Mencken's article appeared in 1936, the situation seems to have become no less—and perhaps more—confusing as an additional rule appears to be in force: To wit, people in a place tend to decide what they will call themselves, whether they be *Angelenos* (from Los Angeles) or *Haligonians* (from Halifax, Nova Scotia). And if any new rule suggests itself, it is that as one moves eastward around the globe from Europe there seems to be an increasing likelihood that an *-i* will be added to one's national name.

In this matter, North Americans are not the only unruly citizens. This is demonstrated by the British Isles, populated by the likes of *Liverpudlians, Oxonians, Dundonians, Mancunians,* and *Cestrians* (who hail respectively from Liverpool, Oxford, Dundee, Manchester, and Chester). Residents of the Isle of Man are *Manx,* a term applied to men, women, and cats.

Then there is the matter of France. In an article "*D'où Êtes-Vous?*" (*Word Ways,* May 1986), Don Laycock writes, "Every French town of any size or antiquity, and every identifiable region, has a particular form for designating someone who comes from there, and knowledge of such forms provides the basis for French cocktail-party conversation." Laycock then goes on to list rules "riddled with exceptions" and "extraordinary specimens of Gallic illogic," such as *Carpiniens* for residents of Charmes, *Longoviciens* for residents of Longwy, *Mussipontains* for residents of Pont-à-Mousson, and *Vidusiens* for residents of the town of Void.

But there is more. In a follow-up article "*D'où Êtes-Vous* Revisited" (*Word Ways*, August 1986), "The Word Wurcher" Harry Partridge claims that "it is the poorly-behaved names that are really consistent and well behaved because, like so many French city-inhabitant names, they are etymological in origin—that is, they are derived from the name from which the present name of the city is derived." The author points to such examples as Saint-Cloud's *Clodoaldiens*, Épinal's *Spinaliens*, and Épernay's *Sparnaciens*. Saint-Cloud was named for Cloud, a sixth-century religious who was also known as *Clodoald;* Épinal's ancient name was *Spinalium;* and Épernay's ancient name was *Sparnacum.*

What is most fascinating about these resident names, however, is that they sometimes take generations to create. A few of them still cause sleepless nights for those people who insist that everything have a proper proper name. The reason for this is that tradition, folklore, and custom are in full play here. How else could one explain the fact that a common name for a resident of Schenectady, New York, is *Dorpian*? *Dorp* is a Dutch word meaning "village," and is an old name for Schenectady that reflects Dutch history in the area.

Consider the long-burning question of what one calls a person from Connecticut. The late Professor Allen Walker Read of Columbia University once researched this topic and found an impressive list of early attempts to name residents of this state: *Connecticutensian, Connecticutter, Connecticutian, Connecticutite,* and—from Cotton Mather in 1702—*Connecticotian.* In addition to these serious suggestions Read found six jocular alternatives: *Quonaughicotter* (from H. L. Mencken), *Connecticutey, Connecticanuck, Connectikook* (from Read himself), *Connectecotton,* and *Connecticutist.* A fellow writer (and a New Yorker) recently suggested to me that *Connecticutlet* had a nice ring to it, and one can always side with Mark Twain, whose label for a character from the state was "Connecticut Yankee."

Although the issue is still unresolved, Read concluded that the most popular solution to the Connecticut quandary was *Nutmegger,* based on the *Nutmeg State* nickname. By the same token there are many who have avoided the tongue-twisting *Massachusettsite* by offi-cially calling themselves *Bay Staters* after the state nickname *Bay State*. One rule of thumb that seems to be in force is that the longer a resident name becomes, the less likely it is to show up in print. This means that *Bay Stater* will get more use. In some cases the news me-dia resort to generic names—"local man," for instance—over a mouth-ful like *Minneapolitan*.

Then there is the case of Michigan, where the issue was resolved politically. In 1979 the state legislature voted to make *Michiganian* the official name for a resident. The bill was introduced at the behest of newspaper editors, who were confused with a variety of names, in-cluding *Michigander, Michiganite,* and *Michiganer*. Some citizens, however, continue to call themselves *Michiganders,* a term that, leg-end has it, was created by representative Abraham Lincoln during the 1848 presidential campaign, when he opposed the nomination of a general from Michigan. *Michigander* is also the name given by H. L. Mencken in *The American Language. Michiganite* is given in sev-eral reference books—including the U.S. Government Printing Office *Style Manual*—not published in Michigan.

All other concerns of this type seem to pale in comparison with the peculiar case of the word *Hoosier,* which transcends the simple mat-ter of usage and form and stirs the emotions. For instance, one thing that will prompt letters to the editor of any newspaper in the country is to use the word *Indianan* in print. A quick letter by a son or daugh-ter of Indiana will inform the paper in no uncertain terms that the proper native term is *Hoosier*. A letter published in the April 11, 1987, *Washington Post* is typical: "A Sports headline March 27 referred to 'Indianans.' My husband is in the service, and in all of our travels, this is the first time I've heard the term 'Indianan.' Please try to get it right next time."

With full realization that these questions are not among the great issues of our time, but that they are important points of local pride and proper usage, I have assembled a collection of resident names.

One nagging detail that accompanied this project was that these terms of residency have no commonly accepted name. Mencken called them *toponyms* but as Allen Walker Read pointed out in a 1991 paper on the subject, that term has often been used simply to mean "place name." The scholar Albert H. Marckwardt used the term *patrial* in a 1952 article: "Every language faces the problem of providing terms designating places of origin; patrials they are sometimes called." However, the term never gained acceptance. Read suggested why when he said that it is somewhat pretentious: "It implies a background of a 'fatherland,' and for terms like Brooklynite, Staten Islander or Tribecan hardly applies." (A *Tribecan* lives in *Tribeca,* or *TriBeCa,* an area of Manhattan that derives its name from "*tri*angle *be*low *Ca*nal [Street].)

Although I had not learned of these earlier attempts at naming these local labels or names for natives, I needed to give my file a name, so I thought that until something better came along I would label it *domunyms* (from *domus,* Latin for "home," and *-nym* for "name"). There were other suggestions—including *hailfrom* (as in, "Where do you hail from?") from writer and editor Bruce O. Boston of Reston, Virginia, and two suggestions from Monique M. Byer of Springfield, Virginia: *locunyms* (from the Latin word *locus* for "place") and *urbanyms* (from the Latin *urbs* for "city")—but I stuck with *domunyms*.

After publishing several articles on my collection, including one that appeared in the March 1988 *Smithsonian* magazine, I received several letters noting that I could use some help with my neologism. The most compelling case was made by George H. Scheetz, director of the Sioux City (Iowa) Public Library and a member of the American Name Society and the North Central Name Society, who has actually made a study of words with a *-nym* ending. Scheetz wrote:

> All but two historically occurring words ending in *-nym* actually end in *-onym,* and all but approximately six percent are formed from Greek root words.
>
> In other words, the Latin root *dom-* (from *domus*), more correctly forms *domonym*. However, the Greek root is already in use as a combining form, *domato-* (from *domatos*), which forms *domatonym*. Literally, both these combinations mean "a house name." The names Tara and The White House are domatonyms.

A better word for the name, derived from a place name, for residents of that place, is *demonym,* from the Greek *demos,* "the people, populace." The names Utahn and Sioux Cityan are demonyms.

An earlier work on this subject entitled *What Do You Call a Person From . . . ?* (Facts on File, 1990) used *demonym,* which occasioned no less an authority than Allen Walker Read to comment that it met with his liking.

Then a second precursor to this work was published as *Labels for Locals: What to Call People from Abilene to Zimbabwe* (Merriam-Webster, 1997) and the term was again used in the book but also repeated by a number of writers. "Demonym is a much needed word," wrote Richard Lederer in his "Looking at Language" column (*The Patriot Ledger,* Quincy, Mass., September 20, 1997), "because people really care about what they are called."

Increasingly the term has become the word for the members of a people or the inhabitants of a place in many places. It is being used widely in print and on the World Wide Web—over 1,900 demonomous citations showed up on one search engine in August 2005—and is used extensively by the online encyclopedia: *Wikipedia.* Immodestly it is hoped that the publication of this book will gain dictionary entry for the term. And if not? It is still a good serviceable word. As Erin McKean, senior editor for Oxford University Press's American English dictionaries, has stated, "You don't have to be in the dictionary to be a word [any more than] you don't have to be a purebred to be a dog."

Finding demonyms has become something of a minor obsession. I once actually got hold of a Kentucky newspaper for the single purpose of making sure that local preference was for *Louisvillian* over *Louisvillan.* Of late I have taken to writing to friends and associates around the country to find out what they call themselves. The best answer to date has come from South Dakotan Bill McKean: "People from Sioux Falls are called PEOPLE FROM SIOUX FALLS. There *are* limits."

Several correspondents asked me for help, including a resident of Sanibel Island, Florida, who wanted to know if she was a *Sanibelian,* a *Sanibelyan,* or a *Sanibelan.* The author of a letter to the *Elmira* (New York) *Star-Gazette,* Geof Huth, wrote of the dilemma of living in Horseheads, New York: "I've been living in Horseheads for over a year, but I haven't heard anyone use a word that means 'someone from Horseheads.' What could that word possibly be?" As it became apparent that there was no central source for these geographical names, the collection seemed to take on a new cast. Why not use it as the basis for a full-fledged reference book on the subject?

But a few anecdotes do not a reference book make, so I decided to approach it in a comprehensive manner by relying on a variety of sources. These ranged from such entities as the U.S. State Department and the Central Intelligence Agency, which have grappled with the issue officially, to newspapers and newspaper editors, who have dealt with it locally. After all, if the *Cedar Rapids* (Iowa) *Gazette* uses the term *Cedar Rapidian* to describe its subscribers, there is no need to look any further.

A major source of information in this quest was the Tamony Collection, stored with the Western Historical Manuscript Collection at the University of Missouri in Columbia. This is the nation's prime archive of unconventional American English—slang, jargon, and regionalisms— and it brims with references bearing directly on this project. I have also solicited letters from linguists, folklorists, and residents of far-flung spots on the globe. One of the reasons for all of this correspondence was to get a sense of what term is preferred and used locally. The principle at work here is that of "home rule." If the people of Albany, New York, choose to be known as *Albanians,* so be it, even though their choice tends to confuse the residents of that city with the people of far-off Albania. Such choices make the neologism *demonym* all the more appropriate, because it stems from the same root as *democratic.*

Despite this, it must be pointed out that many of the demonyms from non-English-speaking areas are analogous to *exonyms,* which are place names given by foreigners that do not correspond to the native names. In English, the names *Naples* and *Vienna* are exonyms because in Italy and Austria those places are called *Napoli* and *Wien.* In fact, *Italy* and *Austria* are exonyms for *Italia* and *Österreich.*

Periodically, an effort is launched to iron out these inconsistencies, but it never seems to work. The problem was demonstrated in 1967 when the United Nations held a conference on name standardization in Geneva, which, depending on where a delegate came from, was called *Genf, Genève, Ginevra, Geneva,* and *Ginebra.* This collection is unabashedly exonymic and does not attempt to propose any reforms.

The one great exception to the use of *exonymia* by speakers of English is the tendency of these same people to use authentic French demonyms. The reason for this is not clear; perhaps it has something to do with a custom that began because of the nearness of England to France. The French examples also tend to be among the most complex, so they may have held a particular fascination for tourists, travel writers, and Francophiles.

What has emerged from this effort is a book meant to be used by those who want to find the proper form—or forms—of address or reference for people in a particular locale. And if one accepts the conclusion that people *do* care about what they are called, whether it be in person or in print, then the collection should be useful. I was once told by an executive of Merriam-Webster, that one of the great services a reference book can accomplish is to help people "keep egg off their faces." This collection was assembled with that worthy premise in mind.

How to Use This Book

$\mathcal{L}$*abels for Locals* is organized as a simple dictionary. Most entries are for the name of a place; these appear in boldface roman type. Generally this kind of entry is followed immediately by its demonym, appearing in lightface italic type. Thus, one finds what a resident of Dallas is called by looking at the entry for that city:

Dallas, Texas. *Dallasite.*

Sometimes the demonym is followed by commentary on its origin, its alternatives, or other matters of interest.

Some entries appear in boldface italic type. Generally these are for demonyms that are not formed by the simple rules of suffixation discussed earlier and thus fall alphabetically more than two entries away from the entry for the place name:

Angeleno. Resident of Los Angeles, California. *Angelino* appears on occasion but is clearly without significant support.

This kind of entry too may include commentary of various kinds.

Entries for places are alphabetized according to the main geographical term that appears in the headword of the entry, with what follows (such as the name of the state in which a city is found) taken into account only when the first part of two or more successive entries is identical. Hence **Dayton, Ohio,** appears before **Daytona Beach, Florida,** because *Dayton* is earlier alphabetically than *Daytona Beach*. On the other hand, **Saint Petersburg, Florida** appears before **Saint Petersburg, Russia,** since what follows the main terms must be used to order the entries.

The criteria used to decide what to include were simple and subjective. I wanted (1) to deal with all nations, major cities, states of the Union, and Canadian provinces, and (2) to deal with small places that pose unusual problems (what do you call residents of the French village of Y?) or that are small but noteworthy. (There is, for example, an entry for Pitcairn Island, which at last count had only 62 residents but which is often written about because those 62 souls descend from the crew of the H.M.S. *Bounty* that mutinied about 200 years ago.) There are so many unusual French examples that only the most important ones could be listed. Fortunately, these French examples are fully documented in the Larousse dictionaries (the *Petit Larousse* contains more than 700).

Although the book shies away from ethnic slurs, it does include slang words, nicknames, and slurs based on geography. Inevitably, this includes some terms like *Okie, Cracker, Canuck,* and *Herring Choker* that are regarded—or can be regarded in certain contexts—as derogatory. The idea here is not to offend anyone or venerate mean slurs but rather to put such terms in context and give the reader some idea of when and to what degree they are offensive. For an exploration of how a term becomes a slur, see the long entry **Dutch.**

Although the bulk of the words in the book are nouns, an attempt has been made to list adjectives of nationality that differ from the noun, as in this entry:

Burundi (Republic of Burundi). *Burundian.* Adjective: *Burundi.*

As this example also shows, a common national name is followed by the official name of the country in parentheses if the official name is different from the common name.

In addition, some common and traditional nicknames for places and residents have been included to add to the reference value of the book. For instance, it would leave a senseless gap to discuss New York City and not mention *the Big Apple* and *Gotham*. Historic and slang nicknames for residents of the American states are entered individually and at the entry for the state under the label "Traditional personal nicknames." Some of these are clearly more current than others, but all are colorful examples of native or interstate naming. State nicknames, even those that have become archaic, are included for the same reason. Some derivative forms of place names are also given and discussed. The terms *Africana* and *Africanist*, for instance, appear under the **Africa** entry.

In the same vein, entries for places whose names have changed since World War II have been annotated to include the former name. Selected obsolete names are included, as well as some generic terms on the order of *citizen, resident, mainlander,* and *exurbanite*. Some planets have been included. This was done not just because they make interesting entries but for the practical reason that they have already provided their share of controversy, as can be seen under the entry for the planet Venus.

There are also some words discussed that a more highly disciplined compiler might have left out as not absolutely belonging to the species in question. However, it was reasoned that these were terms that were very likely to be confused with the real thing, and that it was a good idea to enter them as linguistic bonuses. Therefore there will be an occasional impure entry on the order of **Hoya, Pennsylvania Dutch,** and **Utopia.**

A few large essay-style entries merit special mention here as detailed case studies that are intended to explore the dynamics of geographic nouns of person and geographic adjectives. These entries are the ones for *Connecticut* (a complex case of reluctant demonym-giving), *Texas* (for multiple names with historic distinctions), the term *Okie,* the case of *Dutch* as a slur, the nickname *Hoosier* (and the passions it invokes), and the fascinating case of *Earth,* which takes us into the business of what one calls an inhabitant of the home planet. Also, anyone looking for a small collection of humorous and playful demonyms to browse through should check the entry for *Bunnie.*

LABELS
FOR
LOCALS

What to call
People from Abilene
to Zimbabwe

@. Common typographic symbol, which is commonly called the "at sign," reinforced by its use in e-mail addresses. It has now been given a new significance as a nongendered ending to such terms as Chicano/Chicana, Latino/Latina. For instance, the University of Wisconsin at Madison offers a certificate program in "Chican@ and Latin@ Studies." Thus far the drawback to this innovation is that there appears to be no way to pronounce Chican@.

Aaland Islands, Finland. *Aalander.*

Abilene, Texas. *Abilenian.*

Abkhazia. *Abkhasian.* Region of the Russian Caucasus that is formally an autonomous republic within Georgia but is de facto independent. The demonym also refers to a small ethnic group living within the area and distinct from the Georgians.

Aberdeen, Scotland. *Aberdonian.* Residents of Aberdeen, Washington, and Aberdeen, South Dakota, use the same demonym.

Aborigine. One of several names for first inhabitants of a country along with native and aboriginal. The word *aboriginal* means "from the original" (Latin: *ab origine*) and is a generic word for any group of people who have descended from the first people of a continent or region. Indigenous people also have variously been referred to as "natives," "Aborigines," and "Aboriginals." The term is routinely applied in many nations to noncolonial people with the notable exception of the United States. Taiwan, for instance, recognizes twelve aboriginal tribes, which, among other things, since June 2005 have their own aboriginal television channel.

In Australia, where the term has been used most commonly, it is now defined by the cultural values, rather than physical appearance. An Aboriginal person is someone who has some Aboriginal biological descent, who identifies as Aboriginal, and who is accepted as Aboriginal by an Aboriginal organization.

"Indigenous person" is now the officially agreed upon term for the country's first inhabitants and refers to anyone of Aboriginal or Torres Strait Islander ancestry who identifies as such.

Many indigenous Australians prefer to be referred to by their local group names, such as Western Australia's Nyoongar, Wongi, and Yamitji people and the Koori people of southeastern Australia.

Abu Dhabi, United Arab Emirates. *Emirian.*

Abyssinia. *Abyssinian.*

Acadia. *Acadian. Acadia* was the earlier name for Nova Scotia. Today the term *Acadian* applies to all French Canadians in the Maritime Provinces of Canada. There is a Center for Acadian Studies in New Brunswick and Saint John, New Brunswick, is the site of the annual Acadian Games. A quote from the *Boston Globe* of July 8, 1996: "They are the other French-Canadians, the Acadians of the Maritime Provinces: devoted to Canada and hostile to Quebec's separatist movement, but passionately committed to keeping francophone culture alive in North America." *Acadian* is also synonymous with *Cajun* (q.v.), which denotes a Louisianian of Acadian ancestry and is an alteration of *Acadian*.

Accident, Maryland. *Accidental.* This small town is the only place named *Accident* in the United States, according to the *Washington Post* (May 5, 1985).

Accra, Ghana. Although one would expect the term for a resident of this capital city to be *Accran*, it is listed as *Gas* in the demonymic *Liverpudlian* published by the Marquis Biographical Library Society.

Ada, Oklahoma. *Adan.*

Adrian, Michigan. *Adrianite.*

Afghanistan (Islamic Republic of Afghanistan); *formerly* Democratic Republic of Afghanistan. *Afghan.* The term *Afghanistaner* has appeared in print, but it is a rarity without wide support. A demonstrator at a rally in 1987 for Oliver North (then under fire for his role in the Iran-Contra scandal) was quoted in the November 6, 1987, *National Review* as asking some anti-North protesters, "When was the last time you went to the Soviet embassy to protest the slaughter of Afghanistaners?" The adjective is either *Afghani* ("U.S. Soldier, Three Afghanis Are Killed" headline in *Tulsa World,* October 11, 2005) or *Afghan.*

A curious derivative of *Afghanistan* is a word that has a long history in the newspaper business: *Afghanistanism.* Since before World War II it has denoted an excessive interest in foreign affairs, or as Turner Catledge, former executive editor of the *New York Times,* explained in 1980, "the coverage of far-off places at the expense of local news." Murry Marder of the *Washington Post* was quoted in the same article (*San Francisco Examiner,* January 27, 1980; Tamony Collection) with this definition: "writing about a place or subject so offbeat, that nobody knows if you're right or wrong." The term seems to have lost its relevance after Soviet troops moved into Afghanistan in late 1979.

Africa. *African.* At one point *Afric* was a common adjective, but it has been displaced by *African.* Interesting derivatives include *Africana* for African lore and culture ("He was stuffed, crammed, chock full of Africana," wrote Robert Ruark in *The Honey Badger*), and *Africanist* for one who studies African languages and cultures or who forges a strong bond with the continent. (David Robinson, son of baseball great Jackie Robinson, was quoted in the August 6, 1987, *Houston Chronicle* as saying, "My father was not a great Africanist.")

In late 1988 the Reverend Jesse Jackson announced that *African American* was what a large number of black Americans preferred to be called (62 percent of the respondents to a call-in survey conducted by the *Chicago Sun-Times* said they preferred that name to *black*). It was argued that the term suggested roots in the manner of parallel terms like *Chinese American* and *Italian American.*

Aggie. Student or graduate of Texas A&M University in College Station. Female students and alumnae are sometimes called *Maggies.* Though *Aggies* is what A&M students call themselves, the term is used derogatorily in the context of a never-ending series of "Aggie jokes" that depict the A&M student as hopelessly inept—for example, "Did you hear about the Aggie who lost his job as an elevator operator? He couldn't learn the route." Texas writer C. F. Eckhardt adds that there is also a geographical aspect to this term: "Anyone from a fifty mile radius of Bryan and College Station is automatically an Aggie, from Texas Agricultural and Mechanical College (now Texas A&M University), which started as a cow college at a whistlestop train station called College Station, down in the blackland of the Brazos [River] bottom."

Aiken, South Carolina. *Aikenite.*

Aire-sur-L'Adour, France. *Aturin.*

Aix-en-Provence, France. *Aixois* or *Aquisextain.* The ancient name of this city was *Aquae Sextiae.*

Aix-les-Bains, France. *Aixois.*

Akron, Ohio. *Akronite.* (*Akron* fosters its share of local wordplay. Akronite C. H. Fleming wrote to the author to point out that "anyone born and raised in Akron is obviously an Akronite, but someone that has moved to Akron from elsewhere—and remained—should be considered an anachronism.")

Alabama. *Alabamian* or *Alabaman.* In their *Harper Dictionary of Contemporary Usage,* William and Mary Morris say that "natives of Alabama overwhelmingly prefer *Alabamian.*" They add: "Indeed, the editor of the *Dothan* (Alabama) *Eagle* went on record with this statement: 'If there is any merit in the rule of spelling a proper name just as the possessor spells it, then we are *Alabamians.*'" Most citations show *Alabamian,* though it is possible to find an occasional *Alabaman* in print. For example, in *The Whisper of the Axe,* Richard Condon refers to a "conversation between a Vermonter and an Alabaman" (citation from Charles D. Poe).

Traditional personal nicknames: *Lizard, Yallerhammer,* and *Yellowhammer.* These traditional nicknames and many of those that follow in this book are listed in Lester V. Berrey and Melvin Van den Bark's monumental *American Thesaurus of Slang,* which contains an important section on slang "inhabitants."

State nicknames: *Heart of Dixie, Yellowhammer State,* and *Cotton State.*

Alameda, California. *Alamedan.*

Alamosa, Colorado. *Alamosan.*

Alaska. *Alaskan.* While the demonym is well established, there is some resistance to its use as an adjective. "I have heard from some Alaskan journalists and read in some of their style sheets the claim that *Alaskan* should be used only as a noun referring to a person and should never be used as an adjective," writes Russell Tabbert in his *Dictionary of Alaskan English* (1991), adding, "However, this rule certainly doesn't fit Alaskan usage, including much journalistic usage."

State nickname: *The El Dorado of the North.*

See also CHEECHAKO and SOURDOUGH, names respectively for newcomers and old-timers in Alaska and northwestern Canada.

Alaska Native. Term preferred by the Eskimos and Aleuts of Alaska as opposed to American Indian or Native American.

Albania (Republic of Albania); *formerly* **People's Socialist Republic of Albania.** *Albanian,* also an adjective.

Albany, New York. *Albanian.* Robert Joseph Powers of Shreveport, Louisiana, wrote to this demonymist to recall: "Many years ago an acquaintance of mine remarked that, on moving there [to Albany], he was struck by a sign in the display window of a downtown edifice: '20,000 Albanians Bank Here.' He spent some time marveling over the size of this unique ethnic group before the light turned."

Alberta, Canada. *Albertan.*

Albert Lea, Minnesota. *Albert Lean.*

Albuquerque, New Mexico. *Albuquerquean.*

Aleutian Islands. *Aleut* (pronounced "al-leey-oot")

Alexandria, Virginia. *Alexandrian.*

Algeria (Democratic and Popular Republic of Algeria). *Algerian,* which is also an adjective.

Algiers, Algeria. *Algérois. Algerine* once enjoyed popular use for a native of Algiers or Algeria, and it can be found in the writings of Thomas Jefferson and George Washington, who had to deal with the problem of piracy off the Barbary Coast of North Africa. *Algerine* was also once a common adjective, as in reference to naval vessels (like "an Algerine corsair") from Algiers, and in this naval sphere it was also used as the name of a minesweeper, the H.M.S. *Algerine,* which sank in 1942 but inspired generic use of *algerine* as a noun for other British and Canadian minesweepers of its class. The noun *Algerine* also developed several slang meanings that drew on the piratical connotations resulting from the "Algerine Wars" against the pirates. It was applied most notably to a faction in Rhode Island politics in the 1840s that dealt rather roughly (as via the state militia) with a movement to liberalize suffrage led by Thomas W. Dorr. This contest became the *Algerines* against the *Dorrites.* A theater-world sense of *Algerine* is recorded in old slang dictionaries like J. S. Farmer and W. E. Henley's *Dictionary of Slang* (1890), where an *Algerine* is defined as "A member of a [theater] company who, when 'the ghost' cannot be induced to walk, *i.e.,* when the exchequer is low, and salaries are not paid, 'remonstrates' with the manager. The term is also used to designate the hard-up borrower of petty sums." There is evidence as well of an old dialect sense of *algerine* in Pennsylvania-area timber culture. The noun denoted someone who intercepted logs flowing down the river, sawed off the ends bearing the brand of the owner, and affixed a bogus "pirate" brand. In *The American Language,* Supplement II, H. L. Mencken reported a Pennsylvania verb "*to algerine:* to cut timber on another's land."

Alhambra, California. *Alhambran.*

Allegheny Mountains region. *Alleganian* is traditional but *Alleghenian* is now common in print. The term is used throughout the region, and the weekly newspaper in Cumberland, Maryland, was once *The Alleganian.*

Allentown, Pennsylvania. *Allentonian.*

Alligator. Traditional nickname for a resident of Florida.

Alton, Illinois. *Altonian.*

Altoona, Pennsylvania. *Altoonan.*

Amarillo, Texas. *Amarilloan.*

Amazonia. One who lives in Amazonia (the Amazon River region) is an *Amazonian,* and should not be confused with an *Amazon,* one of a race of fierce female warriors in Greek mythology. However, according to *Merriam-Webster's Geographic Dictionary,* 3rd edition, the region is called *Amazonia* because early Spanish explorers "thought they saw female warriors" on the banks of the Amazon, thus known in Spanish as *Río de las Amazonas,* "river of the Amazons."

Amerasian. A person of American and Asian descent, especially the offspring of an American soldier who served in Asia (as in Vietnam) and had a relationship with an Asian woman.

American. Resident of the United States. The name has long irked those who think that *American* should cover anyone from North to South America; however, the practice is so deeply rooted that it is hard to imagine it changing. For a list of some of the alternative terms that have been suggested, see UNITED STATES OF AMERICA.

    American as an adjective shows up in constructions ranging from *American cheese* to *American plan* and in such derivatives as *Americana* and *Americanize*. See also AFRICA (for discussion of *African American*), COLUMBIAN, and HYPHENATED AMERICAN.

American Samoa. *American Samoan.* Samoan, closely related to Hawaiian and other Polynesian languages, is spoken here along with English.

Amerindian. Term for all Indians throughout the Americas created to distinguish those called Indians in the Western Hemisphere from the people of India. "The choice of some Indianists, mostly in governmental and anthropological businesses," according to Suzan Shown Harjo, president and executive director of the Morning Star Institute, a tribal advocacy group, "it never gained wide usage, happily."

Ameropean. Blend of *American* and *European* for an American expatriate living in Europe. The term is little used today but experienced a vogue in the late 1960s with the publication of *Another Way of Living* by John Bainbridge, which profiled 44 Americans living in Europe. Bainbridge used the term *Ameropean* and it was widely quoted.

Ames, Iowa. *Amesite.* Onomastician George H. Scheetz reports, in an article entitled "Amesite with Derring-Do," that the term was in use as early as 1960.

Amexica. The zone where the United States and Mexico share a border, culture, language, and economic conditions. Writing in the March 2004, *Foreign Policy,* Samuel P. Huntington states: "Charles Truxillo of the University of New Mexico predicts that by 2080 the southwestern states of the United States and the northern states of Mexico will form *La Republica del Norte* (The Republic of the North). Various writers have referred to the southwestern United States plus northern Mexico as 'MexAmerica' or 'Amexica' or 'Mexifornia.' 'We are all Mexicans in this valley,' a former county commissioner of El Paso, Texas, declared in 2001."

Amityville, New York. *Amityvillian.*

Amsterdam, Netherlands. *Amsterdamer* or *Amsterdammer.*

Amsterdam, New York. *Amsterdamian.*

Anaheim, California. *Anaheimer.*

Anchorage, Alaska. *Anchorageite.*

Andalusia, Spain. *Andalusian.* A slang alternative is *Andaloo.* A story by Holly Roth, "The Spy Who Was So Obvious," in *Ellery Queen's 20th Anniversary Annual,* speaks of Gibraltarians who speak Spanish with "a strong Andaloo accent" (from Charles D. Poe).

Andes Mountains region. *Andean,* better known as an adjective.

Andorra (Principality of Andorra). *Andorran,* also an adjective.

Angeleno. Resident of Los Angeles, California. *Angelino* appears on occasion but is clearly without significant support.

Anglo- Prefix that has come to mean "English" in such terms as *Anglo-American, Anglo-Indian, Anglo-Irish,* and *Anglo-Catholic.* It is also used in words like *Anglomania, Anglocentric, Anglophile, Anglophobia,* and *Anglophonic.*

Angola (Republic of Angola); *formerly* **People's Republic of Angola.** *Angolan,* also an adjective.

Anguilla. *Anguillan.*

Annapolis, Maryland. *Annapolitan.* "An Esteemed Annapolitan Dead," read an early headline in the *Washington Post,* October 22, 1881.

Ann Arbor, Michigan. *Ann Arborite.*

Anniston, Alabama. *Annistonian.*

Ansonia, Ohio. *Ansonian.*

Antarctica. *Antarctican,* as in "Antarcticans on the Web." *Antarctic* is the adjective, as in the *Antarctic Circle.*

Antelope. Traditional nickname for a resident of Nebraska.

Antibes, France. *Antibois,* also *Antipolitain* (the city's ancient name was *Antipolis*).

Antigua and Barbuda. Both *Antiguans* and *Barbudans* live here, according to the Central Intelligence Agency's *World Factbook.*

Antipodes. Term for opposite sides of the earth. The Antipodes are a group of small uninhabited islands southwest of New Zealand that were so named because they are antipodal to Greenwich, England. A person located on the other side of the earth from another would be an *antipode* or an *antipodist.* The proper adjective would be *antipodal,* although *antipodean* is used. *Antipodes* is also used as an informal name for Australia and New Zealand, while the noun *Antipodean* sometimes denotes an Australian.

In his *Good Words to You,* the late John Ciardi gave this etymology of *antipode,* which emerged in metaphysical geography when people were still trying to deal with the new concept of a spherical Earth: "Like noses pressed against plate glass at the same point but from opposite sides, the feet of persons 'down under' were said to oppose those of a person on this side <Gk. *anti,* opposite; *pous,* foot, *podes,* feet."

Antipolitain. A resident of Antibes, France (q.v.).

Anzac. Name for a resident of Australia or New Zealand. The term originated during World War I when ANZAC was an acronym for the Australian-New Zealand Army Corps, the official name for the antipodal unit of the British army. The heroic 1915 Anzac landing on the Gallipoli Peninsula during the war was commemorated by renaming the landing area *Anzac Cove.*

Appalachia. This region of the United States stretches through the Appalachian Mountains from New York State into Alabama, and one who lives there is an *Appalachian.* One cannot discuss the connotations of this name without mentioning Appalachin, New York, which was the site of a meeting of 60 underworld characters in November 1957. When the meeting was raided by the police, it was big news, and the town's name took on a special crime connotation. A meeting of underworld figures in 1960 in Buffalo, another in 1965 in Palm Springs, California, and still another in Queens, New York, were each immediately dubbed "Little Appalachin." A raid on a teenage gang meeting in Brooklyn, New York, in 1960 was termed "Jr. Appalachin."

Appleknocker. Affectionate nickname for a person from an apple-growing area such as the orchard-rich counties of upstate New York and Washington State. Bing Crosby, singer and native Washingtonian, was often referred to as one. On the other hand, *Time* reported in 1937 that the Wenatchee Valley (Washington) Chamber of Commerce petitioned the Motion Picture Producers and Distributors of America to eliminate use of *appleknocker* in films on the ground that the term heaped "ridicule and contempt" on the region's apple workers.

    Appleknocker is an interesting term because it began its life as an insult for a rustic or rube of the laziest type: one who would knock apples off trees instead of picking them. It is now used with a degree of affection rather than disdain. In another slang sense it has denoted one who is beginning a new job (as in logging or mining).

Aquisextain. Resident of Aix-en-Provence, France (q.v.).

Arabia. One who lives on this peninsula, which includes Saudi Arabia, Yemen, and the Persian Gulf states, is an *Arabian*. The adjective *Arabian* is used in the term *Arabian horse* and the title of the book *The Arabian Nights*. An interesting related term is *Arabesque*, which is used to describe, among other things, an intricate style of ornamentation and a well-known ballet posture. Closely related to *Arabian* in meaning and just as old is *Arab*. According to *Merriam-Webster's Collegiate Dictionary*, 11th edition, an *Arab* is "a member of the Semitic people of the Arabian peninsula" or "a member of an Arabic-speaking people."

Arab Republic of Egypt. See EGYPT.

Arcadia. *Arcadian.* Arcadia is a mountainous region of ancient Greece, a town in Florida, another town in Nebraska, a city in southern California, and a real or imagined place of innocence and simplicity.

Ardmore, Oklahoma. *Ardmorite.*

Argentina (Argentine Republic). *Argentine,* but the term *Argentinian* commonly finds its way into print. "The Argentinian sat opposite Daughtry, crossed his long willowy legs and lit a small panatella," wrote Herbert Lieberman in *Night Call from a Distant Time Zone*. The term *Argie* sometimes appears in print in Britain—"Now It's Time to Talk to the Argies" was a headline in the *London Telegraph* on April 5, 1987—but it appears to be an impolite nickname owing something to the Falkland Islands war between Britain and Argentina in 1982. A true rarity is *Argentiño,* the most recent citation for which is from 1940.

Arizona. *Arizonan* (which is also an adjective) is currently preferred, but one finds examples of *Arizonian,* including a 1935 western movie, *The Arizonian,* starring Richard Dix. William Safire pointed out in his *New York Times Magazine* column of

June 6, 1982, "Federal style is *Arizonan,* and that is what Senator Barry Goldwater calls himself, but many locals will fight for *Arizonian.*" In a 1947 article for *American Speech,* "Names for Americans," H. L. Mencken noted that *Arizonian* was used by Walt Whitman in one of the early editions of *Leaves of Grass.*

Arizonian seems to be used in more formal applications, as demonstrated by a plaque described in the *Phoenix Gazette* for September 16, 1995: "In the town square [of Sacaton, Arizona] about 50 feet apart is a memorial to Ira Hayes, a Sacaton resident who helped raise the American flag on Iwo Jima and a stone obelisk bearing the inscription: 'Dedicated to the memory of Mathew B. Juan, First Arizonian killed in the World War, Battle of Cantingy, May 28, 1918, erected 1928.'" The demonym is, however, increasingly rare: an electronic search of the *Phoenix Gazette* for the year 1990 yields 241 uses of the term *Arizonan* versus 2 for *Arizonian* and a sweep of the newspaper for 1995 shows 152 versus 2. The first newspaper in the state was the *Weekly Arizonian,* which began publishing in 1859 in Tubac. This and other evidence suggests that the *-ian* ending was much more common before World War II. The *Arizona Republic* for April 26, 1934, carries this comment by an official on the building of the Boulder Dam: "Irrespective of what he may think of the idea of building the dam at all, any Arizonian who fails to see it under construction will miss one of the greatest spectacles ever conceived in the mind of man and executed by his hands. The mind refuses to comprehend what the eyes can see."

Returning to Arizonans, one of the games they play in Arizona is Arizonans versus Californians, which involves comparisons of the residents of these neighboring states. Here are a few such comparisons from Sam Lowe's January 17, 1995, column in the *Phoenix Gazette:*

>—*A Californian will buy a Mercedes because of its classic lines and elegant styling. An Arizonan will buy one because it'll look real cool when you cut off the rear end and put in a truck box.*

—A Californian gets extremely uncomfortable when things go bump in the night. An Arizonan blames it on the jalapeños.

—In California, it's called "sushi." In Arizona, it's called "coyote bait."

—A Californian will say, "The rain in Spain stays mainly on the plain" with a distinct British accent. An Arizonan will say, "Rain?"

The odd term *Arizo-Mex* is used to describe food prepared with a combination of Arizonan and Mexican influences. The word is clearly modeled on the more familiar *Tex-Mex.*

Traditional personal nicknames: *Sand Cutter* and *Apache*, a name that was once common but would probably be regarded with disfavor by American Indians if used today. See also ZONIE.

State nickname: *Grand Canyon State.* Arizona has also been called the *Valentine State,* since it was admitted to the Union on February 14, 1912.

Arkansas. *Arkansawyer,* also *Arkansan* or, more rarely, *Arkansawyan.* In their book *Down in the Holler,* Vance Randolph and George P. Wilson noted that the newspapers often use *Arkansan,* "but one never hears a hillman pronounce it to rhyme with Kansan." As H. L. Mencken pointed out in *The American Language,* Supplement II, "Indeed, there are Arkansawyers who argue spitefully that Kansas itself should be *Kansaw.*"

The term *Arkansawyer* lends itself to a folksy turn of phrase. "At times it was so muddy, as an Arkansawyer put it, that a buzzard would mire down in its own shadow," wrote Everett Dirk in *The Dixie Frontier* (1948). An August 23, 1926, letter to *Time* said: "Please discontinue my subscription at once. *Time* is too hi-toned for me, a one-gallused, terbacker-chewin' Arkansawyer." Nevertheless, one finds a *Washington Post* headline proclaiming, "Arkansan Sentenced to Death in 2 Murders" (May 13, 1988).

Randolph and Wilson noted that *Arkansawyan* is a compromise between the *-awyer* and *-an* endings. In that spirit, on February 16, 1945, State Senator Julien James introduced a bill designating the people as *Arkansawyans,* but the assembly would have none of it.

The basis for *Arkansawyer* is deeply traditional, following the pronunciation of the state's name. Mencken reported that the "saw" pronunciation became a matter of state law by an act of the legislature approved on March 15, 1881. However, the name of the Arkansas River is also pronounced along the lines of *Kansas.*

A line in Walt Whitman's *Leaves of Grass* used *Arkansian* but the word is exceedingly rare today. The full line—"Not only the free Utahan, Kansian or Arkansian"—contains three demonyms that have seen very little use since the poem was published in 1855.

The authors of *Down in the Holler* reported use of *arkansaw* as a verb meaning "to cheat, to take advantage of. When a hunter shoots a quail on the ground, the bird is said to be *arkansawed.* My neighbor told me that a banker was trying to *arkansaw* him out of his farm." Randolph included a recollection that might give the Dutch some solace: "Postmaster McQuary, of Galena, Mo., ate lunch with me in a little restaurant. I reached for the check. 'No,' said he positively, 'we'll go *arkansaw,*' meaning that each man pays for his own food."

Arkansas toothpick is a long-established name for the Bowie knife, and is used in early legislation such as an 1838 Tennessee law outlawing the knife. *Arkansiana* is the accepted term for things relating to the history and culture of the state, as in "old and rare books and Arkansiana."

Traditional personal nicknames: *Goober Grabber, Josh, Toothpick,* and *Razorback* (q.v.). See also ARKIE.

State nickname: *Land of Opportunity.* Older nicknames are *Bear State* and *Bowie State.*

Arkansas City, Arkansas. *Arkansas Citian.*

Arkie. Nickname for a person from Arkansas, considered derogatory. In the Depression era it was used widely in reference to those itinerant agricultural workers from Arkansas who migrated west along with the Okies and others. An Associated Press news item of November 14, 1976, underscores the burden carried by the term. It begins: "LITTLE ROCK, Ark.—In the past 22 months, Frank White has traveled 142,000 miles around the world promoting Arkansas. His worst problem, he says, isn't the recession or the energy crisis—it's the 'Arkie image.'" He went on to say that the mere mention of the name of the state conjured up visions of gun-toting, barefoot hillbillies who shoot outsiders. See OKIE for a similarly negative nickname.

Armenia (Republic of Armenia); *formerly* **Armenian Soviet Socialist Republic.** *Armenian,* which is also an adjective.

Aruba. *Aruban.*

Asbury Park, New Jersey. *Asbury Parker.*

Asia. *Asian. Asiatic* is also used as both noun and adjective, but it is considered offensive by some Asians. This point was underscored by William and Mary Morris in their *Harper Dictionary of Contemporary Usage:* "When a new form of influenza first swept this country, it was called *Asiatic flu.* Then it was pointed out that Asians prefer to be called that—*Asians*—rather than *Asiatics,* a term which many regard as derogatory. So the official medical terminology was changed to *Asian flu.*" Ironically, Robert W. Chapman claimed in his *Adjectives from Proper Names* (1939) that "*Asiatic* has virtually displaced *Asian* as *African* displaced *Afric.*"

Asian. According to a BBC report of August 9, 2005, early immigrants to the U.K. from India, Pakistan, and Bangladesh found themselves saddled with the generic term *Asian.* "And," according to BBC reporter Cindi John, "although it's common to distinguish much more with regards to country of origin, 'Asian' still persists." The 2001 British census contained the category "Asian British," along with "Black British."

Asiental. Asian of unknown or unspecific nationality. It is a blend of Asian and Oriental and seems to be primarily used on Web blogs as a term of description rather than derogation, but it may still have that effect.

Aspen, Colorado. *Aspenite.* The term tends to show up when excesses are discussed: "One Aspenite named her newborn quarter-horse colt Ted Bundy [after the serial killer of that name], saying, 'It'll know how to run'" (quoted in Richard W. Larsen, *Bundy: The Deliberate Stranger*, 1989). The term *Aspenization* is sometimes applied to the process by which a place becomes expensive and chic, as this Colorado town has.

Astoria, Oregon. *Astorian.*

Atchison, Kansas. *Atchisonian.*

Athens, Greece. *Athenian,* also an adjective.

Atlanta, Georgia. *Atlantan.* The variant *Atlantian,* which once had advocates, is little used today and must be considered without any significant support. In his February 1934 *American Speech* note "Names for Citizens," George R. Stewart Jr. pointed out that the city's morning newspaper, the *Atlanta Journal,* used the -*ian* form while the evening paper, the *Atlanta Constitution,* used *Atlantan.* (This same fact was noted by Mencken in *The American Language.*) Today, however, the *Journal* also uses *Atlantan.* The two newspapers share the same style book under the same owner, and on holidays and weekends are published as a single paper, the *Atlanta Journal-Constitution.*

Atlantic City, New Jersey. *Atlantic Cityite.*

Atlantis. *Atlantan* is the demonym used for residents of this legendary island continent. The adjective *Atlantean* is used, as in this small item from the April 1992 *Reason* magazine: "Shirley MacLaine says that in another life she was married to New York City Council President Andrew Stein. Rumor has it that Stein wants to be New York's mayor. The MacLaine connection could help him lock up that all-important 10,000-year-old-Atlantean vote."

Aturin. Resident of Aire-sur-L'Adour, France.

Auckland, New Zealand. *Aucklander.*

Augusta, Georgia. *Augustan.*

Aurora, Illinois. *Auroran.*

Austin, Texas. *Austinite.* "Austinite Crowned Miss Teen Texas," headlined the *Corpus Christi Caller-Times* on November 28, 2005.

Australasia. *Australasian.* Term for Australia, New Zealand, and the many smaller islands in the vicinity, most of which are the eastern part of Indonesia. It is an old term that survives as a descriptor of an ecological area rather than a cultural one. The name was coined by Charles de Brosses in *Histoire des navigations aux terres australes* (1756), who created it from the Latin for "south of Asia."

Australia (Commonwealth of Australia). *Australian,* also an adjective. The nicknames *Aussie* and *Ozzie* are used broadly and are applied in a friendly, nonderogatory manner. *Australia* has a number of derivatives, including *Australiana,* for that which is characteristic of the place; *Australianness,* for Australian qualities; and *Australianism,* for a characteristic of Australian English.

Austria (Republic of Austria). *Austrian,* which is also an adjective.

Avon, England. *Not* "Avon Ladies and Gents," which was puckishly suggested by an ad in Britain for the Computer People that plays on the door-to-door perfume-selling "Avon Lady," but *Avonian.*

Azerbaijan (Republic of Azerbaijan); *formerly* **Azerbaijan Soviet Socialist Republic.** *Azerbaijani,* which can be used as a plural though *-s* is sometimes added. Sometimes the term is spelled *Azerbaidzhani.* Research by Charles D. Poe shows that there are two different approaches to pluralizing the short form (*Azeri*) of this demonym. Some news accounts use *Azeries* (*USA Today* discussed a feud between "Christian Armenians and Moslem Azeries" [June 24, 1988]), but others use *Azeris* (an Associated Press piece in the *Houston Chronicle* [May 31, 1988] talks of violence between "Armenians and Azeris"). An article in the Fall 1996 issue of *The Lamp,* published by Exxon, is titled "The Azeris: A Short History." Exxon's use of the plural noun is significant because its oil interests in Azerbaijan are so significant that it sponsored production of an Azerbaijani-English dictionary. The nation's official Web site, Azerbaijan International (www.azerbaijan.com), says that all three demonyms (*Azeri, Azerbaijani,* and *Azerbaijanian*) are acceptable but that in most cases, people in Azerbaijan use *Azeri* to refer to a person and *Azerbaijani* to refer to the language. It adds: "Not many young people use 'Azerbaijanian,' perhaps because it's so long and more difficult to pronounce. However, each of the terms can refer to the person or the language."

Azores. *Azorean,* which is also an adjective.

Babylonia. *Babylonian,* also an adjective.

Baghdad, Iraq. *Baghdadi.*

Bahamas (Commonwealth of the Bahamas). *Bahamian,* which is also an adjective; the creolized English of the Bahamas is often called *Bahamian dialect* or *Bahamian English,* and less often simply *Bahamian.*

Bahrain (State of Bahrain). *Bahraini,* which is also an adjective.

Bailiwick of Guernsey. See GUERNSEY.

Bailiwick of Jersey. See JERSEY.

Bajan. Resident of Barbados, also called a *Barbadian.*

Baked Bean. Traditional nickname for a resident of Massachusetts.

The Balkans. *Balkan.* "Dimitri is Greek, Bulgarian and Macedonian . . . a true Balkan man" (Jennifer Dunning, "Dancing to an

Ethnic Beat; Where to Dance to an Ethnic Beat: How to Get There," *New York Times:* June 9, 1978).

Balkanization is a geopolitical term originally used to describe the process of fragmentation or division of a region into smaller regions that are often hostile or noncooperative with each other. The term has arisen from the Balkan conflicts in the 20th century up to and including the Yugoslav Wars (1991–2001), a series of violent conflicts in the territory of the former Yugoslavia. The term is also used to describe other forms of disintegration, including, for instance, the subdivision of the Internet or the breakup of language into dialects.

Balsero. Person from the Caribbean who arrives in the United States by raft or boat.

Baltic States. The Baltic States consist of Estonia, Latvia, and Lithuania. Individuals are usually called by the specific demonym for their country (*Estonian, Latvian,* or *Lithuanian*), but the term *Balt* is often used generally for Baltic nationals. A letter to the *Washington Post* on the subject of the Soviet deportation of "the Balts" said, "The presence of Latvians, Lithuanians and Estonians is so prevalent in the Soviet gulag that the term 'Balt' has become a slang term for all political prisoners" (letter from Louise McManus, November 21, 1987).

Baltimore, Maryland. *Baltimorean.* Though the *-ean* form shows up virtually without exception, there is evidence that the term *Baltimorian* was used by some in the 19th century. David Shulman found this line in H. B. Fearon's *Sketches of America* (London, 1818): "the Baltimorians themselves lay claim to a superior reputation for hospitality, enterprise, and bravery." *Baltimorean* is often used as an honorific, as in this *Baltimore Sun* article of February 3, 1995, alluding to a piece in *Life* magazine on the 20th century: "Their conclusion was to list [Babe] Ruth among the 100 most important Americans of the 20th century—the only Baltimorean or Marylander so honored." Readers of the *Sun* editorial page will recognize the phrase "Baltimoreans worth the name," used on issues of local import. Arguing for local acceptance of the Canadian Football League (the city had a CFL team before it got the NFL Ravens in 1996) and invoking the name of the man who took the beloved Colts out of Baltimore, the *Sun* said, "The CFL has no Robert Irsay—Baltimoreans worth the name should love the league on that basis alone." In local parlance *Baltimorean* is often pronounced as if it were spelled "Bawlmeran."

Baltimoron, a seeming slur, can be used with affection in attempts at self-deprecation by local residents. In a *Baltimore Sun* editorial of October 12, 1994, titled "A 'Baltimoron' Claims a Nobel," we are told that "the career of Dr. Martin Rodbell, a self-described 'Baltimoron,' is the stuff of small-boy science-whiz dreams-come-true." The fact that a Nobel laureate can so label himself is part of the easygoing local culture that justifies the city's self-administered nickname *Charm City.*

The term *Baltimore Countian* is used widely to distinguish residents of Baltimore County from those of the city. The *Sun* referred to the book *A Heartbeat Away: The Investigation and Resignation of Vice President Spiro T. Agnew* (by Richard M. Cohen and Jules Witcover) as the "definitive account of the downfall of this infamous Baltimore Countian."

Banana-Bender. Nickname for a resident of Queensland, Australia; *Bananalander* is also used, with Queensland being *Bananaland.* Writer and folklorist W. N. Scott, himself a *Queenslander,* discusses a group of Australian state nicknames that he says are mostly used in a derogatory sense, "though not usually as intentional insults." He points out in a 1989 letter to the author that it is all a matter of context:

> *For instance, two lines of a poem by Graham Jenkin are as follows: "So I grabbed me gear and off I went with a sense of national pride, / To show these Yabbies how it's done on the old crow-eating side . . ."*

Now Jenkin is a South Australian hence himself a Crow-eater, but his hero's description of the Cabbage-patchers, or Yabbies (which are synonymous) shows that a South Australian does not necessarily object to the description of himself as a Crow-eater. It has become simply a name for an inhabitant of the State of South Australia. Nevertheless, in other circumstances it could be used as an insult if necessary, and great and even violent exception might be taken to the use of the epithet in other circumstances.

Scott advises anyone not knowing the "rules" of Australian demonyms to refrain from using them, especially in barrooms.

Banff, Alberta. *Banffite.*

Bangkok, Thailand. No common term is in use; however, this important point is made by librarian Joanne Edwards in the introduction to *Liverpudlian:* "While researching the material, we noted with interest that some regions have no identifying verbal concept of themselves as a unit of people residing together in a specified area. Thus, according to a governmental representative of Thailand, an inhabitant of Bangkok does not identify his place of residence as being that of a city within a country—as say a Londoner might—but rather as a countryman of Thailand, i.e., a Thai."

Bangladesh (People's Republic of Bangladesh). *Bangladeshi,* according to the Central Intelligence Agency's *World Factbook,* which lists the adjective *Bangladesh.*

Bangor, Maine. *Bangorean.*

Baraboo, Wisconsin. *Barabooian.* A note from Charles R. Lancaster of Sarasota, Florida, reminds us that John Ringling, the circus man, couldn't wait to leave this town, which he cynically said was filled with "hick Baraboobians."

Barbados. *Bajan* or *Barbadian.*

Barbareno. Resident of Santa Barbara, California, although *Santa Barbaran* may be more common.

Barcelona, Spain. *Barcelonian* or *Barcelonese.*

Basotho. Plural word for the residents of Lesotho (q.v.).

Basutoland. See LESOTHO.

Baton Rouge, Louisiana. *Baton Rougean.*

Battle Creek, Michigan. *Battle Creekian.*

Bavaria. *Bavarian,* which is also an adjective, as in *Bavarian cream.*

Bay City, Texas. *Bay Cityan.*

Bayonne, New Jersey. *Bayonneite.*

Bay Stater. Resident of Massachusetts, as in a *Boston Herald* headline for August 29, 2005: "Transplanted Bay Stater Will Ride It Out." *Bay State* is the usual nickname for Massachusetts, as in the "Bay State Games."

Bean-eater/Beantowner. Traditional, sometimes scornful nicknames for a resident of Boston, Massachusetts. Both derive from the traditional link between Boston and the consumption of baked beans. In the early Puritan days brown bread and baked beans were served as the regular Sunday meal because they could be prepared on the Saturday before.

Bear. Traditional nickname for a resident of Kentucky. It is said to come from a concentration of bears in the state in its early days.

Béarn, France. *Béarnais. Béarnaise* (from the French feminine adjective) is a culinary term for something prepared in the style of Béarn. *Béarnaise sauce* includes egg yolks, butter, shallots, vinegar, wine, and seasonings. King Henry IV of France was a native of Béarn, and so acquired a demonymic nickname, *Le Béarnais* or *The Béarnais*. In *The Spanish People* (1901), Martin A. S. Hume wrote, "But the great Béarnais was struck down (May 1610) by the dagger of Ravaillac. . . ."

Beatrice, Nebraska. *Beatrician.*

Beaufort, South Carolina. *Beaufortian.*

Beaumont, Texas. *Beaumonter.*

Beaver. Traditional nickname for a resident of Oregon, also used for athletes at Oregon State University.

Bechuanaland. See BOTSWANA.

Bedfordshire, England. *Bedfordian.*

Beefhead. Traditional nickname for a resident of Texas.

Beijing, China. *Beijinger.* An article in the *Houston Chronicle* of November 17, 1991, tells of a novel of great popularity in China titled *A Beijinger in New York.* The name of the city was changed from *Peking* after the Chinese government in 1979 adopted a new system, pinyin, for romanizing the names of Chinese people and places; pinyin replaced the Wade-Giles system.

Beirut, Lebanon. *Beiruti.* In Larry Collins's novel *Maze* (1989) the phrase "an occasional Beiruti" occurs.

Belarus (Republic of Belarus); *formerly* **Belorussian Soviet Socialist Republic.** *Belarusian* or *Belarusan,* both of which are also adjectives.

Belgium (Kingdom of Belgium). *Belgian,* which is also an adjective.

Belgrade, Yugoslavia. *Belgrader.*

Belgravia, London. *Belgravian,* which has also been used as an adjective by such writers as Thackeray and Matthew Arnold.

Belize; *formerly* **British Honduras.** *Belizean,* also an adjective. A passage from Donald E. Westlake's 1985 novel *High Adventure:* "A couple of slightly older fellows in neat but casual clothing would be expatriates, gone north for the advantages of American wage scales, home on a visit to show off their solvency, and incidentally to get some relief from the horrible winters of Brooklyn, where so many expatriate Belizeans made their home."

Bellifontain. Resident of Fontainebleau, France.

Belorussian Soviet Socialist Republic. See BELARUS.

Benelux. No evidence of a demonym could be found, although if there was one, it would probably be *Beneluxian. Benelux* was a name created from *Bel*gium, the *Net*herlands, and *Lux*embourg to describe the three countries as an economic and cultural entity. The term first came into play in 1947, according to Kenneth Versand's *Polyglot's Lexicon: 1943–1966.*

Benin (People's Republic of Benin); *formerly* **Dahomey.** *Beninese* (both singular and plural). This area, controlled by the Beni tribe from the 15th to the mid-17th centuries, was colonized by the French and gained its independence in 1960. The name was changed from *Dahomey* to *Benin* in 1975. Former demonyms were *Dahomeyan, Dahoman,* and *Dahomean.*

Benton Harbor, Michigan. *Benton Harborite.*

Berkeley, California. *Berkeleyite.* The nickname that has been used since the 1960s is *Berserkeleyite* or *Berzerkeleyite,* which stems from newspaper columnist Herb Caen's coinage *Berserkeley.* The following statement appeared in *California Living* (the magazine of the *San Francisco Sunday Examiner and Chronicle*) on January 31, 1982: "Berkeley has a certain reputation to uphold. The word Berzerkeley is painted in large black letters along the side of the Cambridge Apartments at Durant and Telegraph. It's been there since I've been here, for three months, so neither city fathers nor street citizens must take particular umbrage."

Berkshire, England. *Berkshireman* or *Berkshirewoman.*

Berlin, Germany. *Berliner.* In an article in the Winter 1989 issue of *The Spectator,* writer Ken Howard told of President Kennedy's famous speech in which he proclaimed in perfect textbook German, "Ich bin ein Berliner," or "I am a Berliner." Howard points out that some natives thought it funny: "The president and his speechwriters had run afoul of an idiom. 'Ein Berliner' is the local idiom for a 'jelly doughnut.'" Reinhold Aman disputes this widely circulated story: "In the context, nobody thought of a doughnut."

Bermuda. *Bermudian,* but sometimes *Bermudan. Bermudian* was a very early demonym, showing up in a North American newspaper, the *American Weekly Mercury,* as early as 1723. The nickname *Onion* is sometimes used, and can be traced to the *Bermuda onion,* which has retained its name even though significant numbers of the vegetable have not been exported since the 1930s. *Bermuda* gets more than its share of attention through *Bermuda rig* (a sailboat), *Bermuda Triangle, Bermuda* grass, *Bermuda cedar,* and *Bermuda shorts,* which are now part of the official uniform of Olympic athletes.

Bermudians are also called *Onions,* which is explained by a native. "Even though Bermuda isn't in the onion business the way it used to be, a born and bred islander is still called an 'Onion,'" writes Darwin Porter in Frommer's *Bermuda 2005.* The term dates from the early 20th century, when the export of Bermuda onions and Easter lilies to the U.S. mainland were the island's major sources of income.

Bern, Switzerland. *Bernese.*

Berruyer. A resident of Bourges, France.

Berry, France. The name for an inhabitant of this former province is *Berrichon.*

Berserkeleyite *or* **Berzerkeleyite.** Nickname for a resident of Berkeley, California (q.v.).

Bethlehem, Pennsylvania. *Bethlehemite.*

Bhutan (Kingdom of Bhutan). *Bhutanese* (singular and plural), which is also an adjective.

Biafra. *Biafran,* also an adjective. Biafra was a portion of Nigeria that seceded from 1967 to 1970.

Biarritz, France. *Biarrot.*

Bible Belt. *Bible Belter.* Describing those in southeastern and midwestern states where fundamentalist Protestantism is prevalent. Among the many nicknames for Nashville is *the Buckle of the Bible Belt.* because there was a time when it was said it had the highest ratios of churches to people than any other American city.

The "belt" terminology is commonly used in the United States to describe regions with a roughly east-west orientation that share a feature, such as the *Rust Belt,* a term to describe declining industrial areas of the Northeast and upper Midwest; the *Sun Belt,* a term for hot-weather states stretching from coast to coast; the *Snow Belt,* areas in the Northeast and northern Midwest prone to lake-effect snow; the *Black Belt,* a region of fertile farmlands in the Southeast now known as a region of persistent poverty with a high ratio of African American residents; the *Corn Belt,* midwestern states where corn is the primary crop. There are crop-defined *Grain, Peach, Cotton,* and *Wheat Belts.* The *Borscht Belt* is a region of Jewish resorts in the Catskill Mountains of New York State, and the *Porn Belt* is a term coined by former Delaware governor Pete DuPont in the *Wall Street Journal* (November 10, 2000) for the coastal states that voted for Al Gore in the 2000 U.S. presidential election. Arguing that the election was, above all, about culture, DuPont saw an eerie resemblance between the election results and a map showing the percentage of sex movies viewed in the home-video market. DuPont's justification for the Porn Belt coinage: "Mr. Gore carried the areas with the highest percentages (40% on the West Coast and 37% in New England and the Middle Atlantic states); Mr. Bush carried the area with the lowest percentage (14% in the South); and they split the rest of the country that had middling sex movie percentages."

Big Bender. Traditional nickname for a resident of Tennessee (q.v.), from the state nickname *Big Bend State.*

Billings, Montana. *Billingsite.*

Binghamton, New York. *Binghamtonian.*

Birmingham, Alabama. *Birminghamian.*

Birmingham, England. *Brummie* or *Brum,* which derive from *Brummagem,* an alternative name for the city that Eric Partridge termed "a local vulgar form of Birmingham." *Brummie* has been sanctioned by a number of sources. For instance, in 1966 it appeared in a list of what to call residents of various spots in the British Isles that was issued by BOAC, the airline now known as British Airways.

Bisbee, Arizona. *Bisbeean.*

Bismarck, North Dakota. *Bismarcker.*

Bizonian. Nickname for a person in the joint British and American zone of Germany immediately following World War II, which was known as *Bizonia* (as in "bilateral zone"). For example, *The Economist* of London reported on December 13, 1947, that "Bizonia's coal is fetching $10 a ton, of which the Germans receive only the equivalent in marks of $3.60. Mr Molotov [the Soviet foreign minister] scents a scandal." Rudolf J. Storz, now of Huntingdon, Tennessee, remembers the place as "The Bizone or, as of 1947 when the French threw in their lot, The Trizone." He adds, "One wit started calling it Trizonesia and came up with an unofficial anthem: we are the natives of Trizonesia, cannibals we are not but as kissers we are hot. It became a hit in no time." The name *Trizonia* for this zone was included in the 1950 Addenda to *Webster's New International Dictionary of the English Language,* 2nd edition, as was *Bizonia.*

Bloomington, Illinois. *Bloomingtonian.*

Bloomington, Indiana. *Bloomingtonian.*

Blue. Traditional nickname for a resident of New Jersey (q.v.).

Bluegrasser. Traditional nickname for a resident of Kentucky (q.v.).

Blue Hen. Traditional nickname for a resident of Delaware (q.v.).

Bluenose. Resident of Nova Scotia, Canada; an affectionate nickname. The province's most famous sailing ship was called the *Blue Nose,* and the term was once applied generically to Nova Scotian vessels in nautical slang.

In his *Good News to You,* John Ciardi pointed out that the term took on a separate meaning in the United States in the late 19th century: "A rigorously puritanical person of Spartan habits. (Generally implies moral snooping into the habits of others, and certainly, disapproval of them.)" The notion of the moralistic bluenose was such that it found limited use as a verb meaning "to reform; to kill joy."

Blue State / Red State. *Blue Stater / Red Stater.*

The terms *red states* and *blue states* entered popular usage in the weeks following the disputed 2000 election as a result of the majority of American mass media outlets using red to indicate Republican-won states, and blue for Democrat-won states. In addition, the term *red stater* or *blue stater* may refer to individuals who vote for, are affiliated with, or otherwise identify primarily with the Republican Party or Democratic Party, respectively. Increasingly common is the practice of referring to residents of *red states* and *blue states* as *red staters* and *blue staters.*

Bogotá, Colombia. *Bogotan* or *Bogotano.*

Bohemia. *Bohemian.* This term has also been applied to artists, writers, and others who live outside the realm of conventional standards. Greenwich Village in New York City and the Left Bank of Paris have been known for their Bohemians. This use of the term apparently stems from the mistaken belief that Bohemia was the European home of the Gypsies. The term *Bohemian* is still applied to anyone—Gypsy or not—who is seen to have different values than the rest of society.

Boise, Idaho. *Boisean.*

Bolivia (Republic of Bolivia). *Bolivian,* which is also an adjective. Bolivia was named after the great revolutionary Simon Bolívar, who helped liberate the country and several of its South American neighbors from Spanish colonial rule. One consequence of this was the unusual development of an adjective formed from a person's name but having geographical application: *Bolivarian* is defined in *Webster's Third New International Dictionary* as "of or relating to the So. American republics of Colombia, Venezuela, Peru, Ecuador, and Bolivia." *Bolivarian* is also used to describe something done in the manner of Simon Bolívar. In *Fidel: A Critical Portrait,* Tad Szulc describes a Castro trip to South America as "his first Bolivarian gesture."

Boll Weevil. Traditional nickname for a resident of Texas.

Bologna, Italy. *Bolognese.*

Bombay, India. *Bombayite.*

boondocks/boonies. Generic terms for an isolated outpost, the back country. *Boondocks,* which comes from the Tagalog *bundok* for "mountain," entered English in the 1920s and gained widespread popularity during World War II for an out-of-the-way place. United States Marines called their rugged boots *boondockers*— presumably because they were fit for mountain terrain. A collection of citations on the term in the Tamony Collection shows it has been applied to a variety of locations, from the suburbs to minor-league baseball towns. It even underwent a brief slang incarnation as a verb meaning "to park, to neck" in the 1950s. A number of other alternative terms exist, including *hick town, whistlestop, sque(e)dunk, jerkwater town, the sticks, a wide spot in the road, East Overshoe, Hicksville, dogpatch, back 40, tank town,* and *Podunk,* which rates a separate entry.

Bordeaux, France. *Bordelais.*

Border Eagle. Traditional nickname for a resident of Mississippi, from the eagle on the state seal. *Warrock's Almanac* of 1846 erroneously entered *Border Beagle* (see Mathews, *Dictionary of Americanisms*).

Borica. Puerto Rican. The term honors the indigenous Taino culture, which called the island *Borinquin.* The National Association of Hispanic Journalists reports that the use of this term has grown in popularity in recent years.

Borinqueño. Nickname for a resident of Puerto Rico. The original name for Puerto Rico was Taino *Boriquen,* rendered by early Spanish explorers as *Borinquén.* Hence the Arawak natives were the *Borinquen,* or in Spanish, the *Borinqueños.* The feminine form appears in the title of the Puerto Rican anthem, "La Borinqueña." *Punta Borinquen,* or *Point Borinquen,* is at the northwest corner of the island.

Bosnia and Herzegovina (Republic of Bosnia and Herzegovina). The nouns (and adjectives) of nationality are *Bosnian* and *Herzegovinian,* but the far more important names within this land of military action and ethnic cleansing are the ethnic divisions of *Muslim, Serb,* and *Croat.* The nation's bitter ethnic strife began in 1992 when this constituent republic of Yugoslavia declared its independence. Bosnia's Serbs took up arms and several years of war and atrocities ensued.

Boston, Massachusetts. *Bostonian.* Nicknames dating back into the 19th century include *Bean-eater, Bowwow,* and *Beantowner.* Because the city's longest-surviving nickname is *The Hub,* Bostonians are often identified as "Hub man" or "Hub woman."

One subspecies of Bostonian is the *Boston Brahmin.* Here is how the term is explained in Francis Russell's *The Great Interlude:* "It was in reaction to these untouchable newcomers [i.e., the Irish] that the tradition of the Boston *hauteur* came into being, the proper Bostonian, the myth of the Brahmin—that term kindly Dr. Oliver Wendell Holmes coined originally to mean no more than a bread-and-water intellectual asceticism and that would now come to mean a class-conscious membership in the Yankee State Street financial oligarchy." Another name for a Boston Brahmin is, as Russell implies, a *Proper Bostonian.*

Boswash. In the 1960s futurists envisioned an immense city that would someday stretch from Boston to Washington, and so we have the demonym *Boswasher. Bosnywash* (with the *-ny-* for *New York*) has also been used for this city.

Botswana (Republic of Botswana); *formerly* **Bechuanaland.** *Motswana* in the singular, but *Batswana* in the plural. The adjective used by the press is *Botswanan.*

Boulder, Colorado. *Boulderite.*

Bourg, France. In the 1986 *Word Ways* article *"D'où Êtes-Vous* Revisited," Harry Partridge points out that the Bourg in Gironde is inhabited by *Bourcais* while the Bourg (also known as *Bourg-en-Bresse*) in Ain is populated by *Bressans* or *Bourgeois.*

Bourges, France. *Berruyer.*

Bowery, New York City. *Boweryite.*

Bragard. Resident of Saint-Dizier, France.

Brazil (Federative Republic of Brazil). *Brazilian.* The same word is used as an adjective but not in the specific case of the *Brazil nut.*

Bressan. Resident of Bourg (in Ain), France, also called a *Bourgeois.*

Bridgeport, Connecticut. *Bridgeporter.*

Bristol, England. *Bristolian.*

Bristol, Virginia. *Bristolian.*

Brit. Informal short form of the demonym *Briton* that has also been used for the adjective *British*—"Why Brits Had Best Behave" (headline in the *Sunday Age* [Melbourne, Australia] January 1, 2006). The term is not derogatory and points to a conclusion made by N. Sally Hass: "It's hard to tell just what makes a shortened demonym insulting. 'Jap' for Japanese is highly offensive, but 'Brit' for Briton is not. The British use it themselves." Not always so, according to an August 9, 1992, article by Anthony Burgess in the *New York Times Magazine:* "I detest that designation with its connotation of brittle, as though we were cashew nuts, but nobody seems to know what we denizens of the United Kingdom of Great Britain and Northern Ireland ought to be called."

Britain. Short for *Great Britain,* which consists of England, Scotland, and Wales. A resident of Britain is a *Briton.*

Britannic. Rare adjective for Great Britain. Robert W. Chapman addressed the word in his *Adjectives from Proper Names* (1939): "It is now hardly used except in the formal 'His Britannic Majesty' and as the name of a ship." There is also the world-famous *Encyclopaedia Britannica,* which employs an original Latin version of the adjective.

British. The collective demonym (*Briton* is used for an individual) and the adjective for Great Britain, consisting of England, Scotland, and Wales. It is used in many terms and proper names, including the *British Broadcasting Corporation* (BBC) and *British thermal unit* (BTU).

British Columbia, Canada. *British Columbian.*

Britisher. Resident of Great Britain, but *Briton* is preferred by the British. This is an informal term that, according to several sources, became popular in the United States during and immediately after the American Revolution and was meant to be derogatory. One theory holds that the term was used as a means of distinguishing a British army of occupation from the English-born colonists. Today it seems to be used ironically as a playful poke at overblown, stuffy titles. In Alistair MacLean's 1960 thriller *Ice Station Zebra* an American character calls an English character a *Britisher* as a friendly tweak. The Briton later talks of "decadent Britishers."

British Guiana. See GUYANA.

British Honduras. See BELIZE.

British Virgin Islands. *British Virgin Islander.*

Briton. Resident of Great Britain. See also BRIT, BRITISH, BRITISHER.

Brobdingnagian. Giant from a land of giants in Jonathan Swift's *Gulliver's Travels.* It is used for anything that is tremendous in size.

Brockton, Massachusetts. *Brocktonian.*

Bronx, New York. *Bronxite.* New Yorkers always refer to this borough as "The Bronx." (William Safire says that the classic apocryphal question from the carpetbagging politician is, "Where are the Bronx?") *Bronx* is sometimes used in rough-and-tumble characterizations on the order of *Bronx bagpipe,* for a vacuum cleaner, and the internationally known *Bronx cheer,* for a flatulent razz. An adjective *Bronxian* is sometimes used, as in this line from Roger Angell's *The Summer Game* (1972) on the firing of Yogi Berra as manager of the New York Yankees: "The Bronxian Dark Ages had begun."

Brooklyn, New York. *Brooklynite.*

Brooklynese. An accent and manner of speaking that can be heard from New Jersey to the middle of Long Island, but which has always been most closely associated with Brooklyn. It is characterized by dropped *g*'s and *r*'s ("talkin' to my fatha") and replacement of the *th* sound by the *t* sound ("toidy-toid" for "thirty-third"). Brooklynese also involves vowels and diphthongs, as the last example witnesses. Charles F. Dery recalls the illustrative anecdote involving the Brooklyn-born Hall of Famer Waite Hoyt, who pitched for Brooklyn in 1938, the last of his 21 seasons as a major leaguer. "As you will no doubt recall," Dery wrote to Peter Tamony, "when Hoyt was injured an anonymous Brooklyn fan cried out: 'Hert is hoit!'"

Brum or **Brummie.** Resident of Birmingham, England (q.v.).

Brunei (State of Brunei Darussalam). *Bruneian,* which is also an adjective.

Brussels, Belgium. *Bruxellois* (French, from the French name for the city, *Bruxelles*). In *Liverpudlian,* Joanne Edwards points out: "An inhabitant of Brussels has no Flemish term to describe himself as a resident of that city. He does, however, use the French term Bruxellois to indicate the same."

Bryan, Texas. *Bryanite.*

Buckeye. Traditional nickname for a resident of Ohio (q.v.).

Buckinghamshire, England. *Bucksian,* from a shortening of the place name.

Buckskin. Traditional nickname for a backwoodsman or rustic in historic American slang, applied especially to a Virginian or southerner, according to Mitford Mathews's *Dictionary of Americanisms.* It derives from the wearing of buckskin garments.

Bucyrus, Ohio. *Bucyrian.*

Budapest, Hungary. *Budapestiek* is often found in print but the informal *Pesti* is common. "A Pesti (pronounced Peshtee) as the local citizens are called," says an April 4, 1989, report in the *Wall Street Journal,* "is a person who believes only half of what he/she sees, then puts that half under a microscope to see in whose interest it is to appear that way."

Buenos Aires, Argentina. *Porteño.*

Buffalo, New York. *Buffalonian,* not *Buffaloan.*

Bug-eater. Traditional nickname for a resident of Nebraska.

Bulgaria (Republic of Bulgaria). *Bulgarian,* also an adjective.

Bunnie. Playful "gag" name for a resident of Cedar Rapids, Iowa, and a play on "See Der Rabbits." It is one of a number of such forms that can be either tongue-in-cheek or insulting: In *The American Language,* H. L. Mencken listed *Chicagorilla, Baltimoron, Omahog,* and *Louisvillin.* There have also been *Hollywoodenheads* and *Madhattaners.* A man from Santa Barbara, California, notes that the facetious *Santa Barbarian* and *Stabarbaran* are used locally. Lexicographer David Shulman has dubbed a loudmouth from Illinois an *Illinoisy.* See also MAINE for a discussion of *Maineiac.*

At another level, some make a game of coming up with lists of punning or whimsical demonyms. For instance, John Masengrab published a list of these in the *Minneapolis/Saint Paul Magazine* based on local towns like Blue Earth (populated by *Blue Earthlings*), Esko (*Eskomoes*), and Proctor (*Proctologists*). Several collections have appeared in *Word Ways,* including one by Vernon Maclaren ("How to Name the Residents," May 1988) that included names for people from Holyoke, Massachusetts (*Holyokels*); Armonk (*Armonkeys*) and Saratoga (*Saratogres*), New York; and Waterloo, Iowa (*Waterloonies*).

Such local wordplay can be quite clever. A note from Emily Harrison Wier of Northampton, Massachusetts, reports: "Residents of Burlington, Vermont, are called—quite predictably—*Burlingtonians*. But supporters of Burlington's socialist mayor Bernard Sanders [who went on to the United States Congress] are referred to—quite ingeniously I think—as 'Sanderistas.'" A few neodemonyms contain a modicum or more of hostility, as displayed in this line from Johnny France and Malcolm McConnell's *Incident at Big Sky*: "That was Resort Montana, an all-season recreational preserve for wealthy Easterners and the tanned Calvin Klein set some of the old ranchers called 'Californicators.'" Reinhold Aman has coined *Waukeshite* for anti-intellectual locals in his community of Waukesha, Wisconsin.

Regarding Iowa names, Gary L. Thompson insists in an article "What Do You Call Residents of Iowa Towns?" (*Des Moines Register*, March 13, 1988) that *What Cheerleaders* is the only appropriate name for folks from What Cheer, Iowa, and that residents of Waterloo, Iowa, can only be called *Waterloons*.

Burgundy, France. *Burgundian.*

Burkina Faso; *formerly* **Upper Volta.** *Burkinabe* (singular and plural), which is also an adjective, although *Burkinan* appears in some news reports.

Burlington, Vermont. *Burlingtonian.*

Burma. See MYANMAR.

Burundi (Republic of Burundi). *Burundian.* As used in the *Chicago Tribune* on October 4, 2005: "Traditionally, Burundians believe that an eclipse marks a time when the Earth and heaven are linked. It is considered an omen for great misfortune." Adjective: *Burundi.*

Butternut. Nickname for a Confederate soldier or sympathizer in the Civil War, also applied to a resident of Tennessee.

Buzzard. Traditional nickname for a resident of Georgia.

Bytowner. Resident of Ottawa, Canada, originally called *Bytown* after John By (1718–1836), a British engineer who designed and oversaw construction of the Rideau Canal, which runs from the Ottawa River to Lake Ontario at Kingston.

Cabbage-patcher. Resident of Victoria, Australia (q.v.), from the state nickname *Cabbage Patch*. See also BANANA-BENDER.

Cadillac, Michigan. *Cadillacite*.

Cairo, Egypt. *Cairene,* also an adjective. "Spring is a glorious season here," read a recent dispatch from Cairo in the *New York Times;* "Cairenes take to the parks and the streets."

Cajun. Louisianian of Acadian-French descent; a slurring corruption of *Acadian* in the same manner that *Injun* was taken from *Indian.* Acadia was the French colony formed at the Bay of Fundy in 1604 and whose residents were expelled by the British Crown in 1755. About one in four residents of Louisiana calls himself or herself a *Cajun.* It is also an adjective, often used in references to food ("Cajun cooking") and music. One early guided missile of the United States was the *Nike-Cajun.*

Calabria, Italy. *Calabrian* (also an adjective) or *Calabrese.*

Calcutta, India. *Calcuttan.*

Pull date: Tue Sep 29 2009

OWUSU AA

MATILDA

508-755-8717

TESHMEN508@YAHOO.COM

Item barcode:	38123000542007
Title:	Labels for locals : what to call people from Abilene to Zimbabwe / Paul Dickson
Author:	Dickson, Paul.
Call #:	422 Dick fi0gn
Pickup location:	Shrewsbury Library
Hold note:	

Caledonian. A resident of Scotland (q.v.), hence synonymous with *Scot;* also an adjective synonymous with *Scottish.*

Calexico, California. *Calexicote.*

Calgary, Alberta. *Calgarian.* Traditional personal nicknames are *Cowtowner* and *Stampeder;* from the city's historic cattle industry. (Calgary has sometimes been referred to as *Cowtown.*) Each year it hosts the "Calgary Stampede," a rodeo and western festival.

California. *Californian* (also an adjective). The term *Californio* is reserved for the area's early Spanish-speaking inhabitants (as in the title of the book *The Decline of the Californios: A History of Spanish-Speaking Californians 1846–1890,* by Leonard Pitt, University of California Press, 1966).

Among the derivatives are the verb *Californianize,* meaning "to be dominated by or to become like California," and the nouns for this process, *Californiazation* or *Californization.* An article in the March 27, 1988, *Roll Call* on the growing congressional delegation from California was titled "The Californiazation of Congress." A crude but popular verb for California-style overdevelopment is *Californicate,* as printed on a series of western bumper stickers that first appeared in the late 1970s: DON'T CALIFORNICATE MONTANA, DON'T CALIFORNICATE OREGON, etc. An article by Norris Yates in *American Speech* titled "The Vocabulary of *Time* Magazine Revisited" (Spring 1981) suggests that this blend of *California* and *fornicate* was created by *Time.* He found a *Time* use of *Californicated* in the August 21, 1971, issue. Many of these words rely on a stereotype (reinforced by advertising) of a land of bean sprouters, bikinis, and people who say "No problem" a lot.

Traditional personal nicknames: *Gold Coaster, Gold Digger,* and *Prune Picker.*

State nicknames: *Golden State* and *El Dorado.*

Calistoga, California. *Calistogan.*

Cambodia (Kingdom of Cambodia) *or* **Kampuchea.** *Cambodian,* also an adjective. Although the country is sometimes referred to as *Kampuchea, Cambodia* and *Cambodian* hold the upper hand in English. The same was true when the country was *Democratic Kampuchea* (1976–90). For instance, the *Associated Press Stylebook and Libel Manual* (1980) said: "Use this name [Cambodia] rather than *Democratic Kampuchea* in datelines. When *Kampuchea* is used in the body of a story, it should be identified as the formal name of Cambodia." While *Merriam-Webster's Collegiate Dictionary,* 11th edition, includes an adjective *Kampuchean,* noun evidence is extremely scarce, and no demonym is shown.

Cambridge, England. *Cantabrigian.* This is customary for both residents of the English municipality and graduates of Cambridge University. *Cantab* is used colloquially. *Cantabrigian* can also be used as an adjective.

Cambridge, Massachusetts. *Cantabrigian,* sometimes *Cantabridgian.* This term is often shortened to *Cantab* in newspapers. Both the long and short form are sometimes applied to students and graduates of Harvard University, located in Cambridge.

Camden, New Jersey. *Camdenite.*

Cameroon (Republic of Cameroon). *Cameroonian,* which is also an adjective. *Cameroon* is sometimes spelled *Camerouns* or *Cameroun* but neither is found in recent American usage.

Canada. *Canadian,* also an adjective. An illuminating note appears in *Colombo's Canadian References* under the entry on *Canadian:* "Before the passage of the Canadian Citizenship Act which came into force on 1 Jan. 1947, a Canadian could not call himself or herself a Canadian citizen because the official designation for a person born or naturalized within the British Commonwealth was British Subject. The Act created the distinct nationality of a Canadian citizen. . . ."

In his *Adjectives from Proper Names* (1939), Robert W. Chapman comments on this term, "I am not clear why *Canadan* was avoided, but *Canadian* is no doubt French." It is in fact modeled after the French form, *Canadien*.

Canal Zone, Panama. *Zonian* is what an American in the area is called.

Canary Islands (Autonomous Community of Spain). *Canary Islander* but *Canario/Canaria* is colloquial.

Canberra, Australia. *Canberran.*

Cantabrigian. Resident of Cambridge, England, or a graduate of Cambridge University; also used for a resident of Cambridge, Massachusetts, or someone associated with Harvard University, located there.

Canton, China. *Cantonese,* also an adjective.

Canton, Ohio. *Cantonian.*

Canuck. A Canadian, and in early use specifically a French Canadian. This is a difficult term to classify absolutely because it is clearly derogatory and offensive in some cases but not so in others. In eastern Canada and northern New England it is seen as an ethnic slur by French Canadians. In western Canada it is used, among other things, as a name for a hockey team: the Vancouver *Canucks.* In his 1987 book *Good Words to You,* John Ciardi termed it "once pejorative, now commonly accepted by Canadians as a fond nickname." Ciardi did acknowledge that it became "more-or-less pejorative" for French Canadians in northern New England. In this regard, the late Senator Edmund Muskie of Maine was accused in a published letter of laughing at the use of the term during his 1972 presidential campaign. He denied the charge and the letter was seen as probably spurious, but it focused attention on the term and left little doubt that it was considered a slur in the northeastern United States. The *Associated Press Stylebook and Libel Manual* calls *Canuck* a "derogatory racial label" and cautions its writers to "avoid the word except in formal names (The Vancouver Canucks . . .) or in quoted matter."

Canadian Philip Chaplin has summarized his attempts to track the etymology of the term: "The *Oxford English Dictionary* (supplement) says apparently from the first syllable of Canada, *Encyclopedia Canadiana* gives that, with an Algonkian ending -uc as one possibility, *Appleton-Century* says 'N. Amer. Ind.', and Vinay [*Dictionnaire Canadien*] ignores the word. *Canadiana* seems to prefer to trace it to a French attempt at Connaught, originally applying to Irish immigrants, but then says it was used first of French-Canadians. *Oxford English Dictionary*'s earliest quotation is dated 1855, but *Canadiana* gives one from the Boston *Transcript* of 1840, and claims the word was in use in 1835" (letter to author, April 2, 1984). The etymology in *Merriam-Webster's Collegiate Dictionary*, 11th edition, is "origin unknown," and it parallels the "origin uncertain" of Walter S. Avis's scholarly *Dictionary of Canadianisms on Historical Principles*.

Cape Cod, Massachusetts. *Cape Codder.* In context from an article in the *Bangor* (Maine) *Daily News:* "So you're a Cape Cod tourist and you can't for the life of you figure out why Cape Codders seem to dislike you so much?" See also WASHASHORE.

Cape Girardeau, Missouri. *Girardean.*

Cape May, New Jersey. *Cape Mayan.*

Cape Town, South Africa. *Capetonian.*

Cape Verde (Republic of Cape Verde). *Cape Verdian;* however, the Central Intelligence Agency's *World Factbook* has *Cape Verdean.*

Caracas, Venezuela. *Caraqueño.*

Carioca. Resident of Rio de Janeiro, Brazil. In the novel *Isle of the Snakes* by Robert L. Fish, a character asks, "Were they from Rio, do you think? Cariocas?"

Carlisle, Pennsylvania. *Carlisler.*

Carmel, California. *Carmelite.*

Carolinian. Resident of North Carolina or South Carolina.

Carolomacérien. Resident of Charleville-Mézières, France (q.v.), also a *Carolopolitain.*

Carolopolitain. Resident of Charleville-Mézières, France (q.v.), also a *Carolomacérien.*

Carpinien. Resident of Charmes, France.

Carson City, Nevada. *Carsonite.*

Cascadia. Cultural, economic "nation" composed of Oregon, Washington, and British Columbia named for the region's imposing Cascade mountain range. The 10 million residents of the area call themselves *Cascadians.*

"An imaginary country called 'Cascadia' is taking shape in the minds of a growing number of visionaries in the Pacific Northwest, and in some ways the fantasy is becoming reality," reported the *Washington Post* in a May 5, 1991, article, adding, "The movement's proponents are not secessionists, and they go to great lengths to emphasize that the 'new regionalism' is based on the economic realities of a changing world and not on a desire to alter the makeup of politically sovereign states or nations." The region's capital, *Portcouver,* is an urban corridor linking Vancouver, Seattle, and Portland. Compare BOSWASH.

Cascadia has also been applied to a hypothetical landmass along the western edge of North America, inspiring the adjective *Cascadian,* entered in *Webster's Third New International Dictionary* and referring to mountain-making movements in the Cenozoic era. However, according to the *Glossary of Geology* (1987), "Most of the evidence adduced for the existence of Cascadia can now be otherwise interpreted," and the authors discount a massive disturbance called the *Cascadian Revolution* that supposedly created the Cascade Range.

Cat. Traditional nickname for a resident of Cheshire, England (q.v.).

Catasauqua, Pennsylvania. *Catasauquan.*

Cavalier. Traditional nickname for a resident of Virginia (q.v.).

Cayman Islands. *Caymanian,* according to the Central Intelligence Agency's *World Factbook,* and it is shown as an adjective and noun in *Merriam-Webster's Collegiate Dictionary,* 11th edition. One can also find examples of *Cayman Islander.*

Cedar Falls, Iowa. *Cedar Fallsan.*

Cedar Rapids, Iowa. *Cedar Rapidian.* There is also the joking term *Bunnie* (q.v.), a pun based on "See Der Rabbits."

Celt. A member of an ancient Indo-European people or a modern person from the Celtic lands, which include Ireland, Highland Scotland, Wales, Cornwall, and Brittany.

Centennial. Traditional nickname for a resident of Colorado.

Central African Republic. *Central African.*

Central America. *Central American.*

Centralia, Washington. *Centralian.*

Cestrian. Resident of Chester or Cheshire, England.

Ceylon. See SRI LANKA.

Chad (Republic of Chad). *Chadian,* also an adjective.

Chamorro. A member of a people of the Mariana Islands, and the original demonym for Guam (q.v.).

Champaign, Illinois. *Champaignite.*

Channel Islands, United Kingdom. *Channel Islander,* although a resident is commonly addressed on the basis of the specific island, such as *Jerseyan, Jerseyite, Jerseyman,* or *Jerseywoman* for the Isle of Jersey.

Charleston, South Carolina. *Charlestonian,* which can be traced back to 1835.

Charleston, West Virginia. *Charlestonian.*

Charlestown, Massachusetts. *Townie.*

Charles Town, West Virginia. *Charles Towner.*

Charleville-Mézières, France. *Carolomacérien* or *Carolopolitain.* An early Latin name for Charleville was *Carolopolis;* it was founded by Charles of Gonzaga in 1606. It merged with Mézières in 1966, and *Carolomacérien* incorporates a demonym of the latter town, *Macérien.*

Charlotte, North Carolina. *Charlottean.*

Charmes, France. *Carpinien.*

Chaseburg, Wisconsin. *Chaseburger.* By the way, Chaseburg is in Hamburg Township. This was verified some years ago by Bill Gold of the *Washington Post,* who went on to ask, "Is Champ, Maryland peopled by 'Champions,' and Childs, Maryland by 'Children?'"

Chattanooga, Tennessee. *Chattanoogan.*

Chautauqua, New York. *Chautauquan.* The term has wider use because an adult education movement started in the town in 1874 and grew into a national institution. Engaged in religious and secular studies as well as the performing arts, local chapters became known as Chautauquas and those involved were known as *Chautauquans.* Chautauqua meetings combined popular entertainment with "uplifting" lectures and concerts.

Chechnya. *Chechen* is commonly used for an inhabitant of Chechnya, or a member of the predominant, traditionally Muslim ethnic group of Chechnya.

    During the collapse of the USSR, the government of the embedded republic declared independence as the Chechen Republic. As of early 2006, their independence has not been recognized by any major state. This declaration has led to armed conflicts between the forces of the self-declared government and other Chechen groups, and the Russian Federal Army.

Cheechako. Newcomer to Alaska or northwestern Canada, especially the Yukon. It was used for those inexperienced would-be miners who rushed into the Yukon Territory during the Klondike gold rush of 1897–99, and so can be found, along with its antithesis *sourdough,* in the writings of Jack London and Robert Service, whose *Songs of a Sourdough* (1907) and *Ballads of a Cheechako* (1909) were "enormously popular," according to *Merriam-Webster's Encyclopedia of Literature.* In Alaska and Canada there are apparently many criteria that can be used to establish when a newcomer has surpassed the status of Cheechako, and the most popular one seems to be the Cheechako's witnessing both the freezing of the rivers in the fall and, after the long winter, their breakup in the spring. *Cheechako* was originally a Chinook jargon word for "newcomer," from *chee* ("new") and *chako* ("come"). Russell Tabbert writes in his *Dictionary of Alaskan English* (1991) that this was once a term of outright contempt but recently has become one of "good-humored condescension."

Cherokee County, Texas. *Cherokeean.* In "What the People of American Towns Call Themselves," H. L. Mencken noted, "In Rusk, the county seat of Cherokee County, there is a weekly called the *Cherokeean.*"

Cheshire, England. *Cestrian.* A traditional personal nickname is *Cat,* from "Cheshire Cat."

Chester, England. *Cestrian.* In Old English, Chester was known as *Cester* or *Ceaster.*

Chester, Pennsylvania. *Chesterite.*

Cheyenne, Wyoming. *Cheyenneite.*

Chicago, Illinois. *Chicagoan* and never *Chicagan.* It is occasionally argued that *Chicagan* would be consistent with demonyms like *San Franciscan* and *Coloradan,* but the counterargument is that these other names are Spanish while Chicago is of Indian origin.

    Chicago has been used in a number of hurly-burly slang constructions, including *Chicago majority* (105 percent of the vote), *Chicago piano* (a machine gun), and *Chicago rubdown* (a thrashing). The late king of neologisms, Walter Winchell, created the term *Chicagorilla* (*Chicago* and *gorilla*) for local goons and gangsters. One who works in Chicago's famous Loop is known as a *Looper,* an example of how these geographical nouns can work down to the neighborhood level.

Chicagoland. *Chicagolander.* Chicagoland is the area in and around Chicago. The term has been widely applied, as demonstrated by this early reference in *Time* (December 1, 1941): "How then explain the [Chicago] *Tribune*'s success?—its gain of 264,000 circulation in the last five years?—its undeniable influence on isolationist sentiment in the five Midwest States which it calls Chicagoland?"

Chicano/a. An American of Mexican descent. In current use this term seems to be preferred over *Mexican-American* by some. The *Associated Press Stylebook and Libel Manual,* however, advises that it should not be used for routine description of Mexican Americans. It adds: "*Chicano* has been adopted by some social activists of Mexican descent, and may be used when activists use it to describe themselves. To apply it to all Spanish-surnamed citizens would be roughly the same as calling all blacks Muslims." *Chicana,* the Spanish feminine form, has established itself as an independent word in English, where grammatical gender doesn't exist for nouns. Compare LATINA.

A term that has been used as an adjective of intensity is *chicanismo.* In her book *Chicano Art: Inside/Outside the Master's House* (Texas, 1997), Alicia Gaspar De Alba describes the lowrider, a customized car that rides low on its wheels and close to the ground, as an "icon of Chicanismo."

According to the authoritative Web site www.azteca.net the term was once derogatory but not after being appropriated by the "Brown Power" movement of the 1960s and 1970s. It adds that among "assimilated" Mexican-Americans the term retains an "unsavory" connotation because of its use by political activists and those preferring to create "a new and fresh identity for their culture rather than to subsume it blandly under the guise of mainstream culture." Both the Merriam-Webster and Encyclopedia Britannica Web sites refer visitors to Azteca.net for questions relating to Hispanic taxonomy.

Chichester, England. *Cisestrian.*

Chico, California. *Chicoan.* In "What the People of American Towns Call Themselves," H. L. Mencken noted that according to the Chico Chamber of Commerce, *Chican* was replacing the earlier *Chicoan.*

Chilango. Resident of Mexico City. An example in print: "But the first weeks of the year are always a particular trial for chilangos, as natives of the Mexican capital are known, because of the regularity and severity of atmospheric inversions" (*New York Times*, January 16, 1988).

Chile (Republic of Chile). *Chilean,* also an adjective. Before World War I, *Chile* was often spelled *Chili,* which made the residents *Chilians.*

Chilmark, Massachusetts. *Chilmarker.*

China (People's Republic of China). *Chinese* (both singular and plural), which is also an adjective. *Chinaman* has become increasingly scarce, because it is widely regarded as a term of condescension and derision. "A patronizing term," says the *Associated Press Stylebook and Libel Manual,* which advises its writers to confine use to quoted matter. (The back-formation *Chinee* is unquestionably derogatory, as it was often used in the 19th-century notion of "heathen Chinee," but has largely passed from use.)

One of the reasons why *Chinaman* is viewed as a slur is its long and varied history in slang. Variously, a *Chinaman* is or has been an illegible figure on a racetrack tote board; to have a *Chinaman on one's back* means to be addicted and is a synonym for a *monkey on one's back;* and a *Chinaman's chance* is no chance.

The personification "John Chinaman," which was used for all Chinese, no doubt contributed because the name was an expression of the idea that all Chinese were alike and without individual identity. The degree to which the term is taken to be offensive is shown in two newspaper clippings from the *San Francisco Sunday Examiner and Chronicle* in the Tamony Collection. The first is about a man who was referred to as a

Chinaman by an official of the sheriff's office and is headlined "Sheriff Probes Racial Slur on Chinese Man" (August 26, 1979), and the second is this from Herb Caen's column: "Nobody asked me, but why is it that the words Frenchman and Englishman are not offensive but the word Chinaman is? And it is. Ask any Chinese" (August 1, 1971).

China (Republic of China). See TAIWAN.

Chinatown. Name for any of a number of Chinese districts in major cities where large numbers of Chinese have settled. The term *Chinatowner* was given a meaning in the New York garment industry that has nothing to do with Chinatowns east or west. It refers to a manufacturer of cheap dresses and probably derives from the fact that such businessmen once paid their workers "coolie wages."

Christmas Island. *Christmas Islander.*

Chuuk *or* **Truk, Micronesia.** *Chuukese* or *Trukese.*

Cincinnati, Ohio. *Cincinnatian.* Residents of the Queen City have also been called *Porkopolitans* and *Rhinelanders* (qq.v.).

citizen. Generic term for a person who has achieved the full civil rights of a nation by birth or naturalization. The *Associated Press Stylebook and Libel Manual* points out that cities and states do not confer citizenship. Therefore it suggests, "To avoid confusion, use *resident,* not *citizen,* in referring to inhabitants of states and cities."

Clam or Clam Catcher. Traditional nickname for a resident of New Jersey.

Clam Grabber. Traditional nickname for a resident of the state of Washington.

Clay Eater. Traditional nickname for a resident of South Carolina.

Cleveland, Ohio. *Clevelander.* Mencken noted in "What the People of American Towns Call Themselves" that there was "a *Clevelander* express train on the New York Central running to and from New York."

Clinton, Indiana. *Clintonian.*

Clodoaldien. Resident of Saint-Cloud, France, named after Cloud, a sixth-century religious figure who was also known as *Clodoald.*

Coal Miner. Traditional nickname for a resident of Pennsylvania.

Cockader. Traditional nickname for a resident of Maryland.

Cognac, France. *Cognacais.*

Cohee or ***Coohee.*** Traditional nickname for a resident of Pennsylvania, and broadly a slang term for an inhabitant of western Pennsylvania and Virginia. See PENNSYLVANIA.

Cohoes, New York. *Cohosier.*

Collioure, France. *Colliourench,* according to "*D'où Êtes-Vous* Revisited" (by the "Word Wurcher," *Word Ways,* August 1986).

Colorado. *Coloradan.* The variant *Coloradoan* shows up in print with some regularity, but it is unpopular with natives of the state. When one considers that the usual practice is to drop the *-o* when creating a demonym from a Spanish name (*Colorado* is Spanish for "colored"), the case for *Coloradan* becomes stronger.

Traditional personal nicknames: *Centennial, Rover,* and *Silverine.*

State nickname: *Centennial State,* because it was admitted to the Union in 1876, America's centennial year.

Colombia (Republic of Colombia). *Colombian,* also an adjective. This is the only New World nation named for Christopher Columbus.

Columbian. A historical name that was sometimes employed for a resident of America, and especially the United States. *Columbia* was once a term for *America*—as when the poet Phillis Wheatley wrote in 1775, "Columbia's scenes of glorious toil I write"—and so its inhabitants were *Columbians,* writing epics like Joel Barlow's *Columbiad.* Christopher Columbus is of course at the root of all this, and *Columbian* is used to describe someone or something that relates to the explorer (such as the 1893 World's Columbian Exposition, held in Chicago to celebrate the 400th anniversary of Columbus's discovery of America).

Columbus, Mississippi. *Columbian.*

Columbus, Ohio. *Columbusite.* The same demonym applies to residents of the Columbuses in Georgia, Indiana, and Nebraska.

Commonwealth of Australia. See AUSTRALIA.

Commonwealth of Dominica. See DOMINICA.

Commonwealth of the Bahamas. See BAHAMAS.

Comoros (Federal Islamic Republic of the Comoros). *Comoran,* also an adjective.

Conch (pronounced "konk"). A lifetime resident of the Florida Keys who was also born there. The term *Freshwater Conch* is used for a person who has lived in the Keys for a decade or more. The term comes from the gastropod that (along with Key lime pie) is integral to the local cuisine. When preparing conch for soup, salad, or fritters, you must beat the tough conch flesh into submission with a mallet or food processor.

Conch was given new relevance as a term of local pride when the Conch Republic was established by secession of the Florida Keys from the United States of America, on April 23, 1982, in response to a United States Border Patrol blockade on highway U.S. 1 at Florida City just to the north of the Florida Keys. Within hours of its placement a 17-mile traffic jam was created as the Border Patrol stopped every car leaving the Keys searching for illegal aliens attempting to enter the mainland United States. The blockade was a detriment to tourism. The day prior to the secession, Key West mayor Dennis Wardlow went to federal court in Miami to seek an injunction to stop the federal blockade, but to no avail. On leaving the federal courthouse, Wardlow, on the courthouse steps, announced to the world, by way of the assembled TV crews and reporters, "Tomorrow at noon the Florida Keys will secede from the Union!"

Wardlow declared independence, which held for a minute, at which point he turned to the admiral in charge of the naval base at Key West and surrendered to the United States, and demanded $1 billion in foreign aid. This created great publicity for the cause and the roadblock and inspection station were soon removed. Since then Conch Independence Day is celebrated every April 23.

Concord, New Hampshire. *Concordite.*

Concordia, Kansas. *Concordian.*

Congo (Republic of the Congo). *Congolese,* which is also an adjective.

Connecticut. *Nutmegger.* The adjective *Nutmegian* is seldom used. There is no hint of derogation in *Nutmegger* despite the fact that it refers to Yankee skulduggery. The demonym takes its name from the long-established state nickname, *Nutmeg State.* The significance of nutmegs was spelled out by William F. Buckley Jr. in the *National Review* (September 16, 1988): "Connecticut traders went out in the seventeenth and eighteenth centuries to sell nutmeg. But when they ran out of the real stuff, they sold sawdust instead, and called it nutmeg; and everyone thought this absolutely hilarious, and Connecticut celebrated its miscreants by nicknaming itself after the symbol of their misdeeds." When New Haven–born George W. Bush became president in 2001, he became the first native of this state to inhabit the White House. The *New York Times* described Bush, who emphasized his Texas roots, as a "reluctant Nutmegger" (December 24, 2000).

A demonym derived from the name of the state has been a matter of long-standing debate and deliberation. For decades the public printer of the United States has used *Connecticuter* in publications created by the Government Printing Office (GPO), but this has been widely ignored and derided outside government ("a display of Federal arrogance" is how William Safire described it in his *New York Times Magazine* column of June 6, 1982).

Columbia University professor Allen Walker Read (who has gone on the record as opposing the GPO's *Connecticuter* with one final *t*) once researched this topic and found an impressive list of early attempts: *Connecticotian* (Cotton Mather, 1702), *Connecticutensian* (Samuel Peters, 1781), and *Connecticutter* (a California periodical, *Land of Sunshine*, 1897). The last reference may have been intended as a slur: "All the gates the [Hartford] *Courant* can put up will not keep the steady stream of Connecticutters from migrating to California."

A number of good writers have used the *-cuter* demonym. Stephen Vincent Benet used it in his 1944 work *America* and a 1948 citation in the Merriam-Webster files from one of its editors notes: "Throughout Van Wyck Mason's *Eagle in the Sky* he uses Connecticuter to designate a person from Connecticut. He also uses Massachusetter a few times."

After these came *Connectican* (1942), *Connecticutan* (1946), *Connecticutian* (1947), and *Connecticutite* (1968). In addition to these serious suggestions Read found six jocular alternatives: *Quonaughicotter* (from H. L. Mencken), *Connecticutey*, *Connecticanuck*, *Connectikook* (from Read himself), *Connectecotton*, and *Connecticutist*. J. Baxter Newgate, a writer known

Historical Society announces the 14th annual Cracker Supper, at which traditional backwoods food is served and newcomers are inducted as honorary Crackers. However, after the popular comic strip *Bloom County* used the term in jest in 1985, the *Washington Post* carried a letter from a man terming the word an "ethnic slur" and "a demeaning and insensitive insult to a large and virtually defenseless group of Americans" (June 4, 1985).

wthumper. Traditional nickname for a resident of Maryland, originally applied to Roman Catholics, who congregated in the state.

ole. A person of French descent native to the American South, especially Louisiana.

te. *Cretan* (also an adjective), sometimes *Crétois,* which is the name used by French speakers.

atia (Republic of Croatia). *Croat* is the demonym while the adjective is *Croatian.*

w-eater. Slang term for a resident of South Australia. Early European settlers in this state are said to have eaten crows when other food was lacking. See BANANA-BENDER, where the sometimes derogatory nature of this term is discussed.

zan. Resident of Saint Croix, Virgin Islands of the United States.

a (Republic of Cuba). *Cuban,* also an adjective.

mberland, England. People from the area of this former county are known as *Cumberlanders* or *Cumbrians,* from *Cumbria,* which was the medieval Latin name of an ancient Celtic kingdom in northwest Britain and is now the name of a modern county that encompasses both the old Cumberland and Westmorland Counties. Hence *Cumbrian* is a regional demonym used long before

for his skillful wordplay, suggested *Connecticutlet.* A letter to the editor of the *Willimantic* (Connecticut) *Journal* (May 20, 1988) from Babs Johnson suggests a blend of *Connecticut* and *Yankee* to form *Connecticutee.* The suggestion *Connecticutup* is made in the May 1988 issue of *Word Ways.* Allan D. Pratt of New Haven, with an eye to the parkways and train lines, has pointed out that "by far the most common term used to describe residents of Connecticut is 'Commuters.'"

Traditional personal nicknames: *Nutmeg, Nutmegger,* and *Wooden Nutmeg.* State nicknames: *Nutmeg State* and *Constitution State;* another notable nickname is less common: *Land of Steady Habits.*

Since 2003, when a series of corruption scandals, including one involving the governor, were revealed, the term *Corrupticut* has come into play along with *Connection-cut* and *Criminalicut.* A *New York Times* headline of March 28, 2003, reads, "The Nutmeg State Battles the Stigma of Corrupticut."

Cook Islands. *Cook Islander.*

Cooperative Republic of Guyana. See GUYANA.

Copenhagen, Denmark. *Copenhagener.*

Cork, Ireland. *Corkonian.*

Cormoros. *Cormoran.* Cormoros is a group of South African islands at the northern mouth of the Mozambique Channel, about two-thirds of the way between northern Madagascar and northern Mozambique. The 2005 CIA *World Factbook* calls Cormoros "unstable," having endured 19 coups or attempted coups since gaining independence from France in 1975.

Corn Cracker. Traditional nickname for a resident of Kentucky; it was also once used generally for a southern "poor white," though original contextual evidence is sparse. In this sense it is synonymous with *Cracker,* and has even been put forth as the origin of that word. Some have claimed that *Corn Cracker* comes from a rural diet of cracked corn, while another view deems it an alteration of *corncrake,* the name of a bird.

Cornhusker. Resident of Nebraska, although *Nebraskan* is allowed. Headline in the *Hill,* the newspaper of Capitol Hill, for August 16, 1995: "Cornhuskers in Congress."

Cornstalk. Resident of New South Wales, Australia. This and other Australian nicknames should be used with caution.

Cornwall, England. *Cornishman* or *Cornishwoman.* Adjective: *Cornish,* as in "Cornish game hen." Jay Ames, who has collected many demonyms, has spotted examples of *Cornwallian* and *Cornwellian.* A common nickname for Cornish individuals is either *Cousin Jack* or *Cousin Jenny.*

Cornwall, Ontario. *Cornwallite.*

Corpus Christi, Texas. *Corpus Christian,* regardless of religious affiliation.

Corsica, France. *Corsican.*

Corvallis, Oregon. *Corvallisian.*

Coshocton, Ohio. *Coshoctonian.*

Costa Rica (Republic of Costa Rica). In English *Costa Rican.* It has been written as one word, *Costarican,* though this form is less common than it once was. Increasingly, however, the colloquial *Tico* is being used by Costa Ricans to describe themselves. The name of the national soccer team is *The Ticos.* The term comes from the habit of rural people to end words or phrases of dimunition with *-ico* rather than the conventional *-ito.* In the

book *The Ticos: Culture and Social Change* enner, 1999) by Mavis Hiltunen Biesanz, Kar Richard Biesanz, the authors state: "Costa R their special country. In 1949 it became the fi Americas to banish its Army, a fact that many cans call themselves, attribute to their tend agreements peacefully through dialog and con

Côte d'Ivoire. See IVORY COAST.

Cotton-Mainie. Traditional nickname for a reside origin is uncertain.

Cottonwood, Arizona. *Cottonwoodite.*

Council Bluffs, Iowa. *Council Bluffsian.*

countian. Generic term used in designating a coun specific name does not exist or is too cumberso article in the *Kansas City Star:* "The Johnso nity College Foundation named Overland Park Johnson Countian of the Year for 2005" (March 11, 1992, *Houston Chronicle* headline reads: ' Trade TV for Tradition, Exit Polls for a Song," county 90 miles north of Houston.

Covington, Kentucky. *Covingtonian.*

Cowboy. Traditional nickname for a resident of Te>

Cowtowner. Traditional nickname for a resident of

Cracker. Southern United States backwoodsman, siding in Georgia and Florida. Like so many type, this one can be regarded as a slur or affe pending on its context. A 1988 notice from th the modern county was formed in 1974; as far back as 1747 it was applied to the inhabitants of ancient Cumbria in historical writing. *Cumberland* derived from *Cumbria,* and so a *Cumberlander* is likewise a *Cumbrian.*

Cumberland, Maryland. *Cumberlander.*

Cyprus (Republic of Cyprus). *Cypriot.* The alternative *Cypriote* is acceptable.

Cytherean. The adjective now generally used to describe the planet Venus and its hypothetical inhabitants, and deriving from Latin *Cytheria,* another name for Aphrodite, the Greek Venus.

Czechoslovak. Now of historic interest, this was the term for the population of Czechoslovakia as a whole, but *Czech* was used for those in the Czech lands (Bohemia and Moravia-Silesia) and *Slovak* for those in Slovakia. It is significant that 300,000 ethnic Slovaks declared themselves citizens of the Czech Republic in 1994 and the European Union in 2004 (according to the Central Intelligence Agency's *World Factbook*). Similarly, over half a million ethnic Hungarians are residents of Slovakia, the demonym for which (*Slovak*) can have specific ethnic application.

Czech Republic; *formerly* **Czech Socialist Republic.** *Czech,* also an adjective.

Dagestan, Russia. *Dagestani.* Dagestan is the most Islamic of Russia's regions. It has the largest proportion of practicing Islamic believers anywhere in Russia, with over 90 percent of its population being practicing Muslims.

Dahomey. See BENIN.

Dakotan. Resident of North Dakota or South Dakota (qq.v.).

Dallas, Texas. *Dallasite.*

The Dalles, Oregon. *Dallesite.*

Danbury, Connecticut. *Danburian.*

Dane. A resident of Denmark.

Danube. People who live along this European river are called *Danubians.*

Danvers, Massachusetts. *Danversite.*

Danzig, Poland. *Danziger.* *Danzig* is the historic and German name for Gdánsk. The territory surrounding and including Gdánsk was a free city between the two world wars.

Darbian *or* **Darbyite.** Resident of Derbyshire, England.

Darwin, Australia. *Darwinian.*

Davenport, Iowa. *Davenporter.*

Davidson, North Carolina. *Davidsonian.*

Dawson, Yukon Territory. *Dawsonite,* according to Doug Bell, publisher of the *Yukon News* in Whitehorse.

Dayton, Ohio. *Daytonian.*

Daytona Beach, Florida. *Daytonan.*

Dearborn, Michigan. *Dearbornite.*

Decatur, Illinois. *Decaturian.* H. L. Mencken noted in "What the People of American Towns Call Themselves" that this was the "name of the student newspaper at James Millikin University, Decatur. But Mr. B. F. Engleman, of the Decatur *Herald,* tells me that it is not used by his paper, which prefers *resident of Decatur.*"

Delaware. *Delawarean.* A June 7, 1992, *Baltimore Evening Sun* article on the town of Delmar (so named because it is half in Delaware and half in Maryland) employs this demonym: "The line of demarcation is State Street, the main east-west town corridor that defines the 960 folks who live on the north side as Delaware-ans and the 1,430 who live on the south side as Marylanders."

Traditional personal nicknames: *Blue Hen* and *Muskrat.*

State nicknames: *First State, Diamond State* (in that it is small and precious), and *Blue Hen State*—from the fact that a Revolutionary War commander liked to bet on cockfights, in which he favored the "blue hen's" chickens. His brigade was soon called the Blue Hen Brigade and the name was later adopted as a state nickname.

Delhiite *or* **Delhite.** Resident of New Delhi, India.

Del Mar, California. *Del Martian* (jocular, but used).

Delmarva. *Delmarvan. Delmarva* is the informal name for the peninsula situated to the east of Chesapeake Bay. The name comes from the names of the three states that have part of the peninsula: *Del*aware, *Mar*yland, and *Vir*ginia.

Democratic and Popular Republic of Algeria. See ALGERIA.

Democratic People's Republic of Korea. See KOREA, NORTH.

Democratic Republic of Afghanistan. See AFGHANISTAN.

Democratic Republic of São Tomé and Príncipe. See SÃO TOMÉ AND PRÍNCIPE.

Democratic Socialist Republic of Sri Lanka. See SRI LANKA.

Denmark (Kingdom of Denmark). *Dane.* Adjective: *Danish,* as in *Danish pastry* or *Danish seine.* Danish as a modifier of pastry has had interesting consequences. In the summer of 2005 when the Canadians threatened to ban Danish pastry over a fishing tiff, a writer to the *Financial Times* (August 4, 2005) noted the ban might not send the intended message, as the Danes call these pastries *Wienerbred.*

Denver, Colorado. *Denverite.* Mencken noted in his article "What the People of American Towns Call Themselves" that "Mr. Lawrence Martin, managing editor of the *Denver Post*, says that his paper 'uses this name sparingly.'"

A common commercial adjective in this "Mile-High City" is *Mile-High.* There are, according to one report, famous examples like Mile-High Stadium and "enough other Mile-High (or -Hi) shops, parks, schools and churches to fill four columns of the Denver telephone directory" (*Washington Post*, May 28, 1985).

Déodatien. Resident of Saint-Dié, France.

Department of Guadeloupe. See GUADELOUPE.

Department of Réunion. See RÉUNION.

Derbyshire, England. *Darbyite* or *Darbian.*

Des Moines, Iowa. *Des Moinesite* or *Des Moineser.*

Detroit, Michigan. *Detroiter.* The language of the American automobile trade has been called *Detroitese* and many references to the city (i.e., "Detroit's thinking on imports") allude to the automobile industry rather than the actual city.

Devonshire, England. *Devonian* or *Devonite.*

Digger. Traditional nickname for a resident of Nevada.

Dijon, France. *Dijonese.*

Dismalite. Resident of the Great Dismal Swamp, the large marshy tract extending from southeastern Virginia well into northeastern North Carolina. Mitford Mathews's *Dictionary of Americanisms* has a citation from 1775.

District of Columbia. *Washingtonian,* not *Columbian,* although one of the common suggestions for the name of the district should it ever become the 51st state is *New Columbia.*

Dixie. Nickname for the United States South. The demonym *Dixieite* has been cited in Mathews's *Dictionary of Americanisms,* but it is rare and the term *Southerner* is almost always used. The opposite is true for the North, where *Yankee* is common for a *Northerner* but the region is seldom called "Yankeedom." As an adjective *Dixie* shows up as a pure synonym for *Southern* (as in "Dixie Mafia" for Southern gangsters) and in compounds such as *Dixiecrat,* the name for the rebellious anti-Truman Southern Democrats of 1948. The title of a 1930 film, *Dixiana,* is probably a play on the term *Americana* ("A circus performer falls for an heir in 1840s' New Orleans during Mardi Gras" is the brief description of the film in a newspaper).

Djibouti (Republic of Djibouti); *formerly* **French Territory of the Afars and the Issas.** *Djibouti.*

Dodge City, Kansas. *Dodge Citian.*

Dominica (Commonwealth of Dominica). *Dominican.* Residents of this small island-nation in the West Indies share this name with residents of the Dominican Republic and members of the Roman Catholic mendicant order founded by Saint Dominic in 1215.

Dominican Republic. *Dominican.*

Dorpian. Resident of Schenectady, New York (q.v.), and an alternative to *Schenectadian.*

Dorsetshire, England. *Dorsetian.*

Dothan, Alabama. *Dothanite.*

Doubting Thomas. Traditional nickname for a resident of Missouri, apparently from the legendary skepticism of the *Show Me State.*

Down Easter. One from Down East, the realm from Boston to the tip of Maine. It is usually applied to Mainers and is so common there that the magazine devoted to the state is called *Down East.* In fact, the *Associated Press Stylebook and Libel Manual* stipulates that it only be used in reference to Maine: "the terms *Down East* and *Down Easter* are not used for anything or anyone not from Maine as they imply a certain traditionalism and local color."

   Several theories have been advanced on the origin of the term. The following one appears in a display of Down East schooners at the Penobscot Marine Museum in Searsport, Maine: "Down East, a nautical term which can be traced to the 1800s. Coastal schooners sailed from Boston to Maine setting their course northeast. They sailed with the prevailing southwest wind or downwind; hence, the term Down East. Down Easter [is a] person or vessel hailing from that region." A second theory, which is described in William and Mary Morris's *Harper Dictionary of Contemporary Usage,* is that it started as a carryover of a British speech pattern in which anyone going to London is going *up* to London and anyone leaving is going *down* to wherever it is he or she is going. This use of *up* and *down* obtains regardless of the direction where one is coming from or going to. The Morrises suggest that this usage was applied to early Boston—the self-described Hub of the Universe—and that to head out of town was to go "down east" or down to Maine.

down-Islander. See ISLANDER.

Down Under. Nickname for Australia and New Zealand together.

Dublin, Ireland. *Dubliner.* From *Lonely Planet Dublin* (Lonely Planet, 2004) by Fionn Davenport and Martin Hughes: "The purest of the species claim to hail from generations all born within the canals, although the label 'Dubliner' perhaps has as much to do with a state of mind as a birthright these days."

Du Bois, Pennsylvania. *Du Boisite.*

Dubuque, Iowa. *Dubuquer.*

Duluth, Minnesota. *Duluthian.*

Dundee, Scotland. *Dundonian.*

Dunelmian. Resident of Durham City, England.

Dunkirk, New York. *Dunkirker.*

Dun-le-Palleteau, Dun-sur-Aurons, *and* **Dun-sur-Meuse, France.** According to the "Word Wurcher" in "*D'où Êtes-Vous* Revisited" (*Word Ways,* August 1986), these three towns have separate demonyms: people from Dun-le-Palleteau and Dun-sur-Aurons are *Dunois* while those from Dun-sur-Meuse are *Duniens.*

Dunmore, Pennsylvania. *Dunmorean.*

Dunois. Resident of Dun-le-Palleteau or Dun-sur-Aurons, France.

Duquesne, Pennsylvania. *Duquesneite.*

Du Quoin, Illinois. *Du Quoinite.*

Durango, Colorado. *Durangoite.*

Durban, South Africa. *Durbanite.*

Durham, North Carolina. *Durhamite.*

Durham City, England. *Dunelmian.*

Düsseldorf, Germany. *Düsseldorfer.*

Dutch. Adjective used for the Netherlands. The corresponding names for individual residents are *Dutchman* and *Dutchwoman.* The term *Dutch* has many legitimate uses; however, it also has a long history as an adjective of derogation. All evidence points to this negative use of *Dutch* originating in the British Isles and then moving to the United States.

Why the good people of the Netherlands have been made to suffer so in English calls for some explanation. The pejorative use of *Dutch* dates back to the 17th century when the British and the Dutch fought over control of the sea and parts of the New World. Not only did the British start the tradition of hostile *Dutch* slurs, but they also wiped out Dutch names when territory changed hands. New Amsterdam became New York as soon as the British took over in 1664. In *The American Language,* Supplement I, H. L. Mencken traced the English use of the derisive *Dutch* back to 1608, but adds that many of the slurs started in the United States, where some may have been aimed at Germans who had been called "Dutch" for generations. This came about because German immigrants referred to themselves as *Deutsch,* German for "German." Those with the nickname *Dutch* were, in fact, seldom from the Netherlands but rather of German background. For this reason, many a Dutch immigrant referred to himself as a *Hollander* or *Netherlander.*

One *Dutch* term, "Dutch courage," appears to have come from an actual facet of Dutch naval life and not just from generalized dislike of an opponent. In their *Naval Terms Dictionary,* John V. Noel and Edward L. Beach give it this definition and etymology: "The courage obtained from drink. Comes from the custom initiated by the famous Dutch Admirals, Tromp and de Ruyter, of giving their crews a liberal libation before battle with the English. The practice was naturally belittled by the English, who nevertheless were forced to admit to the effectiveness of the Dutch Navy."

When you consult slang dictionaries dating back to 1811 and a number of other specialized dictionaries, it becomes apparent how pervasive the long-standing *Dutch* slur has been.

double Dutch = gibberish, also a jump-rope term for jumping with two ropes

Dutch act = suicide

Dutch auction = one that starts with a high bid and works down

Dutch bargain = a one-sided deal, not a bargain at all

Dutch barn = a barn without sides

Dutch bath = an acid bath used in etching

Dutch book = a bookmaker's account book

Dutch brig = a cell in which punishment is meted out

Dutch build = a squat physique

Dutch cap = a condom

Dutch cheese = baldness

Dutch clock = a bedpan

Dutch comfort = consolation typified by the line "It could have been worse" (also known as "Dutch consolation")

Dutch concert = a concert in which everyone plays a different tune or sings a different song (also known as a "Dutch medley")

Dutch courage = bravery inspired by drinking

Dutch daub = a mediocre painting, ironic since there have been so many great Dutch painters

Dutch defense = surrender, no defense at all

Dutch drink = emptying a glass in one gulp

Dutch elm disease = not the same kind of slur as the others, but it goes to show how unlucky the Dutch are when it comes to naming

Dutch feast = a dinner at which the host gets drunk before the guests do or, worse yet, one where the host is drunk before the guests arrive

Dutch fit = a fit of rage

Dutch gleek = liquor

Dutch leave = absence without leave, a term that became popular during the Spanish-American War

Dutch nightingale = a frog

Dutch palate = coarse taste

Dutch pink = blood, a boxing term

Dutch pump = a sailor's punishment in which he is thrown overboard and must pump to keep from drowning

Dutch reckoning = guesswork or a disputed bill

Dutch rod = a Luger

Dutch roll = combined yaw and roll in an aircraft, which is something to be avoided as it can cause a plane to go out of control. It proves that some of these *Dutch* terms are new because the earliest reference that could be found to it was in a 1950 issue of *Popular Science*.

Dutch route = suicide

Dutch row = a faked altercation

Dutch rub = an intense painful rubbing with the knuckles usually of the scalp

Dutch silver = silver plate

Dutch steak = hamburger

Dutch tilt = the tilting of a television or movie camera from the horizontal for dramatic effect

Dutch treat = a meal or entertainment whose price is shared by host and guests, not a treat at all

Dutch uncle = one who reprimands severely

Dutch wheelbarrow = taking someone by the legs as he or she walks with the hands

Dutch widow = a prostitute

Dutch wife (or "Dutch husband") = a feather pillow, a poor bed companion, or more recently an inflatable rubber sex partner

Dutchifying = converting square-sterned ships into round; frequently done to men-of-war in the early 19th century

Dutchman = a piece of wood or stone used to fill a hollow space

Dutchman's anchor = anything left at home, from the tale

of a Dutch sea captain who explained after he had lost
his ship that he had a good anchor but left it at home

Dutchman's breeches = a small blue patch in the sky. A
note from James Elsaesser of Cincinnati says: "You
may be interested to know that a friend, now old,
who grew up on a farm near here, calls the delicate,
little blue and white wildflowers which peep up in
early spring as Dutchman's breeches." This term for
a plant elsewhere called *bleeding heart* is common
in the Northern and North Midland dialect areas of
the United States.

Dutchman's cape = an imaginary land

Dutchman's drink = a draught that empties the vessel

Dutchman's headache = drunkenness

Dutchy = slovenly

In addition there are *Dutch* phrases like the following:

as drunk as a Dutchman

Well, I'll be a Dutchman's uncle = an expression of
surprise

It beats the Dutch = applied to anything that is
monstrous, startling, or inexplicable

to do a Dutch = to run away

to get one's Dutch up = to arouse one's temper. Charles
Earle Funk points out in his book *Heavens to Betsy!*
that this is, in fact, a reference to the Pennsylvania
Dutch, who are of course not Dutch but German.

to be in Dutch = to be in trouble

The Dutch have done little to fight back. Noah Jacobs tells us
in his book *Naming Day in Eden* that they do refer to a dirty
trick in the Netherlands as a "German trick" and have been
known to refer to the Scots in references to extreme cheapness.
The only other response, according to Stuart Berg Flexner in
I Hear America Talking, was in 1934 when the government of

the Netherlands ordered its public officials to stop using the name *Dutch* because of its connotations and stick to *the Netherlands*.

If there is any consolation to the Dutch it is that they have been left out of the recent round of ethnic, geographical, and college jokes (with *Newfie, Polack, Aggie,* etc.) and that there are other ethnic slurs and characterizations. In 1944, Abraham Roback published *A Dictionary of International Slurs,* which contained scads of them.

Many terms incorporating geographic adjectives are not slurs but simple, neutral descriptions used in everyday speech (*French toast, Danish pastry, Chinese checkers, Siamese twins, Cuban heels, Canadian bacon, English muffins,* and so forth). Many may well be misnomers—Danish pastry is Vienna bread in Denmark and the English are unfamiliar with what Americans call English muffins—but they are hardly disparaging. On the other hand, we do have:

> American tweezers = burglary tools
> Arizona tenor = a cougher (who has gone to the
>   Southwest for health reasons)
> Chinese fire drill = pandemonium
> German tea = beer
> Indian gift = a gift that one expects to have returned
> Italian perfume = garlic
> Mexican carwash = leaving one's car out in the rain
> Mexican strawberries = beans
> Norwegian Jell-O = lutefisk, so called because it is
>   rubbery and gooey after being soaked and cooked.
>   It has been called far worse names.
> Russian boots = leg irons
> Scotch organ = a cash register
> Spanish padlock = a chastity belt
> Swedish fiddle = a cross-cut saw
> Turkish medal = an unbuttoned fly

See also PENNSYLVANIA DUTCH.

Earth. *Earthling* seems to be the currently preferred demonym. *Earthly* is a common adjective, though *terrestrial* and *world* are often used as well. *Earth* shows up in constructions ranging from songs ("Earth Angel") to NASA satellites like EROS (Earth Resources Observation Satellite). The term is capitalized when it refers to the name of the planet ("the satellite went into Earth orbit"), but not in applications like "down to earth."

Earthling has been the preferred demonym for many years. Here is an example from the March 1966 *Westways:* "When and if a colony of earthlings are established on the moon or Mars, their capacity to re-use waste water may be the one factor that determines how long they can remain to explore those moistureless environments." However, it should be noted that not all *Earthlings* are thrilled with that name; for instance, there are those who are content to be called *human.* And other possibilities do exist. Futurist Ralph E. Hamil may have spoken for a number of people when he wrote to the Central Intelligence Agency, which has prescribed *Earthling,* to comment: "I think of myself as an Earthman. As a noun, Earthling has a diminutive tone; as an adjective, it is derogatory. I am more comfortable with it as a plural noun where the only alternative seems to be Earth People." Hamil came up with a list of alternatives, including the standard English terms *Earthman/Earthwoman, Terrestrial,* and *Earth People,* along with a number from science fiction, including the popular *Terran, Solarian* (a demonym also good for inhabitants of nearby worlds), *Terrestrial Being,* the facetious *Blue Planeteer,* and the derogatory *Earthworm.* Sci-fi terms for the planet include *Terra* (used poetically like *Dixie* or *Columbia*), *Sol III, Blue Planet,* and *Spaceship Earth.* Charles D. Poe has found a number of science-fiction demonyms, including the compounds *Earth-person* and *Earth-human* and the rather nice-sounding *Earther.*

East Asia. *East Asian.* The term *East Asia* is a synonym for *Far East* but less Eurocentric—the "far" in *Far East* is an allusion to its distance from Europe.

East Hampton, New York. *Bonackers,* from the name of the Accabonac Harbor. Originally a name for local fishermen who first settled here in the 17th century, but now used for one born there or having at least one parent from there. It has been puckishly suggested that those who live here as full-time residents but do not qualify for the name get to be called "Year-Round Summer People."

East Timor. *East Timorese.* A nation that came into being in May 2002.

Easterner. One who lives in the eastern United States.

Easton, Pennsylvania. *Eastonian.*

Ecuador (Republic of Ecuador). *Ecuadorean,* also an adjective. One finds examples of *Ecuadoran* and *Ecuadorian* in print, and all three terms can be used as adjectives. The nation takes its name from Spanish *ecuador,* for "equator," which runs through the country, so the demonyms imply the idea of an equatorial person.

Edgartown, Massachusetts. *Edgartonian.*

Edinburgh, Scotland. *Edinburgher.*

Edmonton, Alberta. *Edmontonian.* A common personal nickname is *Oiltowner.*

Egypt (Arab Republic of Egypt); *formerly* **United Arab Republic.** *Egyptian,* also an adjective. Besides the nation in the Middle East, this demonym has been applied to residents of the southern part of Illinois around the city of Cairo, which sits at the confluence of the Ohio and Mississippi Rivers. In George Earlie Shankle's *State Names, Flags, Seals, Songs, Birds, Flowers and Other Symbols,* we are told that the sobriquet was given to the Illinoisians "in all probability, both on account of the fertility of the soil in and around Cairo, Illinois, which resembles that around Cairo, Egypt, after the Nile has flooded, and on account of the fact that the people of southern Illinois are dark-complexioned; thus resembling the inhabitants of Egypt."

Eire. See IRELAND.

El Centro, California. *El Centran.*

Elizabeth, New Jersey. *Elizabethan.*

Elkhart, Indiana. *Elkhartan.*

Ellice Islands. See TUVALU.

Elmira, New York. *Elmiran.*

El Paso, Texas. *El Pasoan.* H. L. Mencken noted that in demonyms for American towns with Spanish names ending in -*o* it is customary to drop the -*o* and add -*an* (*San Franciscan, Palo Altan, Sacramentan,* etc.), and he reported that *El Pasoan* was the only exception he could find.

El Salvador (Republic of El Salvador). *Salvadoran* (also an adjective), although there is some use of *Salvadorian.* The name of the republic means "the Savior" in Spanish, and *San Salvador,* the name of its capital, means "Holy Savior."

Elsewhereian. This term was created by former California governor Goodwin Knight for residents of the state born outside it (elsewhere). It sounds useful enough to have become a generic term, but it does not appear to be used outside the Golden State.

Emirian. Resident of the United Arab Emirates.

Emporia, Kansas. *Emporian.*

England. *Englishman* or *Englishwoman.* Adjective: *English,* which appears in a number of compounds, from *English sparrow* to *English muffin* to *English disease,* an unflattering reference to chronic discontent and declining productivity. From this adjective we get *Englishness,* also known as *Englishry,* defined in *Merriam-Webster's Collegiate Dictionary,* 11th edition, as "the state, fact, or quality of being English."

There has been some question as to when it is proper to use the term *England* and its derivatives when talking or writing about Great Britain. For instance, when *Forbes* magazine wrote about the Germans, Japanese, English, and French in an editorial, a reader wrote to point out, "It is incorrect to call Britain 'England,' just as it would be to refer to Germany as Prussia, France as Burgundy, or Japan as Hokkaido" (December 15, 1986).

Perhaps the best explanation appears in Henry Bradley and Robert Bridges's tract *Briton, British, Britisher:* "the names *England* and *English,* the proper terms that differentiate the southern part of the island and its inhabitants from the northern Scotch and western Welsh parts and their inhabitants, have come to be used for the whole island and all the inhabitants thereof—thereby causing offence to those who wish to maintain their distinctive racial titles unobscured; *England* being thus like the name of the founder or predominant partner in a firm, which may hold onto his name even after his decease."

Englewood, New Jersey. *Englewoodite.*

Épernay, France. *Sparnacien.* The ancient name of this town was *Sparnacum.*

Épinal, France. *Spinalien.* This town was originally called *Spinalium.*

Equatorial Guinea (Republic of Equatorial Guinea); *formerly* **Spanish Guinea.** *Equatorial Guinean* or *Equatoguinean,* which is also an adjective. In the *Wilson Quarterly* (Winter 1991), Robert Klitgaard wrote, "The average Equatoguinean can't expect to live past 45, and every year about 90 percent of the population contracts malaria."

Erie, Pennsylvania. *Erieite.*

Eritrea (State of Eritrea). *Eritrean,* also an adjective.

Escondido, California. *Escondidan.*

Estonia (Republic of Estonia); *formerly* **Estonian Soviet Socialist Republic.** *Estonian* or *Esthonian,* which is based on a less preferred rendering of the country as *Esthonia.* The shortened *Esth* is found in crossword puzzles (four-letter word for "native of Tallinn") but it seems to have little use outside that realm.

Ethiopia. *Ethiopian,* which is also an adjective.

Eu, France. *Eudois.* In "*D'où Êtes-Vous* Revisited" (*Word Ways,* August 1986), the "Word Wurcher" is fascinated by this name because *Eu* began as *Augusta,* which has been whittled to a single vowel sound by linguistic attrition.

Eufaula, Alabama. *Eufaulian.* H. L. Mencken adds in "What the People of American Towns Call Themselves": "Mr. H. L. Upshaw, of the Eufaula *Tribune,* told me that *Eufaulan* is also heard, but only rarely."

Eurasian. A person of European and Asian descent.

Eureka, California. *Eurekan.*

Euro-. Prefix meaning "European," and which appears in seemingly countless coinages along the lines of *Eurosclerosis* (European economic slowdown), *Europessimism* (worries about Europe's economy), and *Eurobashing* (criticizing things European).

Europe. *European.* The question raised by this term is exactly which countries are "European." Are, for instance, Great Britain and Iceland included? The answer varies depending on who is giving it, but according to *Merriam-Webster's Geographical Dictionary,* 3rd edition, those places are indeed part of Europe.

European Union. *Europeans,* in general, but *EU People* is sometimes used to distinguish those whose identity is tied to the EU.

Eurozone. *Eurozoner.* Rare demonym defined by currency. Eurozoners are those living in nations that have accepted the euro as their standard currency. On January 1, 1999, the euro became the national currency for 11 countries in the eurozone. On that date the rate of exchange among currencies of Austria, Belgium, Finland, France, Germany, Holland, Ireland, Italy, Luxembourg, Portugal, and Spain were fixed. Greece joined the euro as the 12th member on January 1, 2001.

Evanston, Illinois. *Evanstonian.*

Evansville, Indiana. *Evansvillian.*

Everglader. Traditional nickname for a resident of Florida.

Exeter, England. *Exonian.* The term is also used for students and graduates of schools with *Exeter* in their name, such as Phillips Exeter Academy in Exeter, New Hampshire.

Extraterrestrial. A being from outside the Earth's atmosphere; it is used as an adjective for anything that is not of Earth.

exurbanite. Generic term for a person living beyond the suburbs in the country who maintains urban ways. It gained popularity in the wake of a book, *The Exurbanites*, by A. C. Spectorsky (1955). His *exurbanites* were a displaced New York couple, disdainful of the suburbs, who moved farther out of town to live beyond their means. It spawned associated terms, such as *ex-exurbanite* for one who returns to the city to live.

Faeroe Islands *or* **Faroe Islands.** *Faeroese* or *Faroese.*

Fairmont, West Virginia. *Fairmonter.*

Falkland Islands. *Falkland Islander.* This possession of the United
Kingdom off the coast of Argentina has been disputed territory
since 1833. The islands are administered by the British but claimed
by the Argentines, who call them *Islas Malvinas.*

Fall River, Massachusetts. *Fall Riverite.*

Far East. *Asian* is much more common than any derivative of *Far
East. Far Eastern* is used as an adjective. *East Asia* is a synonym for *Far East,* and is preferred by those who see an element
of Eurocentrism in the "Far" (from Europe) of *Far East.* This
designation, along with *Near East* and *Middle East,* is not official, but it generally applies to the easternmost portions of Asia.
In order to bring order to vagueness, the National Geographic Society specified the Far East in 1952 as "China, Mongolian Republic, Korea, Japan, the Philippines, Indochina, Thailand, Burma,
Malaya and Indonesia."

In recent years the *Far Eastern Economic Review,* a Dow Jones magazine devoted to analysis about Asia and Asian issues, has been challenged as to appropriateness of the use of, as a reader from Singapore put it in a letter that appeared in the March 15, 2001, issue, "*Far Eastern* is an anachronism based in a time when Britannia ruled the Waves." As of this writing the name remains.

Fargo, North Dakota. *Fargoan.*

Federal Islamic Republic of the Comoros. See COMOROS.

Federal Republic of Germany. See GERMANY.

Federal Republic of Nigeria. See NIGERIA.

Federative Republic of Brazil. See BRAZIL.

Fejø, Sweden. *Fejbattinger.*

fellow. A generic term that is demonymic in a phrase like "fellow Americans," beloved of recent presidents who have often addressed their audiences as "my fellow Americans." Occasionally, after this term is used by the president, the question is raised in newspaper letters and op-ed pages as to whether the adjective is one that excludes women because of the meaning of the word *fellow* for a man, boy, or beau. One letter to the *Washington Post* after the term had been used by President Ronald Reagan suggested the alternative "my associate Americans" (August 26, 1987). If one is to base an answer to this question on the meanings given in standard dictionaries, it must be concluded that there are clear meanings of the term *fellow* that are not linked to gender, in the sense of a *fellow* as a peer, comrade, or associate.

An interesting use of *fellow* is in the term *fellow traveler,* a translation of a Russian word used by the Communist leader Leon Trotsky for a person who goes along with communism without declaring himself: a closet Communist. In his syndicated column "Words," Michael Gartner reveled in the irony of a form letter from a travel agency that began "Dear Fellow Traveler."

Fenwayite. Baseball fan who frequents Boston's Fenway Park. It is an example of a special-case demonym.

Fergus Falls, Minnesota. *Fergusite.*

Fife, Scotland. *Man of Fife* or *Woman of Fife.* People from this area often refer to their realm as "the Kingdom of Fife."

Fifty-first Stater/51st Stater. Facetious reference to any citizen of a nation whose politics and culture appear closely aligned with the United States. This term is used in self-deprecation, or to malign. Usually applied to Canadians, the term can also be used to describe Australians, British, or Israelis.

Fiji (Republic of Fiji). *Fijian.* Sometimes *Fiji* is used as an adjective, as in "Fiji rebels," but *Fijian* is more common.

Filipino. Resident of the Philippines.

Finland (Republic of Finland). *Finn. Finlander* is at best a rarity—*Finn* is overwhelmingly favored. Adjective: *Finnish.* (*Finnish* is well suited to punning headline writers who use it as a play on *finish,* as in "Finnish Line"—the title of a *New Republic* article on a boycott by Finnair pilots [October 31, 1983].) The term is inevitably linked to the word *sauna*—as in the headline "Americans Warming Up to Finnish Saunas." Because of Finland's Cold War relationship with the former Soviet Union, the term *Finlandization* has come to mean keeping a balance between independence and subservience.

Flagstaff, Arizona. *Flagstaffian,* according to H. L. Mencken in "What the People of American Towns Call Themselves." He added, "Mr. James D. Walkup, of the Flagstaff Chamber of Commerce, tells me that this is not used by residents, but seems to be accepted in other parts of the state. Flagstaffite is never heard."

Flanders, Belgium. *Flemish,* also an adjective.

Flatlander. Term used by people in hilly or mountainous areas to describe those on level ground. For instance the people on the Upper Peninsula of Michigan call their southern Michigan counterparts *flatlanders.* The term was given currency in the long-running *Barney Google and Snuffy Smith* comic strip in which Snuffy, a moonshine-making loafer who lives in Hootin' Holler, is always having to deal with "Flatland Furriners." In a typical strip, a flatland art dealer comes to buy quilts made by Snuffy's wife Loweezy. The dealer insists they are pieces of history. Snuffy demurs: "Well, if you say so, but as I recall . . . thar mostly pieces of pants!!"

Flickertail. Traditional nickname for a resident of North Dakota, from the state nickname *Flickertail State,* which in turn derives from the flickertail, a squirrel found in the area that flicks its tail.

Flin Flon, Manitoba. *Flin Floner.*

Flint, Michigan. *Flintite.*

Florence, Italy. *Fiorentini* is what the natives call themselves. A headline in the *Toronto Star* for March 15, 1997, read, "Renaissance City: When Florence Overwhelms, Do as the Fiorentini Do—Take a Gelati Break."

Florentine is the common English adjective for the city that is called *Firenze* in Italy. In culinary parlance, *Florentine* is applied to dishes served or dressed with spinach.

Florida. *Floridian* is clearly proper while the rare *Floridan* is now without any broad support, even though the point is made from time to time that *Floridan* hews to convention and that a *Floridian* should rightly be a resident of a place called *Floridia.* At one time, there were those who strongly favored *Floridan,* but by the time H. L. Mencken wrote his 1947 article "Names for Americans," the majority of the newspapers in the state had adopted *Floridian.*

In 1999 the Florida Chamber of Commerce did a survey and found that 75 percent of the state's 15 million residents were born outside of Florida. Of the nonnatives polled 71 percent said they called themselves *Floridians.* The *Florida Times-Union* said on July 24, 1999, that this flew in the face of the conventional wisdom that said nonnatives felt no particular loyalty to the state.

Traditional personal nicknames: *Alligator, Cracker* (q.v.), *Everglader, Gator, Fly-up-the-Creek,* and *Gulfer.*

State nicknames: *Sunshine State, Gulf State, Flowery State,* and *Saint Peter's Waiting Room* (where, part-time Floridian Ben Willis said, "We senior denizens struggle to keep minds and bodies active while awaiting the Great Flight").

Fontainebleau, France. *Bellifontain.*

Formosa. The demonyms *Taiwanese* and *Chinese* are much more common than *Formosan* for residents of Formosa, the main island of Taiwan that is usually called *Taiwan.* See also TAIWAN.

Fort Scott, Kansas. *Fort Scotter.*

Fort Wayne, Indiana. *Fort Waynite.*

Fort Worth, Texas. *Fort Worthian.* However, the less popular and less awkward-sounding *Fort Worther* has been cited in print and *Fort Worthan* has been spotted as close to the place in question as the *Houston Post* (June 27, 1988). Here is an example of the *-ian* ending from the *Dallas Morning News* of December 17, 1994: "Former Fort Worthian Betty Buckley also received Bum Steer recognition for her recent Dallas concert during which she forgot the words to the tune she made famous on Broadway in Cats. The song was Memory."

Fox. Traditional nickname for a resident of Maine.

France (French Republic). *Frenchman* or *Frenchwoman.* Adjective: *French.* In the English-speaking world the word *French* has been associated with sex, as in *French kiss, French disease* (syphilis), and *French letter* (a condom).

Franco-Canadian. A French Canadian (q.v.).

Franco-Ontarian. A Canadian of French ancestry living in Ontario, a province whose population is predominantly British in ancestry. "Marchand was born in Shawinigan, Que., but has lived most of his 47 years in Ontario, Europe and Asia. He says he thinks of himself as a Franco-Ontarian." *The Guelph Mercury,* October 11, 2005.

Frankfort, Kentucky. *Frankfortian.*

Frankfurt, Germany. *Frankfurter.*

Franklin, Pennsylvania. *Franklinite.*

Frederick, Maryland. *Frederictonian.*

French Canadian. Resident of Canada whose ancestry and/or whose native tongue is French; sometimes replaced by *Franco-Canadian. French Canadian* is spelled without a hyphen, according to the *Associated Press Stylebook and Libel Manual* and *Merriam-Webster's Collegiate Dictionary,* 11th edition, making it an exception to the normal practice of hyphenating terms of dual ethnicity.

French Guiana (Department of French Guiana). *French Guianese* or *French Guianan.* Both terms are also adjectives.

French Guinea. See GUINEA.

Frenchman/Frenchwoman. Resident of France.

French Polynesia (Territory of French Polynesia). *French Polynesian,* which is also an adjective.

French Republic. See FRANCE.

French Territory of the Afars and the Issas. See DJIBOUTI.

Fresno, California. *Fresnan.*

Friscan *or* **Friscoite.** Terms applied to residents of San Francisco, California, who probably view them with the same disdain they reserve for those who call the city *Frisco.* Writing under a San Francisco dateline, George Vecsey of the *New York Times* reported on October 11, 1987, "The locals call it The City and it's a $500 fine for any yokel who calls it Frisco."

Futuna Islands. *Futunan.* See also WALLIS AND FUTUNA islands.

Gabon (Gabonese Republic). *Gabonese,* which is also an adjective.

Gadsden, Alabama. *Gadsdenite.*

Galena, Illinois. *Galenian.*

Galesburg, Illinois. *Galesburger.* When Allen Walker Read, Professor Emeritus of English at Columbia University, was interviewed on the subject of Illinois names, he noted that you could buy a hamburger called a *Galesburger* in a restaurant here.

Galicia. *Galician.* Researcher Charles D. Poe has found the alternative *Galicianer* in print: "Undeniably, Galicianers were also clever, resourceful and determined . . ." (George Jonas, *Vengeance,* 1984). Poe also found *Galitzianer* in Leo Rosten's *The Joys of Yiddish,* for a Jew from Galicia. *Galician* itself has had the specialized sense of "a Galician Jew from Poland" (*Webster's Third New International Dictionary*).

Galilee. *Galilean. Galilean* is also an adjectival derivative of the name *Galileo.*

Gallipolis, Ohio. *Gallipolitan.* H. L. Mencken quotes the *Gallipolis Tribune* (May 18, 1944): "The term we usually use to designate residents of our town is Gallipolitan. One of our editors, a few years ago, referred to them as *Gallipots,* but that was irritating to some of our leading citizens. Gallipolisian might be more logical, but we newspaper folk are always trying to find shorter words."

Galloway, Scotland. *Gallovidian,* though *Galwegian* is often seen.

Gallup, New Mexico. *Gallupite.*

Galveston, Texas. *Galvestonian.* A July 14, 1990, article in the *Dallas Morning News* on boxer Jack Johnson describes a World War I monument with his name on it: "Underneath the line, four names were separated from the rest of their fellow Galvestonians with the word, 'Colored.'"

Galway, Ireland. *Galwayman* or *Galwaywoman.*

The Gambia (Republic of The Gambia). *Gambian,* which is also an adjective.

Gary, Indiana. *Garyite.*

Gas. Resident of Accra, Ghana.

Gaspé Peninsula, Canada. *Gaspésian.*

Gator. Traditional nickname for a resident of Florida.

Gaza Strip. *Gazan.* As the Gaza border crossing with Egypt reopened in 2005, the *Kansas City Star* reported, "Gazans go to Egypt for vacation, to study or to receive medical care, and ties have long been close" (November 26, 2005).

Geneva, Switzerland. *Genevan* or *Genevese.*

Genoa, Italy. *Genoan* or *Genovese.*

Geordie. A resident or native of northeastern England and especially Tyneside, the district on each side of the Tyne River that includes the cities of Newcastle upon Tyne and Gateshead. (*Geordieland* is an affectionate local label for the area.) *Geordie* is a diminutive form of *George,* but why it was applied to coal miners, other Tynesiders, Scots, and even a ship for transporting coal is something of a mystery.

Georgia. *Georgian.*

Traditional personal nicknames: *Buzzard, Cracker, Goober Grabber,* and *Sandhiller.*

State nicknames: *Peach State, Empire State of the South,* and *Cracker State.* The name *Peach State* was adopted officially in 1939 by the Georgia General Assembly, which boasted that the state produced "more peaches than any state east of the Pacific Coast with California only leading her in the peach industry."

Georgia (Republic of Georgia); *formerly* **Georgian Soviet Socialist Republic.** *Georgian.*

Germany (Federal Republic of Germany). *German,* also an adjective. The adjective *Germanic* can mean "German" but has specific linguistic application as well.

Germans from the Rhine River area are sometimes called *Rhinelanders* and this term is sometimes incorrectly applied generally to any German. *German* has led to many other words, including *Germanism, Germanize,* and *Germanophile. Germania* is an ancient Latin name for the region that Adolf Hitler wanted to give Berlin after it had been modernized.

Of historic interest are the terms *West German* and *East German,* which had wide use before the reunification of West Germany and East Germany in 1990. The use of *East German* was politically sensitive as East Germans did not refer to themselves this way.

Gettysburg, Pennsylvania. *Gettysburgian.*

Ghana (Republic of Ghana). *Ghanaian,* also an adjective.

Gibraltar. *Gibraltarian.*

Gilbert Islands. See KIRIBATI.

Glasgow, Scotland. *Glaswegian.* Here is the term in a letter that appeared in the *Times* of London on September 5, 1996: "Sir, Glaswegians have known how to pronounce Edinburgh for over 20 years. The correct version is 'Embrer' . . ."

Glassport, Pennsylvania. *Glassporter.*

Glendale, California. *Glendalian.*

Goa, India. *Goanese,* though *Goan* is sometimes used.

Gold Coaster. Traditional nickname for a resident of California.

Gold Digger. Traditional nickname for a resident of California.

Goober Grabber. Traditional nickname for a resident of Arkansas or Georgia.

Gopher. Traditional nickname for a resident of Minnesota.

Gothamite. Resident of New York City. In his *Phrase and Word Origins,* Alfred H. Holt claims that this term was first applied to New Yorkers in 1805 by Washington Irving. (Mathews's *Dictionary of Americanisms* has an Irving citation from 1807.) Holt explains *Gotham* for New York thus: "The inhabitants of Gotham, in England, had long been celebrated as fools (though one story has it that they got their reputation by playing the fool intentionally to avoid the expense of having to entertain the king). Irving's satirical application of the name to New York was an allusion to the Manhattanite's traditional air of 'knowing it all.'" Gotham City is the home of comic book hero Batman, and across the river is New Guernsey.

Grand Duchy of Luxembourg. See LUXEMBOURG.

Grand Forks, North Dakota. *Grand Forker.*

Grand Island, Nebraska. *Grand Islander.*

Grand Rapids, Michigan. *Grand Rapidian,* though H. L. Mencken reported use of *Grand Rapidsite.*

Grasshopper. Traditional nickname for a resident of Kansas.

Great Britain *or* **Britain.** *Briton.* See also BRIT, ENGLAND, SCOTLAND, and WALES.

Great Dismal Swamp. *Dismalite* (q.v.).

Great Plains. One who lives on these United States prairie lands that extend from the Missouri River to the Rocky Mountains and from North Dakota to Texas is a *Plainsman* or *Plainswoman.*

Greece (Hellenic Republic). *Greek.* Adjective: *Greek* or *Hellenic,* with the latter term referring especially, though not exclusively, to ancient Greece.

Greenland. *Greenlander.* Adjective: *Greenlandic.*

Greensboro, North Carolina. *Greensburgher.*

Greenville, South Carolina. *Greenvillian.*

Grenada. *Grenadian* or *Grenadan;* both are also adjectives.

Grosse Pointe, Michigan. *Grosse Pointer.*

Guadalajara, Mexico. *Tapatío,* also an adjective and nickname for
the place, as in the Hotel Tapatío.

Tapatío is a brand of hot sauce produced in Vernon, California, that can be found at most grocery stores in the United States.
Many Mexican restaurants feature a bottle of Tapatío on the
table. According to the company's Web site "Jose-Luis Saavedra
Sr. started the Tapatío Hot Sauce Company in 1971 as a privately
held business and it continues being that way. The product's
name *'Tapatío'* means a person born in Guadalajara, capital of
the state of Jalisco in Mexico." The hot sauce is used in a number
of foods and drinks including the *Martini Tapatío* or *Tapatío
Dirty Martini.**

Guadeloupe (Department of Guadeloupe). *Guadeloupian* or
Guadeloupean; both are also adjectives.

Guam. *Guamanian,* and not *Guaman.* This demonym—with its
double suffix—has an interesting history, which was outlined in a
long letter that appeared in the September 1, 1950, issue of the
Washington Star and was written by Martha L. Jay of the *Guam
Echo.* She wrote in response to a letter to the *Star* asking why
Guamanians were called Guamanians. Her response in part:

The native inhabitants of the Marianas Islands where
Guam is located were originally known as Chamorros. However, after Guam came under the jurisdiction of the United

---

* *Martini Tapatío*

Vodka
Vermouth
Olive juice (hence the name dirty)
2 Olives
2 to 10 shots (drops of Tapatío)

Served in a chilled Martini glass

States in 1898 and after the other Marianas Islands went to the Japanese under a League of Nations mandate at the end of World War I, the people of Guam assiduously cultivated American ways and philosophy. During World War II the Guamanians suffered hideously at the hands of the Japanese because of their loyalty to America and because of their many heroic deeds (not the least of which was the driving of the Japanese from one end of the Island of Guam).

After World War II the people of Guam determined to separate themselves as distinctly as possible from those Chamorros who had been under Japanese jurisdiction between World War I and World War II. It was then that the Chamorros of Guam evolved the desire to be called Guamanians. There was, during the prewar period, some debates as to the relative merits of the names "Guamians," "Guamanians," and "Guamericans." Apparently, it was felt that "Guamanians" was more pleasing to the ear than either of the other two choices.

Beginning with the 1990 United States Census, *Guamanian* is one of nine Asian-Pacific groups that a respondent can check off under the question of race (the others: Chinese, Filipino, Hawaiian, Korean, Vietnamese, Japanese, Asian-Indian, and Samoan).

Guatemala (Republic of Guatemala). *Guatemalan* (also an adjective) is the conventional choice, but *Guatemalteco* is used as well (as William Safire put it in his *New York Times Magazine* column of June 6, 1982, "When you're in Guatemala, do as the *Guatemaltecos* do").

Guernsey (Bailiwick of Guernsey). *Channel Islander;* or *Guernseyman* or *Guernseywoman.*

Guinea (Republic of Guinea); *formerly* **French Guinea.** *Guinean,* which is also an adjective.

Guinea-Bissau (Republic of Guinea-Bissau); *formerly* **Portuguese Guinea.** *Guinea-Bissauan,* which is also an adjective.

Gulfer. Traditional nickname for a resident of Florida.

Gun Flint. Traditional nickname for a resident of Rhode Island (q.v.).

Guthrie, Oklahoma. *Guthrian.*

Guthrie Center, Iowa. *Guthrian.*

Guyana (Cooperative Republic of Guyana); *formerly* **British Guiana.** *Guyanese* (both singular and plural), which is also an adjective.

habitant. According to the *Dictionary of Canadianisms* this term is used for (1) a farmer in French Canada, originally a person holding land from a seigneur, and (2) any French Canadian, especially from rural Quebec. Capitalized and plural it is a nickname of the Montreal Canadiens hockey team, often shortened to *Habs*.

Hackensack, New Jersey. *Hackensackite.*

Hagerstown, Maryland. *Hagerstowner.*

The Hague, Netherlands. *Hagenaar.*

Haiti (Republic of Haiti). *Haitian*, also an adjective.

Halifax, Nova Scotia. *Haligonian.* This North American demonym has a long history. Researcher David Shulman has found it in print as early as 1840: "[In] those days Haligonians were proverbial for their hospitality" (*The United Service Magazine*). Shulman also found an example from 1859 in which the term was spelled with two *l*'s, but this must be considered an error or ephemeral variation.

Contemporary nicknames for the city are *The Fax* and *Hali*.

Halluner Moat. Resident of Helgoland (q.v.), the tiny North Sea island that was called "Hitler's Gibraltar" during World War II.

Hamburg, Germany. *Hamburger.*

Hamilton, Ontario. *Hamiltonian* or *Hambletonian.* A traditional slang name is *Steeltowner.* Hamilton in contemporary Canadian slang is often referred to as *The Hammer.*

Hammond, Indiana. *Hammondite.*

Hampshire, England. *Hantsian.*

Hamptonite. Person who lives or vacations in one of the "Hamptons," several towns on the east end of Long Island, New York.

Hanover, Germany. *Hanoverian.* The German ducal house of Hanover produced the British royal House of Hanover, which began with George I's accession to the throne in 1714 and lasted until Queen Victoria's death in 1901. *Hanoverian* was established as an adjective with senses relating to the ducal and royal houses. The noun *Hanoverian* is a demonym for a resident of the city and has stood for a member or supporter of one of the aforementioned houses. The word is also widely used for "a breed of horses developed by crossing heavy cold-blooded German horses with Thoroughbreds" and for "any animal of this breed," according to *Webster's Third New International Dictionary.* For those with an interest in this horse there is even an American Hanoverian Society.

Hanover, Pennsylvania. *Hanoverian.*

Happy Camp, California. *Happy Camper.* "No one today is quite sure how the team got its name," said an article on the town in the *Los Angeles Times* of November 5, 1995, "but it most likely dates to 1852, when the first prospectors found gold in the river and proclaimed themselves exceedingly happy . . . To this date the locals call themselves 'Happy Campers.'"

Hardboot. Traditional nickname for a resident of Kentucky.

Hard Case. Traditional nickname for a resident of Oregon, reportedly from the ruggedness of the early settlers. In *The American Language,* Supplement II, H. L. Mencken claims that the old nickname *Hard-Case State* refers to "the large number of evil characters who flocked into the Oregon country in the early days."

Hardhead. Traditional nickname for a resident of Tennessee.

Harrisburg, Pennsylvania. *Harrisburger.*

Harrovian. Student or graduate of the famous Harrow School, Middlesex, England.

Hartford, Connecticut. *Hartfordite.* In "What the People of American Towns Call Themselves," H. L. Mencken wrote: "Mr. M. S. Sherman, editor of the Hartford *Courant,* tells me that this is 'most commonly applied,' but adds that it is banned from the editorial page of the *Courant.* He says: 'It is, as Artemus Ward would say, 2 mutch.'"

Hashemite Kingdom of Jordan. See JORDAN.

Hatter. Resident of Medicine Hat, Alberta.

Havana, Cuba. *Havanan,* also an adjective.

Haverford, Pennsylvania. *Haverfordian.*

Havre de Grace, Maryland. *Havre de Gracean.*

Hawaii. *Hawaiian* (also an adjective), although *Islander* is often used. For instance, the *World Almanac and Book of Facts* has a category for "Famous Islanders" under the entry for Hawaii. Colloquial term for native born is *kamaaina.* "Airlines and hotels give discounts to residents called *kamaaina* rates," writes James R. Smith in his book *Living and Retiring in Hawaii: The 51st State in the 21st Century* (Universe, 2004).

   State nickname: *Aloha State.*

Hawkeye. Iowa is the *Hawkeye State* and, to a limited degree, an Iowan is a *Hawkeye.* For instance, 19th-century editor and humorist Robert Jones Burdette was known as "the Burlington Hawkeye Man."

Hebrides, Scotland. *Hebridean,* which is also an adjective.

Helgoland, Germany. *Helgolander,* though one finds *Halluner Moat* as a name the islanders call themselves. Helgoland, in the North Sea, was evacuated by Hitler, who used it as a fort, and the islanders were not returned to their battered home until 1952. A 1952 Associated Press article on the return used both *Helgolander* and *Halluner Moat. Helgoland* is sometimes written as *Heligoland* with an *i.*

Hellenic Republic. See GREECE.

Helsinki, Finland. *Helsinkian.*

Herefordshire, England. The demonym for this former county is *Herefordian.*

Herkimer, New York. *Herkimerite.*

Hermian. Term used by Arthur C. Clarke in his *Rendezvous with Rama* for a resident of the planet Mercury and as an adjective descriptive of the planet. This makes sense as Hermes was the Greek equivalent of the Roman god Mercury.

Herring Choker. Slang term for a resident of one of Canada's Maritime Provinces, especially a New Brunswicker. In *Colombo's Canadian References*, John Robert Colombo points out, "So plentiful are herring in the North Atlantic that the Atlantic Ocean was known in the late-seventeenth century as a 'herring pond.'" *Herring Choker* has also been used as a nickname for the Irish from County Galway.

Hertfordshire, England. *Hertfordian* (pronounced "Hartfordian").

Hibbing, Minnesota. *Hibbingite,* but also *Iron Ranger* from the fact that Hibbing is in the Iron Range.

Hibernian. Resident of Ireland. *Hibernian* is also an adjective synonymous with *Irish.*

Hickory, North Carolina. *Hickorite.*

Hilo, Hawaii. *Hiloite.*

Hispanic. Noun and adjective used to describe people of Spanish-speaking ancestry. In North America it is used as a catchall for people with Spanish surnames whose families originally came from Spanish-speaking lands. The term is most useful because it is all-inclusive. In an article in the February 1986 issue of *Word Ways,* the late Dmitri A. Borgmann compiled an admittedly incomplete list of 64 names (friendly, neutral, and derogatory) for various Hispanics found in the United States, including *Afro-Cuban, Chicano* (and the female *Chicana*), *Cuban, Latin American, Mexican, Puerto Rican, South American, Spanish-*

Speaking, and *Spanish-Surnamed.* One must also mention *Latino* and *Latina* (qq.v.).

The term used to describe someone of Latin American descent living in the United States dates back to the early 1970s. According to the *Oxford English Dictionary,* the earliest citation of *Hispanic* occurred in the *New York Times Magazine,* on September 24, 1972: "The fictional melting pot has become a pousse-café in which every layer is jealous of, or hostile to, every other layer; in a fever of ethnicism, Italians, Jews, Orientals, Blacks, Hispanics and others have withdrawn into themselves."

Then as now the drawback to the term is that, in the words of a 1986 *Washington Post* editorial, "'Hispanic' means 'Spanish-speaking,' nothing else." However, it specifically connotes a lineage or cultural heritage related to Spain. In a paper, "Understanding Ethnic Labels and Puerto Rican Identity," posted on the Web page of the Yale–New Haven Teachers Institute, Diana Peña-Pérez noted: "It homogenizes the varied social and political experiences of more than 23 million people of different races, classes, languages, national origins, gender and religions. The term may be cause for offense as to the millions of people who speak Spanish but are not of true Spanish descent."

The National Association of Hispanic Journalists does in fact use the term in its own title but notes that it is controversial among some Latinos who view it as a "government imposed" label used in the 1980 Census concluding that reporters should ask the person or group being written about how they want to be identified.

Hispaniola. *Hispaniolan.*

Hispano. Term preferred by the subpopulation, mostly in the southwestern United States, who identify with the Spanish settlers of the area. *Hispanos* largely populate New Mexico's Rio Grande Valley and Sangre de Cristo Mountains of the same state.

The term is employed for such groups as the Albuquerque Hispano Chamber of Commerce and in allusions to Hispano culture.

Hoboken, New Jersey. *Hobokenite.*

Hogtowner. Traditional nickname for a resident of Toronto (q.v.), sometimes called *Hogtown.*

Ho-Ho-Kus, New Jersey. *Ho-Ho-Kusite.*

Holland. See NETHERLANDS.

Hollywood, California. Despite the importance of this Los Angeles district in the cultural scheme of things, there seems to be no common demonym. *Hollywoodite* is used but rarely, as are *Hollywoodian* and *Hollywooder.*

 The name *Hollywood* inspires other terms based on the idea of Hollywood as a source of glitz, glamour, and fantasy. A *Hollywood ending* is a happy ending and *to Hollywoodize* is to give something added glamour. An interesting use of the verb came into play at the Democratic National Convention of 1960 when the finale (which included the acceptance speeches of John F. Kennedy and Lyndon B. Johnson) was said to be *Hollywoodized.* In the vast file of citations collected by Merriam-Webster one finds *Hollywoodish* (Hollywood-like), *Hollywoodization* (becoming like Hollywood), *Hollywoodery* (the Hollywood spin), *Hollywoodesque* (in the manner of Hollywood), *Hollywoodese* (the jargon and cant of Hollywood), and *Hollywooden* (clumsy and clunky in the style of Hollywood). An interesting play on *Hollywood* is *Bollywood* for Bombay, India's film capital. "Why do I love Bollywood movies? To an Indian, that's like asking why we love our mothers; we don't have a choice. We were born of them" (the *New York Times Magazine,* November 14, 2004).

 Common nickname: *Tinseltown.*

Holyoke, Massachusetts. *Holyoker.*

Homer, Alaska. *Homerite,* but there is some evidence of *Homeroid.* Charles P. Wohlforth writing in Frommer's *Alaska 2005* hints at a native eccentricity that prefers this demonym over something more conventional:

Homer's leading mystic, the late Brother Asaiah Bates, always maintained that a confluence of metaphysical forces causes a focus of powerful creative energy on this little seaside town. It's hard to argue. Homer is full of creative people: artists, eccentrics, and those who simply contribute to a quirky community in a beautiful place. Indeed, Brother Asaiah may have been the quintessential Homeroid, although perhaps an extreme example, with his gray ponytail, extraordinary openness and generosity, and flowery rhetoric about "the cosmic wheel of life." Homer is full of outspoken, unusual, and even odd individualists—people who make living in the town almost an act of belief. I can say this because I'm a former Homeroid myself.

The question of whether or not Homeroid is actually used locally was put to Michael Armstrong of the *Homer News*. "Well, yes and no. It's true that some people from Homer refer to themselves as Homeroids, but this is usually done in jest. We have this tradition here of getting all worked up about some silly issue or another, so when some people from Homer are acting like jerks, they'll say, 'Oh, don't be a Homeroid.' Because of the obvious pun, in polite company we call ourselves Homerites."

Homestead, Pennsylvania. *Homesteader.*

Honduras (Republic of Honduras). *Honduran,* which is also an adjective.

Hong Kong. *Hong Konger,* but sometimes *Hong Kongese* as a group. *Honger* is a term of derogation used primarily in Canada for immigrants from Hong Kong used by Mandarin-speaking and Canadianized Chinese. *Hongcouver* is another negative reference applied to the city of Vancouver, so called because of its high Asian population (especially in reference to the large number of immigrants from Hong Kong).

Honolulu, Hawaii. *Honolulan.*

Hoosier. Resident of Indiana. *Hoosier* stands alone as an American demonym in terms of the concern and controversy it generates. It is a term that, if anything, is more popular today than ever before and is so universally preferred that it has totally eclipsed the old debate as to whether *Indianian* or *Indianan* was preferable.

The name appears everywhere. There are 107 businesses listed in the Indianapolis phone book whose names begin with *Hoosier,* and that does not include the gigantic Hoosierdome. It is the nickname of the Indiana University athletic teams and was the name of an immensely popular movie on Indiana high-school basketball. The Hoosier School of American writing is one that included Booth Tarkington and James Whitcomb Riley, and to be called a "Hoosier's Hoosier" is to be paid the ultimate compliment.

"Hoosier English" is a term applied to the central-southern Indiana variety of English. In 1960 linguist Harold Whitehall, professor and one of the editors of *Webster's New World Dictionary,* predicted that it was just a matter of time ("perhaps 50 years") before it would be the dominant worldwide English accent.

Hoosier has more than one meaning. Before he became vice president, Senator Dan Quayle of Indiana made it very clear that he did not like those other non-Indiana meanings and actually took steps to take charge of the meanings of the term—to rewrite the dictionary definitions of *hoosier.*

The facts are these. On Monday, March 30, 1987, Senator Alfonse M. D'Amato of New York took the Senate floor and predicted that his alma mater, Syracuse University, would win the NCAA men's basketball championship by beating the Indiana University Hoosiers that evening.

Such athletic boasts and jibes are common, and over the years the *Congressional Record* has detailed hundreds of them. However, in this case D'Amato invoked the sacred Indiana word of place, *Hoosier,* and pointed out that according to *Webster's Third New International Dictionary,* it not only meant a native of the state but also described "an awkward, unhandy or unskilled person; especially an ignorant rustic." There was also a verb—*to hoosier*—which is defined as "to loaf on or botch a job." D'Amato used this verb to predict the defeat of Indiana: "I would submit to you that if that is the case . . . the outcome of the game tonight is a foregone conclusion and Syracuse will be victorious."

Neither of Indiana's senators was present for this, but Senator Robert Byrd of West Virginia did interrupt D'Amato to point out that Rule XIX of the Senate stated that a senator could be asked to take his seat if he spoke negatively of another state. Byrd asked D'Amato if he were speaking disparagingly of Indiana. "Of course not," D'Amato replied. "That would never be my intention."

That night Syracuse lost to Indiana by a score of 74-73.

The next day Indiana Senator Dan Quayle rose to the floor of the Senate to offer congratulations to the team and to put forth a nonbinding resolution containing a new definition of *hoosier:* "Whereas, Indiana University's basketball team displayed the real meaning of the word, 'Hoosier,' therefore, be it resolved that a Hoosier is someone who is smart, resourceful, skillful, a winner, unique and brilliant."

The matter could have rested at that point as a matter of spirited Senate tomfoolery in reaction to a championship season. However, Quayle mentioned in his Senate speech that he intended to take up the definition he did not like with the editors of the dictionary. Later in the week, Quayle wrote to William A. Llewellyn, then the president of the company that first published the mammoth *Webster's Third New International Dictionary* in 1961. The company, Merriam-Webster, Inc., of Springfield, Massachusetts, had published the first two editions in 1909 and 1934, and other editions of *Webster's Unabridged* back to 1847. Not without its critics, this dictionary is regarded by many as the authoritative voice of American English. It is periodically updated through addenda.

Quayle asked that the old derogatory definitions of *hoosier* be removed from the dictionary and suggested that his upbeat substitute be inserted. According to Llewellyn, Quayle also said that if the negative definitions could not be removed, then at least a full explanatory discussion of the etymology of the term should appear in the book.

Senator Quayle's office was given a polite but firm no from Llewellyn in a letter that arrived on April 13. He added that the dictionary reflected the way words are used and that the company would be delighted to change the meaning if Quayle's meaning ("smart, resourceful, skillful," etc.) came into common use. Llewellyn later pointed out that his company's big dictionary is a "dictionary of record" and that it contains other entries and definitions that people don't like. He noted that the book contains four-letter words, racial and religious slurs, and words that are regarded as sexist, for the simple reason that these words are part of the language. Llewellyn also stated that the *Third* is not an etymological dictionary and that there was no reason to afford *hoosier* special treatment.

In announcing Llewellyn's original reaction, Quayle's press secretary, Peter Lincoln, made a statement that was reported by the Associated Press: "We, and I'm sure the rest of the citizens of the Hoosier state, will press on with our campaign over time to persuade the folks at Webster's that they don't have it right." He also suggested a new verb, *to webster,* which he said meant "to misdefine a word stubbornly and outrageously." An article by Lynn Ford of the *Indianapolis Star* appeared under the headline "Quayle May Boot Dictionary from His Office" and reported that the book might be banned from Quayle's office. The article quoted Lincoln as saying that a copy of the book was in the office, "but when the senator returns from vacation, I need to ask whether he wants a different dictionary in there." Reached a few days before Quayle was elected vice president in 1988, Lincoln said that the threat of banning the dictionary was done "tongue-in-cheek," but that the rest of the controversy was entirely "on the level." He said that he would stick by his definition of the verb *to webster.*

Llewellyn said he did get about 50 letters on the subject of *hoosier,* of which about half sided with Quayle with the other half commending the dictionary for sticking to its definitions. Several came from people in such places as Kentucky and Missouri who pointed out that *hoosier* was an insult in their neck of the woods and had nothing to do with the state of Indiana. Pamela N. Silva, the Merriam-Webster publicist, did check the company's file of more than 13 million citations on words and word usage and found evidence dating back to the 1850s that showed the word *hoosier* being used in the South for "a lazy rustic."

Ironically, Quayle should have directed his ire at the people of Saint Louis and other places where the meaning of *hoosier* that obtains is close to the meaning that offended the Indiana Republican. If anything, the dictionary treatment is mild compared with the reality in Saint Louis. Listen to Elaine Viets, a popular columnist for the *Saint Louis Post-Dispatch,* who has written puckishly about Hoosier culture and once proposed a Hoosier museum replete with such artifacts as Confederate mud flaps and John Wayne portraits on velvet: "In St. Louis it [*hoosier*] has one meaning and that comes as a shock to people who come here from Indiana. It is highly pejorative and means a low life redneck." She points out that you don't call people *hoosiers* unless you want to get into a fight. "Hoosiers are destroyers: they get into fistfights and people are always calling the police about them. They have a car on concrete blocks in the front yard and are likely to have shot their wife who may also be their sister."

An article by Thomas E. Murray of Ohio State University in the March 1987 issue of *Names: The Journal of the American Name Society* titled "You $#^%?*&@ Hoosier" supports this definition and concludes that in the Gateway City *hoosier* occupies "the honored position of being the city's number one term of derogation."

The extensive file on the term in the Tamony Collection at the University of Missouri contains a number of negative applications of *hoosier,* including use in sea slang (for an incompetent seaman), underworld slang (a sucker or holdup victim), logger slang (fighting word for one who is stupid or cowardly), trade union jargon (anyone who doesn't know his job), and narcotics slang of the 1930s (a *hoosier fiend* is an inexperienced addict who does not know of his addiction until he is deprived of drugs and experiences withdrawal symptoms).

The word *hoosier* is of uncertain origin. A number of theories exist, however, which makes it one of those curiosities that intrigue linguists. Several theories are consistent with the Saint Louis sense of the term, including one that appeared in a handout from the Indiana Department of Tourism. The handout acknowledges a highly fanciful explanation offered by Hoosier poet James Whitcomb Riley, who said the term came from tavern fighting in which men would "gouge, scratch, and bite off noses and ears of their opponents. Then a settler would walk in and see an ear. He would ask, 'Whose ear?'" Another less than flattering theory is that it stems from the idea of a "husher"—a bully who hushes his opponents.

But these are only two of many. Some believe it came from a Cumberland (England) dialect word, *hoozer,* used for anything unusually large (the *humongous* of its time?), others insist that it comes from a canal foreman named Hoosier who would only hire men from Indiana, and still another says that it comes from the exclamation of victory "Huzza!"

In any event, *Hoosier* has a long history. Its first literary appearance was in the *Indianapolis Journal* on January 1, 1833, in a poem by John Finley titled "The Hoosier's Nest." It apparently sprang into use at once.

Hornell, New York. *Hornellian.*

Houston, Texas. *Houstonian.* A test that ran on a Houston-based Web site has an item that states, "You know you're a Houstonian if . . ." You get points if you respond to statements like "Your house of worship has more than 5,000 members or fewer than 100" and "You've chosen between burnt orange and maroon."

Hoya. Nickname for a student or graduate of Georgetown University in Washington, D.C. This term has caused much confusion because the standard definitions for *hoya* are: (1) "a large genus of climbing Asian and Australian shrub" and (2) "a valley or basin high in the mountains." The university nickname stems from an earlier nickname for the football team, the Stonewalls. It seems that the students, with a touch of classic inspiration, renamed them the *Hoya Saxa,* which means "What stones!" This was arrived at from the combination of Greek *hoia,* the neuter plural of *hoios* ("such a" or "what a"), with the Latin word *saxa,* "rocks." Later the name was shortened to *Hoya* or the *Hoyas.*

Hub. Nickname for Boston that is used as a noun ("the Hub") and an adjective, as in "Hub union boss." It comes from the notion of Boston as "Hub of the Universe." Local newspapers use "Hub man" or "Hub woman" as alternatives to *Bostonian.*

Hungary (Republic of Hungary). *Hungarian,* also an adjective.

Huntington, Indiana. *Huntingtonian.*

Huntsville, Alabama. *Huntsvillian.*

Huron, South Dakota. *Huronite.*

hyphenated American. Generic term for Americans of family origin outside the United States. The term is used for such persons even when the compound designation (like *African American*) is not actually hyphenated. *The Oxford English Dictionary* traces the term to 1893 and Farmer and Henly's classic work on slang, *Slang and Its Analogues,* contains this definition: "*Hyphenated American,* a naturalised citizen, as German-Americans, Irish-Americans, and the like."

The hypen was long ago denigrated by former president Theodore Roosevelt, on October 12, 1915, in a speech before the

Knights of Columbus, which became known as his "Hyphenated American Speech." He said in part: "There is no room in this country for hyphenated Americanism. When I refer to hyphenated Americans, I do not refer to naturalized Americans. Some of the very best Americans I have ever known were naturalized Americans, Americans born abroad. But a hyphenated American is not an American at all. This is just as true of the man who puts "native" before the hyphen as of the man who puts German or Irish or English or French before the hyphen."

Roosevelt is cited by the National Association of Hispanic Journalists in their objection to the use of the hypen since it implies a subclass which is not fully American.

Iberia. One who lives on this European peninsula containing Spain and Portugal is an *Iberian. Iberian* is also an adjective.

Ibiza, Spain. *Ibicenco* or *Ibizan.*

Iceland (Republic of Iceland). *Icelander.* Adjective: *Icelandic,* as in *Icelandic Airlines.*

Idaho. *Idahoan,* a term that long ago overwhelmed the little-used and academic *Idahovan.* H. L. Mencken wrote of it in his 1947 article "Names for Americans" in *American Speech:* "About 1925 the learned brethren of the State University at Moscow launched *Idahovan,* and for a while it was used in the university town press, but the rest of the State refused to accept it, and it has been obsolete since 1925." The name of the now defunct Moscow, Idaho, newspaper was the *Daily Idahonian.*

State nicknames: *Gem State* and the *Gem of the Mountains.*

I-Kiribati. A resident of Kiribati.

Illinois. *Illinoisian,* but there is some support for *Illinoisan* and *Illinoian.* The two-*i* *Illinosan* must be considered to be without any significant support.

The three choices here underscore the point that though different demonyms may be technically "correct," only one tends to be used. Confronted with the fact that the *Random House Dictionary,* 2nd edition (1987) lists all three, N. Sally Hass of Sleepy Hollow, Illinois, reacted: "Illinoisian (with the S pronounced) is the one we use around here. I've never heard the others. But the name of the state is *ill-annoy,* not *ill-a-noise.*" The term *Illini* is used for students and graduates of the University of Illinois. Hass, whose daughter attended the university, points out: "You'd think the singular would be Illinus (m.) or Illina (f.), but no. Illini is both singular and plural, masculine and feminine."

A university pamphlet entitled "The 80's Belong to the Illini!" reports: "The state of Illinois was named for an Indian tribe—Illini—which once inhabited the area. The term meant 'Brave Men.' Since the start of athletics at the state university in the late 1800's, the teams have been called the 'Illini,' and more recently 'The Fighting Illini.'" The college newspaper *The Daily Illini* was founded in 1872. A 1925 letter to Merriam-Webster on the subject of this term from Professor Frank W. Scott said in part: "As an adjective or part of a name, the word is widely used and always, I believe, in the same sense as the title 'Illini Poetry,' that is, poetry written by Illini or members of the tribe Illini. It is customary to speak of the Illini team, Illini dances, Illini spirit and so on—but *never* Illini University. I presume that you are aware of the use of the word rather generally throughout the state for matters pertaining to the state." It seems that some Illinois residents are still using *Illini* outside the context of the university. Philip Bateman of Decatur, Illinois, wrote to report that *Illinoisan* is generally regarded as proper, "but I hear Illini some among the general public—used either singular: 'I am an Illini' or plural: 'We are Illini.' Do not know if it will grow in use."

In August 2005, the NCAA, the ruling body of college athletics in 2005, proscribed 18 schools, of its 1,024 member schools, with nicknames deemed "hostile" or "abusive" from appearing in tournaments or postseason play with their logos, nicknames, and mascots. One of the names banned was Illini. Although the mascot, Chief Illiniwek, is indisputably Indian, supporters argued that the nickname "Illini" refers wholly to the university's students and alumni.

Traditional personal nicknames: *Egyptian, Sandhiller,* and *Sucker,* which seems to have been used nonpejoratively in earlier times just as *Hoosier* is used for a resident of Indiana. For more information on all three of these terms, see their individual entries.

State nicknames: *Prairie State, Inland Empire,* and *Sucker State.*

Independence, Missouri. *Independent,* even though H. L. Mencken said in 1948 that there was no demonym for this city.

Independent State of Papua New Guinea. See PAPUA NEW GUINEA.

Independent State of Western Samoa. See WESTERN SAMOA.

India (Republic of India). *Indian,* also an adjective.

Indiana. *Hoosier.* See the entry for this term for a detailed discussion. Despite the intensity of the pro-*Hoosier* lobby the term *Indianan* still shows up in print, although it is usually followed by a letter to the publication in question asserting, as did a letter to the *Washington Post,* that "there is no such word as 'Indianan.'"

State nickname: *Hoosier State.*

Indianapolis, Indiana. *Indianapolitan,* which appeared to be rare enough that by 1996 Marc Allen of the *Indianapolis Daily News* could not recall ever seeing it in print. Allen said that locals are commonly identified as *Hoosiers.*

Indianola, Mississippi. *Indianolan.*

Indigenous Person. Increasingly common and, by most accounts, the preferred term for the approximately 300 million people so identified worldwide. They are so called because they were living on their lands before settlers came from elsewhere; they are the descendants of those who inhabited a country or a geographical region at the time when people of different cultures or ethnic origins arrived, the new arrivals later becoming dominant through conquest, occupation, settlement, or other means. Among many indigenous peoples are the Indians of the Americas (for example, the Mayas of Guatemala or the Aymaras of Bolivia), the Inuit and Aleutians of the circumpolar region, the Saami of northern Europe, the Aborigines and Torres Strait Islanders of Australia, and the Maori of New Zealand. These and most other indigenous peoples have retained social, cultural, economic, and political characteristics that are clearly distinct from those of the other segments of the national populations.

Indochina. *Indochinese,* also an adjective. Indochina (or *French Indochina*) was the former French dependency that became Vietnam, Cambodia, and Laos. *Indochina* is still used to refer to the three countries collectively, and broadly refers to an area that also includes Myanmar, Thailand, and West Malaysia.

Indonesia (Republic of Indonesia). *Indonesian,* also an adjective.

Iowa. *Iowan.* Sometimes *Hawkeye* is used for an Iowan or for a student or graduate of the University of Iowa. This derives from the Sauk and Fox chief Black Hawk, who figured in the early history of Iowa. One alternative to the term is *Iowegian,* which Allen Walker Read has suggested may have developed from the strong Scandinavian influence (*Norwegian,* perhaps, led to *Iowegian*). It has been suggested that there is or once was a bar in northeast Iowa called *The Iowegian.*

State nickname: *Hawkeye State.*

Iran (Islamic Republic of Iran). *Iranian,* also an adjective. *Irani* is also used, but less commonly, and *Persian* is even rarer. Iran was called *Persia* until 1935. The language is *Farsi* but some outside the country still refer to it as *Persian.*

Iraq (Republic of Iraq). *Iraqi,* also an adjective as in *Iraqi War.* The modern nation coincides roughly with ancient Mesopotamia.

Ireland (Irish Republic) *or* **Eire.** *Irishman* or *Irishwoman.* The collective is *Irish.* Adjective: *Irish.* An alternate demonym and adjective is *Hibernian,* and the Irish are sometimes called *Patrick's People,* in reference to Saint Patrick, patron saint of the nation. The name *Eire* has led to derivatives on the order of *Eirophile* (for one who loves Ireland).

　　In a derogatory sense *Irish* has been used in England and the United States for a certain crudeness, as in *Irish confetti* (bricks), *Irish dividend* (an assessment), *Irish draperies* (cobwebs), *Irish parliament* (a noisy argument bordering on a free fight), and *Irish pennant* (a loose thread). On the other hand there is *Irish lace, Irish coffee,* and the *Fighting Irish* of Notre Dame University. *Fighting Irish* was originally the nickname of New York's heavily Irish 69th Regiment.

Iron Mountain, Michigan. *Mountaineer.*

Iron Puddler. Traditional nickname for a resident of Pennsylvania.

Islamic Republic of Iran. See IRAN.

Islamic Republic of Mauritania. See MAURITANIA.

Islamic Republic of Pakistan. See PAKISTAN.

Islamic Republic of Afghanistan. See AFGHANISTAN.

Islamist. Term for those who see Islam as not just a religion but a political ideology known as *Islamism*, which refers to modern movements that developed during the 20th century in reaction to several forces including the belief that Islam was in retreat, and that Western ideas were spreading throughout Muslim society, along with the influence of Western nations. Since the 9/11 terrorist attacks, the term has proved useful in the sense that an *Islamist terrorist* is not the same as an *Islamic terrorist.*

The term has been used in this manner since at least the turn of the century, including *Pan-Islamist* for those who would start an independent Islamist kingdom.

Islander. Generic term for resident of an island, often used in compounds like *Hawaiian Islander* or *Channel Islander.* In the case of Nantucket it would seem that *Islander* in a specific sense is used more often than *Nantucketer. Islander* appears with much more frequency in the island's newspaper, the *Inquirer and Mirror.* In some cases, anyone not from the island in question is known as an *Off-Islander.* On the island of Martha's Vineyard one finds a bifurcation of *Islander* into *up-Islander* and *down-Islander,* since the western part of the island is *up-Island* (there are seven businesses listed in the Martha's Vineyard phone book that begin with *Up Island*), and the eastern, more densely settled part is *down-Island.* Noted Vineyarder Art Buchwald has written humorously on the differences between *up-Islanders,* whose ranks have included Carly Simon and Jackie Onassis, and the less reclusive *down-Islanders.* For example, when a down-Islander is en route to a party at the home of an up-Islander, he or she has to stop along the way and phone for help, at which point the host will recite a bewildering combination of turns and clues to guide the guest to the concealed destination.

Isle of Man. See MAN, ISLE OF.

Isle of Wight. See WIGHT, ISLE OF.

Israel (State of Israel). *Israeli,* also an adjective. When the state of Israel was founded in early 1948, the National Geographic Society put out a press release that began: "Washington, D.C.—The citizen of Israel should be called an Israeli, suggests the Foreign Secretary of the new Jewish state in Palestine. His preference follows an Arab-favored style which makes Iraqis of citizens of Iraq and Baghdadis of Baghdad's inhabitants." The term was accepted immediately and without further debate, but the National Geographic Society could not resist pointing out that many other terms would have worked. It said that an Israeli could just as well have been "called an Israelian, in the manner of the Brazilian, Egyptian, or Babylonian. He could be an Israelese, following the form for the man from China, Japan, Siam, or Portugal. Taking a leaf from the book of the New Yorker, the Asiatic, the Frenchman, or the Nazarene, he could be, respectively, an Israeler, an Israelic, Israelman or Israelene." The society went on to say that even "Disraeli," the family name of the British prime minister, was a plausible alternative, as was the time-honored *Israelite.*

However, the term *Israelite* has been relegated to biblical use and is an increasingly rare term for a Jew in an English-speaking nation. In the late 19th and the early 20th centuries, there was a group of newspapers for American Jewish families named *The Israelites, The American Israelite,* and *The Chicago Israelite.*

Istanbul, Turkey. *Istanbullu,* singular; *Istanbullus,* plural.

Italy (Italian Republic). *Italian.* The common adjective is *Italian,* while *Italic* is used in talking about ancient Italy and its languages and (uncapitalized) a common typestyle.

Ithaca, New York. *Ithacan.*

Ivory Coast *or* **Côte d'Ivoire (Republic of Côte d'Ivoire).** *Ivorian,* also an adjective. There are some who use *Ivory Coaster;* however, sources ranging from the Central Intelligence Agency's *World Factbook* to the *Washington Post* use *Ivorian.*

Jackson, Mississippi. *Jacksonian.*

Jacksonville, Florida. *Jacksonvillian.*

Jakarta, Indonesia. *Jakartan.*

Jamaica. *Jamaican,* which is also an adjective. The definition given in the *Dictionary of Jamaican English* (1980) for *Jamaican* is: "Among the folk: a term used contrastively with Chinese, East Indian, Creole, etc. for a Jamaican negro."

Japan. *Japanese* (both singular and plural), which is also an adjective. The word *Japanese* should not be shortened to *Jap,* since this is now regarded as a slur. The word was used in books and movies of the World War II era, as a wartime insult for a declared enemy. Despite the universal opposition to its use today, the term still finds its way into print as an abbreviation.

In 1986 a concurrent resolution was passed by the House of Representatives in which the use of the abbreviation *Jap* was labeled as racially derogatory and offensive, and it was suggested that *Jpn* be used when an abbreviation is needed. The force behind such a resolution is moral rather than legally binding. Representative Norman Y. Mineta (D-Cal.) made this point in supporting the resolution: "This abbreviation is so pervasive it still can be found in the word games of some major national newspapers, if not in their stylebooks. Newspaper usage is particularly important since most modern dictionaries list the offensive term at issue here as indeed an offensive racial epithet. Yet common usage has a powerful impact on society. And it is that usage we seek to influence with today's action."

Jarocho. Resident of Veracruz, Mexico.

Jayhawker. Common demonymic nickname for a Kansan. Kansas is the *Jayhawk State* and the Jayhawk is the mascot of the University of Kansas. In discussing this term in his *Good Words to You*, the late John Ciardi described the modern mascot as "a nonheraldic cartoon figure or stuffed doll of a nonexistent bird that resembles a miniature pterodactyl with a thyroid deficiency." However, originally the term was anything but comic. It was used before the Civil War during the "Bloody Kansas" era as a nom de guerre for free-soil guerrillas who fought proslavery forces. Some of these original Jayhawkers were nothing more than criminals operating under the cover of an abolitionist crusade.

Because there is no such bird as the jayhawk, there have been many conjectural attempts to determine the inspiration for the mythical bird of prey. In his *Why Do Some Shoes Squeak?*, George W. Stimpson suggests a simple answer: it "may have been derived from a combination of the names of the blue jay and the sparrow hawk, both of which are plunderers."

Jefferson, Texas. *Jeffersonite.* C. F. Eckhardt points to the lack of parallelism here: "Folks from Houston have, since time out of mind, been called Houstonians, though those living in Jefferson for some reason have never been Jeffersonians but Jeffersonites."

Jeffersontown, Kentucky. *Jeffersonian.*

Jerome, Arizona. *Jeromeite.*

Jersey (Bailiwick of Jersey). The Central Intelligence Agency's *World Factbook* lists *Channel Islander,* but the traditional demonyms have been *Jerseyman* and *Jerseywoman.*

Jerseyan. A resident of New Jersey.

Jersey Blue. Traditional nickname for a resident of New Jersey (q.v.).

Jersey City, New Jersey. *Jersey Cityite.*

Jerseyite. Resident of New Jersey.

Jerseyman/Jerseywoman. Resident of the island of Jersey. It appears to be a powerful demonym: Jersey American Philip S. Bentliff in a letter to the *New York Times,* September 30, 1984 notes, "Natives call themselves Jerseymen and Jerseywomen, not Englishmen and Englishwomen."

Jerusalem, Israel. *Jerusalemite.*

Johannesburg, South Africa. *Johannesburger.*

Johnson City, Tennessee. *Johnson Citian.*

Johnstown, Pennsylvania. *Johnstowner.*

Joliet, Illinois. *Jolietan.*

Jordan (Hashemite Kingdom of Jordan). *Jordanian,* also an adjective.

Josh. Traditional nickname for a resident of Arkansas. It apparently originated in the Civil War, and Mathews's *Dictionary of*

State nicknames: *Jayhawk State, Sunflower State, Central State* (from its location on the map), and *Prairie State*.

nsas City, Kansas. *Kansas Citian* or *Kansas Cityan*.

nsas City, Missouri. *Kansas Citian* or *Kansas Cityan*.

uai, Hawaii. *Kauaian*.

ybecker. Northern New England term for a French-speaking Canadian lumberjack working in the United States, which is now used as a jocular reference to someone from Quebec often by a resident writing informally in English. Rather than appear as a term of derogation it seems more like a play on demonyms like *Mainer* and *Vermonter*.

azakhstan (Republic of Kazakhstan); *formerly* **Kazakh Soviet Socialist Republic.** *Kazakhstani*, which is also an adjective. *Kazakh* is still used to denote "a member of a Turkic people of Kazakhstan and other countries of central Asia" (*Merriam-Webster's Collegiate Dictionary*, 11th edition).

t, England. A true oddity because there are two demonyms, depending on where one lives in Kent. As verified by reference librarian David S. Cousins of Canterbury, a *man of Kent* lives east of the River Medway while a *Kentish man* lives west of the River Medway.

tucky. *Kentuckian*. The late Charles D. Poe noted that this term has graced its share of movie titles, including *The Fighting Kentuckian* (with John Wayne, 1949) and *The Kentuckian* (with Burt Lancaster, 1955). The derivative *Kentuckiana*, for that which is typical or characteristic of Kentucky, is in common use—there is, for example, the annual Kentuckiana Antiques Market in Louisville.

Traditional personal nicknames: *Bear, Bluegrasser, Corn Cracker, Hardboot*, and *Red Horse*. While the origin of *Hardboot*

Americanisms includes an explanation by the famed *Overland Monthly* from 1869, which states that when the Tennesseans saw their fellow Rebels from Arkansas coming to join them before the battle of Murfreesboro (1862–63), they yelled, "Thar come the tribes of Joshua!"

Jovian. Adjective for the planet Jupiter. Used as a demonym in Emanuel Swedenborg's *The Earths in the Universe*. Writing about the psychic and medium who lived from 1688 to 1722, Martin Gardner described Swedenborg's Jovians as

> kind and gentle, living on fertile lands where there are many wild horses. Although grouped into nations, warfare is unknown. Those in warm climates go naked except for loincloths. Their tents and low wooden houses have sides decorated with stars on blue backgrounds. When they eat they sit on the leaves of fig trees with their legs crossed. Curiously, they do not walk erect but "creep along" by using their hands.

Swedenborg's descriptions of other inhabitants of the sun's planets are no less curious and humanoid. *Mercurian* women, for instance, are small, beautiful, and wear linen caps. All of these types are described in Gardner's article "Psychic Astronomy," which appeared in the Winter 1987 issue of *Free Inquiry*.

Jug. A short form of the demonyms *Jugoslav* and *Jugoslavian, Jug* could easily be construed as derogatory even though it appears to be used neutrally like *Brit* or *Balt*. "The Jugs denied everything," says a character in Paul Henissart's *Margin of Error*. One would be advised, however, to avoid its use, even if for nothing more than the simple reason that it has a jarring similarity to the defamatory *Jap*.

Jugoslav or Jugoslavian. Alternative forms of *Yugoslav* and *Yugoslavian*, based on the spelling *Jugoslavia*.

Jugoslavia. See YUGOSLAVIA.

Juneau, Alaska. *Juneauite,* but not universally accepted. In an editorial on *JuneauEmpire.com* dated June 24, 2001 Nita Nettleton wrote:

> Juneau, ending with a vowel sound, has a lot of possibilities. I thought I would hear a wide variety of suffixes when I asked around here. Sadly, not. Most people said they call themselves Juneauites, a few Juneauers, and one, whom I won't name, Juneauarian. The question I used for all was, "Since you live in Juneau, what do you call yourself?" The more interesting responses included: crazy, an Alaskan, a Southeasterner, a shootist and Brad. This was harder than it looked. One person allowed that Juneauite sounded Biblical, but that Juneauan was otherworldly, sort of alien. Other people agreed there is an old-fashioned air to Juneauite, but were not very comfortable with Juneauer. The majority I polled called themselves Juneauites.

Kalamazoo, Michigan. *Kalamazooan.*

Kamloops, British Columbia. *Kamloopsian,* accord[ing to] Michele Young of the *Kamloops Daily News.*

Kampuchea. See CAMBODIA.

Kankakee, Illinois. *Kankakeean.*

Kannapolis, North Carolina. *Kannapolitan.*

Kansas. *Kansan* is the formal demonym, but *Jayhaw[ker is the pre]*ferred nickname. Susan Page of *USA Today* used [it in] her commentary on November 6, 1996, the day a[fter the presi]dental election. Her article was on the Kansas jinx i[n pol]itics: "As a fifth-generation Jayhawker, I knew. The[...] that made Bob Dole a Kansan would be his undoi[ng...] campaign."

Traditional personal nicknames: *Jayhawke[r], [Sun]flower,* and *Grasshopper,* in commemoration of a [plague of] grasshoppers that almost destroyed the crops of K[ansas...]

is obscure, more information on the other nicknames listed here can be found at their individual entries.

State nickname: *Bluegrass State,* from the abundant growth of bluegrass on its limestone soil. The legendary Kentucky musician Bill Monroe named his acoustic group the *Blue Grass Boys,* and as a result the distinctive type of country music he popularized became known as *bluegrass.*

Kenya (Republic of Kenya). *Kenyan,* also an adjective.

Kerrville, Texas. *Kerrvillians* to most, but musician and writer Kinky Friedman has called them *Kerrverts.* Writing in the *Houston Post* for March 7, 1991, he maintained: "I've often said about my fellow 'Kerrverts' that the only Jews they know in Kerrville are Kinky Friedman and Jesus Christ, which can be a little tedious at times."

Key West, Florida. *Key Wester.*

Kingston, Ontario. *Kingstonian.*

Kinshasa, Zaire. *Kinshasan.*

Kirghiz. Resident of Kyrgyzstan.

Kirghizia. See KYRGYZSTAN.

Kirghiz Soviet Socialist Republic. See KYRGYZSTAN.

Kiribati (Republic of Kiribati). *I-Kiribati,* which is also an adjective. Kiribati includes the Phoenix Islands, Line Islands, and Gilbert Islands. The Gilbert Islands were formerly part of a British colony, the Gilbert and Ellice Islands, and the demonym *Gilbertese* is also a noun standing for a language spoken in Kiribati along with English.

Kitchener, Ontario. *Kitchenerite.*

Kittanning, Pennsylvania. *Kittanningite.*

Kittitian. Resident of the island of Saint Kitts, in Saint Kitts-Nevis (q.v.).

Kiwi. A New Zealander. The nickname parallels *Aussie* for *Australian.* The kiwi is a flightless bird with hairlike plumage that is native to New Zealand. "Carnival Test for Kiwi All-Stars" (Melbourne *Herald Sun,* January 2, 2006).

In an earlier approach to this topic (*What Do You Call a Person From . . . ?*), the author declared that "kiwi fruit is also native to the nation," which occasioned a letter from Sean Bonner of New South Wales, Australia, who said that the fruit is actually native to mainland China and is known in New Zealand as the Chinese gooseberry. (It was known by that name in the United States until we started getting it from New Zealand.) However, New Zealand now exports the fruit to China.

Knickerbocker. Traditional nickname for a New Yorker, explained at the entry for the state of New York.

Knoxville, Tennessee. *Knoxvillian.*

Kokomo, Indiana. *Kokomoan.*

Korea, North (Democratic People's Republic of Korea). *North Korean.*

Korea, South (Republic of Korea). *South Korean.*

Kosovo, Serbia. *Kosovar.* It is often seen in tandem with a further descriptor, as in *Kosovar Albanian.* Sometimes *Kosovan* is used instead of *Kosovar.*

Kosrae, Micronesia. *Kosraean.*

Kuril Islands. *Kurilian.*

Kuwait (State of Kuwait). *Kuwaiti,* which is also an adjective.

Kyrgyzstan (Kyrgyz Republic) *or* **Kirghizia;** *formerly* **Kirghiz Soviet Socialist Republic.** *Kyrgyz* or *Kirghiz. Kirghiz* is a long-established word for "a member of a Turkic people of Kyrgyzstan and adjacent areas of central Asia" (*Merriam-Webster's Collegiate Dictionary,* 11th edition). There is evidence of *Kyrgyzstani* as an adjective, but sometimes it is used as a metaphor for something distant and confusing: "A smiling blond saleswoman named Tera Jamesen explained the time share (they don't call it that), stressing the plan's 'flexibility,' which is more confusing than a Kyrgyzstani menu" (*Philadelphia Daily News,* September 27, 2005).

L.A. Common abbreviation/nickname for Los Angeles. It leads to some offbeat names like *L-Alien* and *Lalaland.*

Labrador, Canada. *Labradorean* or *Labradorian,* both of which are also adjectives.

Ladakh, India. *Ladakhi,* also an adjective.

Lafayette, Indiana. *Lafayettean.*

La Junta, Colorado. *La Juntan.*

Lake Placid, New York. *Lake Placidian.*

Lancashire *or* **Lancaster, England.** A resident of this county is a *Lancastrian,* and the same is true for the city of Lancaster. (*Lancashire* was formed by combining *Lancaster* and *shire,* "county.") However, Roger B. Appleton of West Glamorgan, Scotland, points out that *Lancastrians* and *Yorkists* do not necessarily come from Lancaster or York, since the terms have special historical meanings.

John of Gaunt (1340–99) was the duke of Lancaster and fathered Henry IV, often called Henry of Lancaster in his own time. The royal House of Lancaster held the English throne from 1399 to 1461 (Henry IV, Henry V, and Henry VI), but battled the House of York in the famous "War of the Roses." (The York kings were Edward IV, Edward V, and Richard III.) *Lancastrian* is both a noun for a member or supporter of the Lancaster camp and an adjective that describes something of or relating to it. *Yorkist* is a noun and adjective for the other side.

Lansing, Michigan. *Lansingite.*

Laos (Lao People's Democratic Republic). *Lao* or *Laotian.* Both terms are also adjectives, and the plural of *Lao* is *Lao* or *Laos.* For purely "national" reference, *Laotian* may be the better choice, since the Lao are a Buddhist people who can also be found in Thailand. *Lao* is also the name of their language, which is the official language of Laos.

Lapland. One who lives in this Arctic area extending through northern Scandinavia and Russia is a *Laplander.* The name *Lapp* is used for a member of the people native to the area, and for one or all of their various related languages. *Lappish* is an adjective that has also been used as a noun synonym of *Lapp.*

Curiously enough, a *Laplander* is also a person living on the Missouri-Arkansas border where Missouri "laps over" into Arkansas. In their book on Ozark folk speech, *Down in the Holler,* Vance Randolph and George P. Wilson wrote, "The 'bootheel' country in southeast Missouri has long been known as Lapland and is the subject of many dull jokes."

Laramie, Wyoming. *Laramieite.*

Laredo, Texas. *Laredoan.*

La Salle, Illinois. *La Sallean.*

Las Cruces, New Mexico. *Crucen.*

Las Vegas, Nevada. *Las Vegan.* Resident Robert J. Throckmorton points out that the term *Vegasite*, which consciously apes the word "parasite," is used pejoratively and selectively. *Las Vegan* has a certain ring to it that is displayed in this line from the May 1983 *Sunset* magazine: "Such complete control may be just as well for the thousands of visiting Las Vegans, Angelenos and Phoenicians who on weekends consider the calm waters of the lower Colorado their back-yard swimming pool."

Latina. A female Latin American, or a female of Latin American ethnicity living in the United States. It is also an adjective.

Latin America. *Latin American.*

Latino. A Latin American, or a person of Latin American ethnicity living in the United States. It is also an adjective. The term gradually replaced the earlier Latin (as in "Latin lover") in the years following the Second World War.

Latvia (Republic of Latvia); *formerly* **Latvian Soviet Socialist Republic.** *Latvian,* also an adjective. A much less common demonym is *Lett* (from German *Lette* for a Latvian), and the adjective *Lettish* is also less favored.

Laurel, Mississippi. *Laurelite* or *Laurelian.*

Lausanne, Switzerland. *Lausannois.*

Laval, Quebec. *Lavaller* or *Lavallois. Lavalier* is the term for a jeweled pendant worn on a chain around the neck. *Lavalier microphones* are small microphones that can be clipped onto a person's shirt to record their voice.

Lawrence, Kansas. *Lawrentian.*

Lawrence, Massachusetts. *Lawrencian.*

Lawton, Oklahoma. *Lawtonian.*

Leatherhead. Traditional nickname for a resident of Pennsylvania. According to George Earlie Shankle's *State Names, Flags, Seals, Songs, Birds, Flowers, and Other Symbols,* the term "alludes to the great hide and tanning industries of Pennsylvania, particularly those in the Northwest part of the State."

Leavenworth, Kansas. *Leavenworthean.*

Lebanon (Republic of Lebanon). *Lebanese,* which is also the plural form and an adjective. This demonym got an interesting workout in the fall of 1996 when Ellen DeGeneres raised the possibility that her television character, Ellen Morgan, would come out of the closet on the show *Ellen.* As she made the talk show circuit she had a pat response: "The character does find out—and this is where the confusion comes in—that she is Lebanese."

Lebanon, Pennsylvania. *Lebanonian.*

Leningrad, Russia. See SAINT PETERSBURG, RUSSIA.

Lesotho (Kingdom of Lesotho); *formerly* **Basutoland.** *Mosotho* is the singular form while *Basotho* is plural. Adjective: *Basotho,* though *Lesothan* is also used. The language of the Basotho people is *Sesotho.*

Lett. Resident of Latvia (q.v.).

The Levant. *Levantine.* The term applies to the lands and islands of the eastern Mediterranean.

Lewiston, Idaho. *Lewistonian.*

Lexovien. Resident of Lisieux, France (q.v.).

Liberia (Republic of Liberia). *Liberian,* also an adjective.

Libya (Socialist People's Libyan Arab Jamahiriya). *Libyan,* also an adjective.

Liechtenstein (Principality of Liechtenstein). *Liechtensteiner.*

Lille, France. *Lillois.*

Lilliputian. A tiny person from the fictional Lilliput of Jonathan Swift's *Gulliver's Travels,* or someone whose size evokes comparison with the inhabitants of that island.

Lima, Peru. *Limeño.*

Limey *or* **Lime-juicer.** Increasingly uncommon American terms for an Englishman. They appear to have been inspired when American sailors noted the compulsory British practice of giving sailors lime juice as an antiscorbutic, although some support the notion that *limey,* at least, derives from the expletive "Gor blim'y" (for "God blame me," or the more powerful "God blind me"). From an American standpoint, the term seems to have begun as a seagoing slur but later was more commonly used with some degree of affection, such as during the two world wars. Both terms can refer to a British sailor or an Englishman, while *lime-juicer* has also been used as a slang term for a British ship. In recent times, the term has been used mostly as an adjective—"limey food," "limey accent."

Limoges, France. *Limougeaud.*

Lincoln, Nebraska. *Lincolnite.*

Lincolnshire, England. *Lindunian* in some circles, according to the research of Jay Ames, but *Lincolnian* in others.

Lisbon, Portugal. *Lisboan,* from the Portuguese name for the city, *Lisboa.*

Lisieux, France. *Lexovien.* This word comes from the name of an ancient Celtic people, the Lexovii, who lived in northern Gaul.

Lithuania (Republic of Lithuania); *formerly* **Lithuanian Soviet Socialist Republic.** *Lithuanian,* also an adjective.

Little Rock, Arkansas. The prevailing name for a resident of Little Rock is *Little Rockian.*

Liverpool, England. *Liverpudlian,* which is conventional, but the slang nicknames *Scouse* and *Scouser* are also in use. *Liverpudlian* is apparently based on "a jocular substitution of *puddle* for *pool*" in the name *Liverpool,* with the addition of an *-ian* ending, according to the *Oxford English Dictionary,* 2nd edition. The oldest citation given is from 1833. One finds some cases in which it is spelled *Liverpuddlian,* such as Robert W. Chapman's *Adjectives from Proper Names.* A good example of the term in use as an adjective is an advertisement for Cockburn's Port: "At a monastery in Lamego, Portugal more than three hundred years ago, sat the two sons of a Liverpudlian wine trader and a Jolly Abbot they had befriended."

Philip Chaplin, who has done research on *Scouse* and *Scouser,* reports that "Lobscouse is the name of a dish of salt beef biscuit and onions formerly common in British merchant ships. I believe the American equivalent was cracker hash. Shortened it means a native of Liverpool, which is, of course, a major commercial port."

Logger. Traditional nickname for a resident of Maine.

Loggerhead. Traditional nickname for a resident of Pennsylvania.

London, England. *Londoner.*

Long Beach, California. *Long Beacher.*

Long Beach, Indiana. *Beacher.*

Long Beach, New York. *Long Beacher.*

Long Branch, New Jersey. *Long Brancher.*

Longhorn. Traditional nickname for a resident of Texas, also used for sports teams at the University of Texas. The *Texas longhorn* is a specific breed of cattle, though the term is also used synonymously with *longhorn* for a broader category of long-horned bovines.

Long Island, New York. *Long Islander.* Compare HAMPTONITE.

Longwy, France. *Longovicien.*

Looper. Someone who works in Chicago's Loop.

Lorain, Ohio. *Lorainite.*

Los Altos, California. *Los Altan.*

Los Angeles, California. *Angeleno* and *Angelino* are the most commonly used terms, but one also finds *Los Angeleno* and *Los Angelean.* Derivatives are rare, but one finds examples of *Losangelize* for creating something in the image or style of the city. Motion picture director Mike Nichols described his 1967 film *The Graduate* as being about "the Losangelization of the world" (*San Francisco Examiner,* July 24, 1967). There was also a bumper sticker selling in Marin County, California, in the mid-1970s that read DON'T LOSANGELIZE MARIN; this, in turn, prompted a counter-sticker, DON'T MARINATE LOS ANGELES.

Los Angeles has attracted a number of nicknames ranging from the mild *City of Angels* to the deprecating *Lotusland,*

Lotusville, and *Lalaland.* The *Lotus-* names and *Lalaland* are often used in the context of a grotesque event. The *San Francisco Chronicle* used to have a column that ran such items as stories about fistfights between Hollywood stars under the rubric "Life in Lotusland Department." One of the oddest nicknames for the city was *Double Dubuque,* a put-down popular from the years following World War II through the 1960s. See also HOLLY-WOOD.

Los Gatos, California. *Los Gatan.*

Louisiana. *Louisianian* or *Louisianan.* Most press and book citations favor *Louisianian,* but one can find *Louisianan* in many newspaper reports: "Distressed Louisianan Nureka Jacobs was told she and her five children couldn't stay in the Astrodome because it was reserved for victims coming in on buses only" (*Houston Chronicle,* September 11, 2005). One historic nickname is *Pelican* because of the numerous pelicans found throughout the state and the fact that this bird is depicted on the state seal. See also CAJUN.
    State nicknames: *Pelican State* and *Creole State.*

Louisville, Kentucky. *Louisvillian.*

Lowell, Massachusetts. *Lowellite.*

Lower Peninsula, Michigan. *Trolls,* because they live beneath the Mackinac Bridge. See UPPER PENINSULA.

Lubbock, Texas. *Lubbockite.*

Lumberman. Traditional nickname for a resident of Maine.

Lusitania. See PORTUGAL.

Luxembourg (Grand Duchy of Luxembourg) *or* **Luxemburg.** *Luxembourger* or *Luxemburger.* The French version is

Luxembourgeois, which appears in the *Oxford English Dictionary. Luxembourgian* and *Luxemburgian* are both adjectives. The *Oxford English Dictionary,* 2nd edition, shows some past use in English of the French noun and adjective *Luxembourgois,* but it is clearly not a common English form.

Lynn, Massachusetts. *Lynner* or *Lynnian.* But sometimes derogatorily *Sinner* because this is a city bedeviled by an old couplet known to many who have never been to Lynn.

> *Lynn, Lynn, city of sin. You never come out the way*
> *you came in.*
> *Ask for water, they give you a gin . . . it's the darndest*
> *city I ever been in.*

The "City of Sin" label caused a 1997 effort by city solicitor Michael Barry to propose renaming the city "Ocean Park," but this initiative was withdrawn after receiving widespread ridicule (opponents came up with a new rhyme, *"Ocean Park, Ocean Park, you'd better get out before it gets dark"*).

Lyons, France. *Lyonnais.* The adjective *lyonnaise* is used in a culinary context for food prepared with onions, and *Credit Lyonnais* is a global bank whose name (in French, *Crédit Lyonnais*) indicates its origin in this city.

Macao *or* **Macau.** *Macanese* (both singular and plural).

Macedonia (Republic of Macedonia). *Macedonian.*

Macon, Georgia. *Maconite.*

Madagascar (Republic of Madagascar). *Malagasy* (both singular and plural); it is also a well-established adjective. Another accepted noun and adjective is *Madagascan.*

Magdalen Islands, Quebec. *Madelinot.*

Madison, Wisconsin. *Madisonian.* Like *Jacksonian* and *Jeffersonian,* this is one of those demonyms identical to great presidential adjectives.

Madras, India. *Madrasi.*

Madrid, Spain. *Madrilenian* (also an adjective) or *Madrileño.*

Maggie. A female *Aggie* (q.v.).

Maine. *Mainer* or *State of Mainer* (sometimes *Maine Stater*). The term *Maineiac* (or its alternatives *Mainiac* and *Maine-iac*) is used affectionately for summer residents who fall in love with the place or for immigrants who stick around. An anecdote in the December 1983 *Reader's Digest* from a Hampden, Maine, man described a native explaining the difference between *Mainer* and *Maine-iac*: "A 'Mainah' is a pehson who likes Maine so much that he decides to stay through the wintah. A 'Maine-iac' is a pehson who is so devoutly in love with Maine that he decides to stay a second wintah." In his incomparable *Maine Lingo* (1975), John Gould notes that "*Maineiac* is more used by out-of-staters than by bona fide residents of the Pine Tree Precinct, but the latter are capable of tossing it off to describe themselves when it suits, and with more than a little pride." A parodic newspaper published in Maine since 1987 is called the *Maineiac Express.*

Traditional personal nicknames: *Fox, Logger, Lumberman, Maineiac,* and *Pine Treeman.*

State nicknames: *Pine Tree State, Down East State,* and *Lumber State.* See also DOWN EAST.

mainland. *Mainlander.* Term used by islanders to describe those on the mainland. For reasons that are unclear, it is especially common in Canada where the *mainland* variously: (1) refers to all of British Columbia except the islands; (2) is used in Cape Breton, Nova Scotia, to refer to the rest of Nova Scotia; (3) is used by Newfoundlanders to refer to a person from mainland Canada, often used in the derogatory.

Majorca *or* **Mallorca, Spain.** *Majorcan* or *Mallorcan.*

Malaga Islandite. A demonym with a special meaning in Maine, where it once was euphemistic for a misfit. It shows up in John Gould's *Maine Lingo* with the following explanation: "About the turn of the century unpleasant conditions among the residents of

Malaga Island in eastern Casco Bay forced the state welfare authorities to resettle them by families in numerous Maine communities. It was a social-betterment project well ahead of its time. Historically, Malaga Island had been a dumping place for odd people brought to Maine from the waterfronts of the world, with consequent confusion."

Malagasy. Resident of Madagascar, also the plural form.

Malawi (Republic of Malawi); *formerly* **Nyasaland.** *Malawian,* also an adjective.

Malaysia. *Malaysian,* which is also an adjective.

Maldives (Republic of Maldives). *Maldivian,* also an adjective.

Mali (Republic of Mali); *formerly* **Sudanese Republic.** *Malian,* also used as an adjective.

Malibu, California. According to the editor of the *Malibu Surfside News:* "The current prevailing term is *Malibuite.* Plural—*Malibuites. The Malibu Surfside News* pioneered the term in the 1970s. Years previously, many had used the term *Malibueno.* Plural—*Malibuenos.* "

Malouïn. Resident of Saint-Malo, France.

Malta (Republic of Malta). *Maltese* (both singular and plural); the adjective was immortalized in the film *The Maltese Falcon.*

Mamaroneck, New York. *Mamaronecker.*

Man, Isle of. *Manxman, Manxwoman,* or the collective *Manx* (q.v.), which is an alteration of *Maniske,* from an assumed Old Norse word *manskr,* from *Mana,* "Isle of Man."

Manchester, Connecticut. *Manchesterite.*

Manchester, England. *Mancunian.* Sometimes shortened to *Mancs.* The term has been said to derive from *Mancunium,* the name of a Roman fort on the site, though the *Encyclopaedia Britannica* only mentions another known form, *Mamucium.* Other old names include *Mancunio* and *Mameceaster.*

Manhattan, Kansas. *Manhattanite.*

Manhattan Island, New York. *Manhattanite,* as in "Manhattanites with takeout menus in the fridge" (*Philadelphia Inquirer,* December 4, 1988). The derivative *Manhattanization* describes the process of becoming like the island between the Hudson and East Rivers. The specific meaning varies with the context, but it is often used to describe an increase in the number of high-rise buildings in a city. It has also been used to mean "urban decay." See also GOTHAMITE.

Manila, Philippines. *Manilite.*

Manitoba, Canada. *Manitoban.* Common nickname is *Manisnowba* referring to the harsh winters with a large average snowfall.

Manitou Springs, Colorado. This matter prompted one of the most interesting letters relating to the demonym project. It came from Susan Elizabeth Musick of Norman, Oklahoma, and it reads:

> *As one who has moved around the country a bit, I've had a fair number of . . . "demonyms." I was born an Illinoisan—a Lockporter to be exact—and it was early impressed on me that the S in Illinoisan is silent.*
>
> *I've been a San Franciscan—which is by no means your run-of-the-mill Californian, and almost a different species from an Angeleno. I've been an Oregonian, but was told by some there that I ought to call myself a Webfoot. For*

nineteen years I was a Coloradan, putting in time as a Denverite, a Colorado Springsite, and a Cripple Creeker in addition to the time I spent in Manitou Springs. Then last year I became an Oklahoman, or, as many insist, a Sooner. But my favorite of all demonyms is what my neighbors in Manitou Springs called themselves: Manitoids.

Manx. The people of the Isle of Man (a British crown dependency), a Celtic language of the island, and the name of a breed of cat that has a bump where its tail should be. The cat originated on the island and many are still bred there at the government-owned Manx Cattery in the Manx capital of Douglas. *Manx* is also an adjective, as in the previous sentence.

Manxman/Manxwoman. Resident of the Isle of Man.

Maplewood, New Jersey. *Maplewoodian.*

Mariel, Cuba. *Marielito,* the name given to any of the 125,000 Cubans who were sent from Mariel, a city on Cuba's west coast, to the United States in 1980 as "outcasts." The vast majority of the *Marielitos* have been assimilated into American society, but the term is still used to identify those who were in the mass boatlift.

Marin County, California. *Marinite.*

Marion, Indiana. *Marionite.*

Maritime Provinces, Canada. *Maritimer;* also the slang term *Herring Choker.*

Mars. *Martian.*

Marseilles, France. *Marseillais.*

Marshall, Texas. *Marshallite.*

Marshall Islands (Republic of the Marshall Islands). *Marshallese* (both singular and plural), also an adjective.

Martha's Vineyard, Massachusetts. *Vineyarder.* See also ISLANDER.

Martinique. *Martiniquais* (both singular and plural), which is also an adjective along with *Martinican.*

Maryland. *Marylander.* Coming off the tongue of a native, this demonym, which appeared in print as early as 1723, sounds more like "Merl-lander" than "Mary-lander." The derivative for that which is typical or characteristic of the state is *Marylandia.*

Traditional personal nicknames: *Cockader, Crawthumper, Old Liner, Oyster,* and *Terrapin.*

State nicknames: *Free State* and *Old Line State.* The latter name comes from colonial days, when Maryland refused to alter its boundaries to please Lord Baltimore and William Penn.

Massachusetts. *Bay Stater,* which according to the *Boston Globe* of June 26, 2005, is the official designation as per Section 35 of Chapter 2 of the General Laws of the Commonwealth (Arms, Great Seal, and Other Emblems), which states plainly, "Bay Staters shall be the official designation of citizens of the commonwealth."

The debate is still fraught with emotion and the urge to call themselves something other. An early scholar who looked at demonym-formation in 1859 threw up his hands and announced that Massachusetts, Connecticut, and Arkansas refused to yield to the process. Attempts have been made to give names on the order of *Massachusettite* and *Massachusettsan* but they have not taken. Newspapers in the commonwealth occasionally yield examples deriving directly from its name, but they seem to be created for effect or alliteration, as in the phrase "meddlesome Massachusettsensian" spotted in the *Boston Herald.* The *National Review* referred to Senator Ted Kennedy as the "inevitable Massachusettsian."

Then there is the 18-letter mouthful *Massachusettensian,* which was addressed by Henry Austin in the June 4, 1908, issue of

Town Topics: "Although the term Massachusettensian has the august authority of John Adams, our second president, I prefer Massachusettsian and submit as a reason therefor that President Adams derived his from a Latinized adjectival of an Indian word which improperly drops the final 's.' If this long form should be preferred by scholars, or by the people—the ultimate authority in language, the deleted sibilant logically should be restored. But Massachusetts is already overburdened with anserine sounds, and the shorter the derivation, the sweeter, apart from the consideration of economy in space." Compare *Massachutensian* (in *Modern Music,* 1942), which drops out "set" from the state name.

Despite all of this, the official name used by the U.S. Government Printing Office is *Massachusettsan,* which rankles *Bay Staters,* who have local law on their side. Those who insist on using *Massachusettsan*s do so at the peril of public ridicule. When in 2003 during the course of the presidential primary campaigns, Democratic hopeful John Dean issued a press release thanking the "6,000 Massachusettsans" who contributed to his campaign (and repeated the term twice again in the release), the *Boston Herald* proclaimed in an October 26, 2003, editorial, "Dean is one odd Vermontarian."

Traditional personal nicknames: *Baked Bean, Old Colonial,* and *Puritan.*

State nicknames: *Bay State, Old Bay Colony, Old Colony,* and *Taxachusetts* for its supposedly higher-than-average tax rates. On July 17, 1990, the *Boston Globe* addressed the veracity of this handle in this way: "According to William Ahern of the Tax Foundation in Washington, the Bay State ranks 30th among the 50 states and the District of Columbia on combined state and local tax levies—at least until the state Legislature's new tax package takes effect."

Massillon, Ohio. *Massillonian.*

Mauch Chunk, Pennsylvania. *Chunker.*

Maui, Hawaii. *Mauian.*

Mauritania (Islamic Republic of Mauritania). *Mauritanian,* also an adjective.

Mauritius (Republic of Mauritius). *Mauritian,* which is also an adjective.

Mayberrian. Demonym applied to members of the Andy Griffith Show Appreciation Society and other fans of the long-running and still popular situation comedy set in the fictional town of Mayberry, North Carolina.

Mayotte (Territorial Collectivity of Mayotte). *Mahorais* (singular and plural); the adjective is *Mahoran.*

McAlester, Oklahoma. *McAlesterite.*

McKeesport, Pennsylvania. *McKeesporter.*

Medicine Hat, Alberta. *Hatter.*

Melanisia. *Melanisian.* This designation includes the island of New Guinea, the Bismarck and Louisiade Archipelagos, the Admiralty Islands, and Bougainville Island (which collectively make up the independent state of Papua New Guinea); the Solomon Islands, the Santa Cruz Islands (part of the Solomon Islands); New Caledonia and the Loyalty Islands; Vanuatu (formerly New Hebrides); Fiji, Norfolk Island; and various smaller islands.

Melbourne, Australia. *Melbournite, Melbournian,* or *Melburnian.* The last two are also adjectives, as in this quote from *The Age,* a Melbourne newspaper, on November 21, 1996: "The first person to touch Michael Jackson after he stepped on to Melbournian concrete in black slip-ons for the first time since 1987 was Tony Pugliese, a 23-year-old Ansett baggage handler. While 100 or more fans screamed impotently in the departure lounge upstairs, Mr. Pugliese . . . cried 'G'day mate,' stepped forward and shook Jackson's hand."

Memphis, Tennessee. *Memphian* or, rarely, *Memphite*. The term *Memphian* rolls off the tongue better than the harsher *Memphite*. Steve Rushin writes in the October 4, 1993, *Sports Illustrated:* "Of course, I am biased in favor of the *Memphians*. I'll admit, I just like the euphony of the word Memphians." The term *Memphisite* shows up in Clive Barker's novel *The Damnation Game* but appears to be contrived.

Mercury. *Mercurian*. Adjective: *Mercurial*.

Meriden, Connecticut. *Meridenite*.

Meridian, Mississippi. *Meridianite*.

Mesopotamia. *Mesopotamian*, also an adjective.

Metz, France. *Messin*.

Mexicali, Baja California. *Cachanilla* after a small, spiny desert shrub.

Mexico (United Mexican States). *Mexican*, also an adjective. In Australian slang, a *Mexican* is one who lives south of the Queensland border (as in New South Wales), or south of the New South Wales border, in Victoria.

Mexico City, Mexico. *Chilango*. In recent years, the city has been called *Chilangolandia* in a construction reminiscent of Chicagoland.

Miami, Florida. *Miamian*.

Michiana. This is the unofficial name for the area surrounding South Bend, Indiana, where northern Indiana and southern Michigan meet. *Michianans* live there. The name *Michiana* is a blend of *Michigan* and *Indiana.* Michiana is a media market, and there are periodicals such as the free weekly tabloid *Michiana Now* and the real estate magazine *Michiana Homes.*

Michigan. *Michiganian* is the official name, but strong support exists for *Michigander.*

In 1979 the state legislature voted to make *Michiganian* the official demonym. The bill was introduced at the behest of newspaper editors who were confused by a variety of names, including *Michigander, Michiganite,* and *Michiganer.* Nevertheless, some citizens continue to call themselves *Michiganders,* a term that, legend has it, was created by Abraham Lincoln in the 1848 presidential campaign, when, as a United States Congressman, he opposed the nomination of a general from Michigan. It is also the name given by H. L. Mencken in *The American Language.* However, because of the *-gander* in the term, its prestige suffers some from those who puckishly insist, "If the men are *Michiganders,* the women are *Michigeese.*"

Michiganite is given in the U.S. Government Printing Office (GPO) *Style Manual* and was put there by the GPO Style Board. This term has been fought by residents for years. An article in the *Christian Science Monitor* from December 19, 1957, pointed out that there were many in the state who wished the government in Washington would leave the name alone. An executive of the Michigan Tourist Council was quoted as saying that *Michiganite* "sounds like something you'd dig out of the ground." That executive, Robert Furlong, favored *Michiganian* because it "just plain sounds better. It has a roll and a savor to it." *Merriam-Webster's Collegiate Dictionary,* 11th edition, includes both *Michiganite* and *Michigander.*

All of this debate over the proper name for a person from Michigan suggests a certain zaniness that was underscored in a 1988 letter from Brooklynite Lillian Tudiver: "I am sure that this is one of many letters you have received pointing out that Michiganer or Michiganah [sounds like a word that] means a crazy person in Yiddish." The word is *meshuggener.*

Traditional personal nickname: *Wolverine* (q.v.), which appears to have been used as a demonym more commonly in the past.

State nicknames: *Wolverine State, Great Lakes State,* and *Automobile State.*

Micronesia, Federated States of. *Micronesian.* This political entity includes the islands of Pohnpei (or Ponape) and Kosrae and the island groups of Yap and Chuuk (or Truk). Respective demonyms are *Pohnpeian* (or *Ponapean*), *Kosraen, Yapese,* and *Chuukese* (or *Trukese*). The Federated States of Micronesia is different from the geographical Micronesia that includes the Caroline, Kiribati, Mariana, and Marshall island groups.

Middle Atlantic States. The U.S. Census Bureau defines these as New York, New Jersey, and Pennsylvania, but some less formal references include Delaware and Maryland. A resident of the area is a *Middle Atlantian.*

Middle East *or* **Mideast.** *Middle Easterner* or *Mideasterner.* The Middle East includes the area once considered to be the Near East, which is now hard to distinguish from it. In 1952, the National Geographic Society, trying to bring order to the three Easts (Near, Middle, and Far), limited its definition of the *Middle East* to India, Pakistan, Afghanistan, Nepal, Bhutan, Sikkim, and Ceylon. The definition used by the United States government in 2005 to describe the Middle East; the Middle East is the area in Asia and Africa between and including Libya in the west, Pakistan in the east, Turkey in the north, and the Arabian Peninsula in the south. The countries included in this area are Afghanistan, Bahrain, Cyprus, Egypt, Iran, Iraq, Israel, Jordan, Kuwait, Lebanon, Libya, Oman, Pakistan, Qatar, Saudi Arabia, Syria, Turkey, the United Arab Emirates, Yemen Arab Republic (North), and Yemen, People's Democratic Republic of (South).

Middle West *or* **Midwest.** *Midwesterner* or *Middle Westerner.* Adjective: *Midwestern* or *Middle Western.*

Midland, Texas. *Midlander.* In an article on the town and its relationship to George W. Bush in the January 30, 2005, New Orleans *Times-Picayune,* "George was considered an old Midlander," O'Neill said of the president, who moved to Houston in his early teens but returned to Midland after completing Harvard Business School. "When he came back, he got a very welcoming response."

Milan, Italy. *Milanese,* also an adjective.

Milwaukee, Wisconsin. *Milwaukeean.*

Miner. Traditional nickname for a resident of Nevada.

Minneapolis, Minnesota. *Minneapolitan,* but also a *Twin Citian* by virtue of the fact that Minneapolis and Saint Paul are the *Twin Cities.*

Minnesota. *Minnesotan.*
>   Traditional personal nickname: *Gopher,* in reference to a large prairie mole.
>   State nicknames: *North Star State* and *Gopher State.*

Mishawaka, Indiana. *Mishawakan.* "The first Saturday of summer will be celebrated by Mishawakans at the 13th annual Summerfest family festival in Merrifield Park," reported the *South Bend Tribune* in a 1996 article.

Mississippi. *Mississippian.*
>   Traditional personal nicknames: *Border Eagle, Mud Cat, Mud Waddler,* and *Tadpole.*
>   State nicknames: *Bayou State* and *Magnolia State.*

Missouri. *Missourian.* Because Missouri is the "Show Me State," the term *Missourian* has been used for anyone who has to be shown proof. An ad in the Tamony Collection for a betting system begins with the line: "ALL MISSOURIANS—DOUBTERS—SKEPTICS—LOSERS!!" (*The National Police Gazette,* September 27, 1924). In Herman Melville's *The Confidence-Man* (1857), set on a Mississippi River steamer, the *Missourian* is a disillusioned frontiersman not inclined toward faith or confidence in charlatans and their claims.

Traditional personal nicknames: *Doubting Thomas* (presumably from the "Show Me" motto) and *Puke* (q.v.), which was extremely common in the 19th century. Still another archaic and pejorative name for a Missourian is *Piker.* It has been suggested that it came from the days of the California Gold Rush because so many Missourians came from Pike County, but it may also be related to *Puke.*

State nickname: *Show Me State.* According to George Earlie Shankle in his *State Names, Flags, Seals, Songs, Birds, Flowers, and Other Symbols:* "The origin of the expression *Show Me* is generally attributed to the late Willard D. Vandiver, former Representative from Missouri. The late speaker Champ Clark credited Vandiver with originating the expression in an impromptu humorous address as a Member of Congress before the Five O'Clock Club in Philadelphia in 1899. 'I come from a country that raises corn, cotton, cockleburs, and Democrats,' Vandiver said in the address. 'I'm from Missouri, and you've got to show me.'"

Mobile, Alabama. *Mobilian.*

Modesto, California. *Modestan.*

Moldova (Republic of Moldova); *formerly* **Moldavian Soviet Socialist Republic.** *Moldovan,* also a well-established adjective. *Moldavian* was the previous demonym.

Moline, Illinois. *Moliner.*

Monaco (Principality of Monaco). *Monegasque* or *Monacan;* both are also adjectives.

Moncton, New Brunswick. *Monctonian.*

Mongolia (Mongolian Republic). *Mongolian,* also an adjective. *Mongol* is more of an ethnic term, while *Mongoloid* is an adjective and noun with reference to an Asian racial group. The use of words like *mongol, mongolianism,* and *mongoloid* in reference to mental retardation is not favored nowadays. The term of reference is *Down syndrome.*

Montana. *Montanan.* "A Montanan who has set up 53 schools in Pakistan and Afghanistan to educate young people, especially girls, urged state residents this week to donate to earthquake relief" (*Great Falls Tribune* [Montana], October 19, 2005).

Traditional personal nickname: *Stubtoe* (see remarks on *Stubtoe State* below).

State nicknames: *Mountain State* and *Treasure State.* Montana has also been called the *Stubtoe State,* and this may have been from the idea of stubbing one's toes on the high mountains in the western part of the state.

Montclair, New Jersey. *Montclairian.*

Montenegro; Serbia and Montenegro. *Montenegrin,* which is also an adjective. Montenegro and Serbia are all that remain of the former Yugoslavia, which included Croatia, Bosnia and Herzegovina, and Slovenia (qq.v.). The current country is a loose federation of two republics called Serbia and Montenegro. The Constitutional Charter of 2003 creating the nation of *Serbia and Montenegro* includes a provision that allows either republic to hold a referendum after three years that would allow for their independence from the state union.

Monterey, California. *Montereyan.*

Monterrey, Mexico. *Regiomontano.*

Montevideo, Uruguay. *Montevidean.*

Montpelier, Vermont. *Montpelierite.*

Montreal, Quebec. *Montrealer.* In "What the People of American Towns Call Themselves," H. L. Mencken added this in a footnote, "Among the French inhabitants *Montrealais* is used, with *Montrealaise* as its feminine form." The correct French spellings are *Montréalais* and *Montréalaise* (the city itself is *Montréal*).

Montserrat. *Montserratian.*

Moon. *Lunarian* has been suggested for a resident but *Selenite* seems to have strong support. (The Greek word for the moon is *sēlenē*.) Futurist Ralph E. Hamil, who preferred the latter, pointed out that *Selenite* is basically the same in French, Spanish, and Russian. The question of whether a lunar demonym is really needed is not as academic as it may seem, because while the population may be zero, it has been as high as two. *Lunar* is the preferred adjective.

Moonraker. Resident of Wiltshire, England. It is one of those British demonyms with a charming story behind it. Local lads were smuggling in some untaxed brandy late one moonlit night when an excise man surprised them. To avoid detection, they were forced to roll the barrels of brandy into a pond. They dumped the brandy in time and the tax man left, but the excise man returned later and caught the lads using their contraband. The smugglers explained that they were dragging the pond for a large cheese they had spotted and pointed to the reflection of the full moon on the surface of the pond. The revenuer left convinced that these men—these moonrakers—were daft.

Moose Jaw, Saskatchewan. *Moose Javian,* used as an adjective in "Moose Javian Screamin Hot Skeeter Wings," the name of a Canadian recipe that appeared in *Cottage Life* magazine. *Moose Jawite* was reported by H. L. Mencken in his 1948 *American Speech* article. In the 1930s this town was given the nickname *Little Chicago* when it was used by such figures as Al Capone to smuggle liquor into the nearby United States during Prohibition.

Morganton, North Carolina. *Morgantonian.*

Morocco (Kingdom of Morocco). *Moroccan,* also an adjective.

Morristown, New Jersey. *Morristonian.*

Moscow, Idaho. *Moscowite.*

Moscow, Russia. *Muscovite.*

Mosotho. A resident of Lesotho; the plural is *Basotho.*

Motswana. A resident of Botswana; *Batswana* is the plural form.

Mount Vernon, New York. *Mount Vernonite.*

Mozambique (Republic of Mozambique); *formerly* **Portuguese East Africa.** *Mozambican,* also an adjective. An article in the *Indianapolis Star* on Christmas in Africa (December 25, 2005) noted, "During the month of December, Mozambicans greet friends with 'Boas Festas,' which is Portuguese for 'Happy Holidays.'"

Mud Cat. Traditional nickname for a resident of Mississippi.

Mudhead. Traditional nickname for a resident of Tennessee.

Mud Waddler. Traditional nickname for a resident of Mississippi.

Muncie, Indiana. *Muncieite.* An interesting note on this came from Baltimorean Melvin H. Wunsch: "When I lived in Muncie, Ind., 45 years ago, I wrote to [H. L.] Mencken about *The American Language.* When he replied, he asked what residents of Muncie called themselves. I checked and told him that 'Muncieite' seemed to be preferred over 'Muncian' and that, years earlier, 'Munsonian' had been suggested. I added that the place had been named after the Munsee tribe of Indians. He expressed surprise at that in his thank you note and added that he had always assumed the city had been named after Frank Munsey, the world's worst editor."

Munhall, Pennsylvania. *Munhallite.*

Muscat and Oman. See OMAN.

Muscovite. Resident of Moscow, Russia.

Muscogee, Georgia. *Muscogean.*

Muskogee, Oklahoma. *Muskogeean.*

Muskrat. Traditional nickname for a resident of Delaware.

Myanmar; *formerly* **Burma.** *Burmese,* also an adjective. The nation was officially known as *Burma* until 1989, but *Burmese* is still the customary demonym and adjective while *Burma* itself is commonly used in place of *Myanmar.* On the other hand, one does sometimes find *Myanmarese* used as a noun and adjective.

Nairobi, Kenya. *Nairobian.*

Namibia (Republic of Namibia); *formerly* **South-West Africa.**
Namibian (also an adjective).

Nantucket, Massachusetts. *Nantucketer* seems to be more popular off the island than on it; a *New York Times* piece of June 5, 2005, said, "Old-time Nantucketers are given to trading what one of them called 'barbarian stories.' Did you hear that Rick Sherlund, a Goldman Sachs partner, annoyed some of his neighbors when he hired Jackson Browne to entertain at his anniversary party? Or that John Winkelried, another Goldman Sachs partner, had the nerve to close off a small road that people had been using for as long as anyone can remember?" An ad for Mitchell's Book Corner (February 17, 1972) begins with the line, "Nantucketers have been dreaming about becoming a separate nation for many years." In his essay "What the People of American Towns Call Themselves," H. L. Mencken reported, "Edouard A. Stackpole, president of the Nantucket Historical Association, tells me that *Nantucketite* is sometimes used by newcomers, but that the natives prefer *Nantucketer.*" *Islander* seems to be preferred today on Nantucket and in the local paper, the *Inquirer and Mirror.* See also OFF-ISLANDER.

Naples, Italy. *Neapolitan,* also an adjective. The ancient name of the city was *Neapolis.*

Nashville, Tennessee. *Nashvillian.*

Natchez, Mississippi. *Natchezian.*

Native American. Term that came into use in the 1960s to denote the groups served by the Bureau of Indian Affairs: American Indians and Alaska Natives (Indians, Eskimos and Aleuts of Alaska). Later the term also included Native Hawaiians and Pacific Islanders in some federal programs.

As its meaning grew, it came into disfavor among some Indian groups and today the Bureau of Indian Affairs has officially distanced itself from the term: "The preferred term is American Indian. The Eskimos and Aleuts in Alaska are two culturally distinct groups and are sensitive about being included under the 'Indian' designation. They prefer 'Alaska Native.'"

An article by Suzan Shown Harjo, president and executive director of the Morning Star Institute, a national Indian rights organization, titled "What Do You Want to Be Called?" published in *Indian Country Today,* July 25, 2001, says that the question about *Indian* versus *Native American* is the question she is most asked. "For decades, my stock answer has been that they're both wrong, so use them interchangeably."

One of Harjo's main concerns with the term *Native American* is that many non-Natives in the United States considered themselves "Native Americans." She alludes to responses to a 1980s' questionnaire given to delegates to the Republican and Democratic conventions who checked the box labeled "Native American" in large numbers. "Nearly all were non-Natives who said in follow-up calls that they thought the term meant born in the United States. Since they weren't immigrants, they said they were Native Americans."

Perhaps the most adamant opponent of the term *Native American* is Russell Means, the Lakota activist and founder of the American Indian movement (AIM), whose January 16, 1998, statement titled "I Am an American Indian, Not a Native American!" said in part:

> I abhor the term Native American. It is a generic government term used to describe all the indigenous prisoners of the United States. . . . I prefer the term American Indian because I know its origins. The word Indian is an English bastardization of two Spanish words, En Dio, which correctly translated means with God. As an added distinction the American Indian is the only ethnic group in the United States with the American before our ethnicity.

> Finally there is the 1995 Census Bureau study of terms of identity (the most recent such study as of this writing ten years later) indicated that 49 percent of those polled preferred American Indian while 37 percent preferred Native American and 5 percent had no preference.

Nauru (Republic of Nauru); *formerly* **Pleasant Island.** *Nauruan,* also an adjective.

Naxalbari, India. *Naxalite.*

Nazareth, Israel. *Nazarene.* A Christian is sometimes referred to as a *Nazarene,* since Jesus was from there though born in Bethlehem.

Neapolitan. A resident of Naples, Italy.

Near East. *Near Easterner.* The term *Near East* has suffered an identity crisis as it is hard to distinguish from the term *Middle East.* As defined by the National Geographic Society, which tried to bring order to the three Easts (Near, Middle, and Far) in 1952, the area includes Turkey, Cyprus, Syria, Lebanon, Israel, Iraq, Iran, Egypt, Jordan, and the nations of Arabia.

Nebraska. *Nebraskan,* although the nickname *Cornhusker* is common. It arose in this century as an epithet for the University of Nebraska football team and was extended to include the state.

Traditional personal nicknames: *Antelope, Bug Eater,* and *Cornhusker.*

State nicknames: *Cornhusker State* and *Beef State.*

Neorican. A Puerto Rican who lives in the continental United States or has lived on the mainland and returned to the island.

Nepal (Kingdom of Nepal). *Nepalese* (both singular and plural), though *Nepali* is used commonly as both a demonym and an adjective.

Netherlands (Kingdom of the Netherlands) *or* Holland. *Netherlander, Dutchman, Dutchwoman, Dutch* (as a collective), or *Hollander.* Adjectives include *Netherland, Dutch* (q.v.), *Netherlandic,* and *Netherlandish.* The news media tend to use *Dutch.*

Netherlands Antilles. *Netherlands Antillean,* also an adjective.

netizen. "Citizen" of the Internet—newcomer and old-timer alike. The term tends to be used in the sense of a collective Net consciousness, as in this line from the May 25, 1995, *Computing* magazine: "Netizens are not deterred by the fear, uncertainty and doubt (FUD) factors related to some alleged snipers or hackers on the highway."

Nevada. *Nevadan.*

Traditional personal nicknames: *Digger, Miner, Sagebrusher, Sage Hen,* and *Silver Stater.*

State nicknames: *Silver State* and *Sagebrush State.*

Nevisian. Resident of the island of Nevis, in Saint Kitts–Nevis. Compare KITTITIAN.

Newark, New Jersey. *Newarker.*

New Braunfels, Texas. *New Braunfelser.*

New Britain, Connecticut. *New Britainite.*

New Brunswick, Canada. *New Brunswicker* is customary, though *Herring Choker* is a common nickname that apparently is not as derogatory as it might sound.

New Brunswick, New Jersey. *New Brunswicker.*

New Caledonia. *New Caledonian.* Because *Caledonia* is the Latin name for Scotland, it would be incorrect to call a resident of New Caledonia a *Caledonian,* which is reserved for Scots.

Newcastle, Australia. *Novocastrian.*

Newcastle upon Tyne, England. Three terms are used: the formal, Latinate *Novocastrian;* the much more popular *Tynesider* (from *Tyneside,* the area on both sides of the Tyne); and *Geordie* (q.v.).

New Delhi, India. *Delhiite* or *Delhite.*

New England. *New Englander* and the nickname *Yankee* (q.v.). *New Englandy* and *Yankee* are adjectives. Singer-songwriter John Gorka, quoted in the July 14, 1996, *Boston Globe,* demonstrates why not all demonyms work alike in his line, "It's nice to be back in New England among the New English."

Newfoundland, Canada. *Newfoundlander.* The alternative *Newlander* was advanced by newspaper writers after World War II, according to an Associated Press dispatch of October 13, 1948, because the residents objected to the informal terms *Newf* and *Newfie*. Despite this, *Newfie* is still in common use, as in informal travel articles like one from the headline of the August 17, 2003, Brisbane *Sunday Mail*, "Newfie Warmth Is No Joke." Although *Newfie* to some might have the sound of a slur, it is used with some affection by Newfoundlanders. Bob Tulk's *Newfie Jokes*, published in 1990 by Corner Brook, Newfoundland, carries this notice: "This book was published, not for the purpose of making fun of Newfoundlanders but to show that most of us can take a joke as well as give one."

New Hampshire. *New Hampshirite.* However, *New Hampshire-man/New Hampshirewoman* and *Hampshireman/Hampshirewoman* are traditional and listed in some dictionaries. *Granite Boy/Granite Girl* is an old slang term for a native in celebration of the state's extensive granite quarries.

State nickname: *Granite State.*

New Haven, Connecticut. *New Havener.*

New Hebrides. See VANUATU.

New Jersey. *New Jerseyan,* which is replacing the former *New Jerseyite.* For instance, a letter from a New Jersey man published in the *National Review* (June 10, 1988) refers to a piece of legislation that "allows New Jerseyans to deduct part of their property tax from their state income tax." Craig Schoonmaker, a New Jerseyan who ran for president in 2000 as the candidate of the Expansionist Party of the United States, which advocates the annexation of Canada by the United States, and claims to have coined the term "gay pride," says that he helped get Merriam-Webster, a major publisher of dictionaries and other reference works (e.g., the *Encyclopaedia Britannica*), to recognize *New Jerseyan* as the preferred term for someone from New Jersey. Quoting from his Schoonmaker 2000 Web site:

When I was young, and to this day in many dictionaries, the only term one could find for a resident of New Jersey was "New Jerseyite." We in New Jersey (my state of birth) never used that bizarre term, so I wrote to Merriam-Webster, the most prestigious dictionary maker, to complain. They said that their entries arise from actual citations in published materials, and that citations for "New Jerseyite" go back over a century and are found in many works. (Of course a term that dictionaries offer would be used by people who have no better information!) I replied by sending a number of citations to written mentions of "New Jerseyan," including a form letter from then-U.S. Senator from New Jersey and present-day presidential candidate Bill Bradley. I also sent off letters to educators and publications in New Jersey asking them to write to Merriam-Webster to point out that in New Jersey, "New Jerseyan" is standard. If you check a recent Webster's *New Collegiate Dictionary,* you'll see that Merriam-Webster now includes "New Jerseyan" first, and only then the hated "New Jerseyite." It really should abandon the ignorant misuse "New Jerseyite," but they may argue that they retain it for readers of older materials—as tho [*sic*] people would be puzzled as to the meaning of "New Jerseyite" if it weren't given in a dictionary!

Jerseyan and *Jerseyite* are sometimes used when there is no chance of confusion with the British Isle of Jersey. Earlier writers often used *Jerseyman* and *Jerseywoman,* which are rare today but used proudly by some traditional natives. *Jersey guy* and *Jersey gal* have a long tradition going as a term of self-description (used by Bruce Springsteen, Frank Sinatra, Bruce Willis, Jack Nicholson, Danny DeVito, Shaquille O'Neal, and Joe Piscipo, among them.) *Jersey boys* was the name taken by a pair of racist radio "shock jocks" in New Jersey who claimed, according to the *Bergen County Record* of April 29, 2005, that they represented "the average guy in New Jersey, blue-collar white people . . ." They rountinely engaged in racial invective giving the name a new and negative meaning.

Traditional personal nicknames: *Blue, Clam, Clam Catcher,* and *Jersey Blue. Jersey Blue* and *Blue* derive from the color of the uniforms worn by New Jersey soldiers in the Revolutionary War.

State nicknames: *Garden State* and *Mosquito State.* The origin of *Garden State* is addressed on the New Jersey State Web site: "Alfred M. Heston, in his two-volume work, Jersey Waggon Jaunts, published in 1926 (Camden, NJ, Atlantic County Historical Society, 1926), twice credits Abraham Browning of Camden with coining the name at the Centennial Exhibition in Philadelphia on New Jersey Day, August 24, 1876. On page 310 of volume 2 he writes: 'In his address Mr. Browning compared New Jersey to an immense barrel, filled with good things to eat and open at both ends, with Pennsylvanians grabbing from one end and the New Yorkers from the other. He called New Jersey the Garden State, and the name has clung to it ever since.'"

"We get the scornful title, the Mosquito State," the state librarian told George Earlie Shankle for his 1941 work *State Names, Flags, Seals, Songs, Birds, Flowers, and Other Symbols,* "because we seem to have our share of these industrious and bloodthirsty insects. As a matter of fact, however, a considerable number of other states have as many, if not more, of these pests."

New London, Connecticut. *New Londoner.*

New Mexico. *New Mexican.* An interesting derivative is *New Mex,* which is a style of cooking that combines New Mexican and Mexican influences in the manner that *Tex-Mex* cooking combines Texan and Mexican cuisine.

State nickname: *Land of Enchantment.*

New Orleans, Louisiana. *New Orleanian* or *Orleanian. Houston Chronicle* partial headline of October 19, 2005: "New Orleanian Busy Dealing with FEMA, Furnishing Her New Apartment." Mencken noted that Thomas Jefferson used *Orleanese* in 1808, and Merriam-Webster has a citation for *New Orleander.* The city is nicknamed the *Big Easy.*

Newport, Rhode Island. *Newporter.*

New Rochelle, New York. *New Rochellean.*

New South Wales, Australia. *New South Welshman* as well as *Cornstalk,* according to Australian folklorist Bill Scott. The latter should be used with caution.

Newton, Kansas. *Newtonian.*

New Ulm, Minnesota. *New Ulmer.*

New York. *New Yorker.* It is occasionally suggested that New Yorkers deserve a more colorful name (on the order of *Hoosier* or *Sooner*), but none has ever come along. *Knickerbocker,* explained below, is traditional but not a common everyday demonym. In this regard, a transplanted New Yorker, Lois H. Jones, wrote to the *Miami Herald* in 1988 asking for a title based on her state of origin. The newspaper's answer was: "The usual nickname for people from New York is simply New Yorker, but if you want to get fancy, maybe you can call yourself an Imperialist, since the state is known as the Empire State." "There's just not a lot of colorful monikers you can hang on yourself," says Jean Palmer, librarian in the Local History Special Collections Department of the Onondaga County Library in upstate New York. "Actually, New Yorkers don't go much for nicknames," she says. "That's why we're mostly called New Yorkers" (*Miami Herald,* October 11, 1988).

Traditional personal nicknames: *Knickerbocker* and *Noo-*

yawker. Knickerbocker originated with *Knickerbocker's History of New York* (1809), which was said to be the work of one "Diedrich Knickerbocker" but was actually written by Washington Irving. The word was soon attached to practically anything related to New York, and became an established noun for descendants of the original Dutch settlers and for New Yorkers in general.

State nicknames: *Empire State* (from its commercial importance and the enterprise of its people) and *Excelsior State* (from the motto on its coat of arms).

New York, New York. *New Yorker.* The names *Gothamite* and *Manhattanite* are also used. H. L. Mencken found that the term *New Yorker* was used by George Washington in 1756. In 1871 author William Dean Howells launched *New Yorkess* as a feminine form, but it did not catch on. A term for that which is typical or characteristic of the city is *New Yorkiana.*

The city is nicknamed the *Big Apple,* a term that etymologist David Shulman traces back to 1909. It has also attracted a number of other nicknames, from O. Henry's *Yaptown-on-the-Hudson* to the fanciful *Alaspooryork,* the winner in a 1971 contest to rename the place in case it seceded from the state and established itself as an independent city-state.

New Zealand. *New Zealander* or *Kiwi* (q.v.).

Niagara Falls, New York. There is no commonly accepted term, but *Niagaran* has been used.

Nicaragua (Republic of Nicaragua). *Nicaraguan,* also an adjective. One finds the shortened *Nic* used in newspaper headlines—"U.S. Pushes to Expel Nic Ambassador," *Boston Herald,* July 14, 1988—but this seems to be a product of space considerations rather than an attempt to create a new term.

Nice, France. *Niçois.*

Niger (Republic of Niger). *Nigerien* is clearly the prevalent demonym and adjective, though *Nigerois* has also been used.

Nigeria (Federal Republic of Nigeria). *Nigerian,* also an adjective.

Niles, Ohio. *Nilesite.*

Ninth Islander. Hawaiian living in any place outside of Hawaii's eight islands that is frequented by a large number of Hawaiians. Las Vegas, Santa Cruz, etc. A May 8, 2002, Associated Press piece read: "Honolulu, Hawaii—May 8: [Hawaii] Gov. Ben Cayetano has slipped off to Las Vegas to participate in the kickoff of the Great Ninth Island Expo, a three-day event to display made-in-Hawaii gifts and products."

Niue. *Niuean.*

Ni-Vanuatu. A resident of Vanuatu; the same form is used for the plural.

Nogales, Arizona. *Nogalian.*

Nome, Alaska. *Nomeite.* "Snow Blower Is a Nomeite's Best Friend" was headline in the January 31, 2002, issue of the *Nome Nuggett.*

Nooyawker. Traditional nickname for a resident of New York.

Norfolk, England. *Norfolkian* or *North Anglian.*

Norfolk, Nebraska. *Norfolkan.*

Norfolk, Virginia. *Norfolkian.*

Norfolk Island. *Norfolk Islander.*

Normal, Illinois. *Normalite.*

Norman, Oklahoma. *Normanite.*

North America. *North American.*

Northampton, Massachusetts. *Northamptonite.*

North Carolina. *North Carolinian* or *Tar Heel* (q.v.). *Carolinian* is used for residents of both North Carolina and South Carolina.

Traditional personal nicknames: *Tarboiler, Tar Heel, Tucko,* and *Turpentiner.*

State nicknames: *Tar Heel State* and *Old North State* (to distinguish it from South Carolina).

North Dakota. *North Dakotan,* although *Dakotan* is used for residents of both North Dakota and South Dakota. On occasion *Nodak* is used as a combination nickname and abbreviation, and *Flickertail* is a traditional slang demonym. In recent years there have been several small attempts to have North Dakota renamed *Dakota*—to fight what has been termed an image of "blizzards and rocks"—but it is doubtful that anything will come of it. (Columnist George Will puckishly suggested that if the state really wants to change its image it should rename itself *Bermuda*).

State nicknames: *Sioux State, Flickertail State, Peace Garden State,* and *Cyclone State.*

Northern Ireland. *Northern Irishman* and *Northern Irishwoman,* or the collective *Irish* and *Northern Irish.*

Northern Rhodesia. See ZAMBIA.

Northern Territory, Australia. *Territorian* or *Top-ender.*

North Korea. See KOREA, NORTH.

North Slope, Alaska. *North Sloper.*

Northumberland, England. *Northumbrian. Northumberland* is from *Northumber* or *Northumbria,* an ancient region of England whose name literally means "north of the [river] Humber." *Northumber* itself was once used as a demonym for residents of this land. For example, Richard Grafton wrote in 1568, "While king William was thus occupied in Normandy, the Northumbers rebelled."

Norwalk, Connecticut. *Norwalker.*

Norwich, England. *Dumplings.* "It is the picture of a bygone England," said *The Guardian* in an October 12, 1991, profile. "There are no modern carbuncles, only the spires of medieval churches. Its cobbled alleyways are bright with flowers. Even the food is of a former age: locals call themselves Dumplings after the traditional dish."

Norway (Kingdom of Norway). *Norwegian,* also an adjective. *Norse* is a synonymous adjective, although it can have specific reference to ancient Scandinavia. The noun *Norse* has senses as a collective demonym for Scandinavians and Norwegians. A *Norseman* is an ancient Scandinavian.

Nova Scotia, Canada. *Nova Scotian,* or the popular slang term *Bluenose* (q.v.).

Novocastrian. Resident of Newcastle upon Tyne, England, or especially Newcastle, Australia, which even has a hotel by this name.

Nunavut. *Nunavummiut* is officially used by the government of Canada, which describes it as a term used to describe all peoples living in Nunavut, and is not limited to the indigenous inhabitants. There are examples of *Nunavumiut, Nunavumiuq,* and *Nunavutian* in use on Canadian Web sites.

Nunavut is Canada's newest territory. Formerly part of the vast Northwest Territories, Nunavut officially separated on April 1, 1999, via the Nunavut Act and the Nunavut Land Claims Agreement Act, though the actual boundaries were established as early as 1993. The capital of Nunavut is Iqaluit (formerly Frobisher Bay) on Baffin Island. Other major communities include Rankin Inlet and Cambridge Bay. Nunavut has a population of only about 27,000 Nunavummiut spread over an area the size of Western Europe. *Nunavut* means "our land" in Inuktitut, the language of the Inuit.

Nutmeg *or* **Nutmegger.** Traditional nickname for a resident of Connecticut (q.v.), as in "a band of far-sighted Nutmeggers" (from *Time,* August 1, 1949). The *Hartford Courant* Sunday magazine, *Northeast,* has a column on local matters that is called *Nutmeggery.*

Nuyorican. A Puerto Rican who lives in New York City.

Nyack, New York. *Nyacker.*

Nyasaland. See MALAWI.

Oakland, California. *Oaklander.* Two negative names are *Joaklander* and *Ughlander.*

Oak Park, Illinois. *Oak Parker.*

Oak Ridge, Tennessee. *Oak Ridger.*

Oaxaca, Mexico. *Oaxacan.*

OBtian. Resident of Ocean Beach, a section of San Diego, California. A demonymic oddity reported by OBtian Ellen Todd, who writes: "I live in the Ocean Beach section of San Diego. We all have a penchant for giving our cities and neighborhoods letter abbreviations 'LA,' 'SD,' and so on; so our community is called 'OB.' We are therefore OBtians, O-B-shuns."

Oceania. *Oceanian.*

Odessa, Texas. *Odessan.*

off-islander. A generic term popular on some islands for people from anywhere but the island in question. It has a strong association with the island of Nantucket because of a Nathaniel Benchley book called *The Off-Islanders* (1961), which was made into the movie *The Russians Are Coming! The Russians Are Coming!* (1966). In addition to tourists and visitors, the term is sometimes used to refer to a person who lives on the island (full- or part-time) but was not born there. The term is also commonly used by residents of the islands of the state of Maine. Jonathan Tourtellot of the National Geographic Society reports a variation: "If you're not Manx but live on the Isle of Man, you're a 'Come-over.'" See also ISLANDER.

Ogden, Utah. *Ogdenite.*

Ohio. *Ohioan,* but the nickname *Buckeye* is sometimes used. It commemorates the abundance of buckeye trees in the state, which produce a horse chestnut that looks like a buck's eye when first cracked open and is thus called a *buckeye.*

Traditional personal nicknames: *Buckeye* and *Yellowhammer,* which was once popular and has also been used for Alabamians.

State nickname: *Buckeye State.*

Okie. Pejorative term for an Oklahoman, mainly because it is so strongly tied to the poor migratory farmworkers from Oklahoma who fled the Dust Bowl. In 1947, H. L. Mencken noted that the term is "not tolerated locally, though it is in wide use elsewhere, especially in California, which received the brunt of the mass migration of 1935, described with poetic fancy in John E. Steinbeck's *Grapes of Wrath.*" The term existed before Steinbeck's 1939 novel, but the classic helped spread it. In 1968, Oklahoma governor Dewey Bartlett began a campaign to renovate the "derogatory title of *Okie*" by using it as the centerpiece of a program in which Oklahoma progress and pride would be recognized through such means as "Okie pins" and "Okie certificates." (Mike McCarville, Bartlett's press secretary, wrote a book called *Okie* [1970] recounting the program.) An association of *Okie* with migrant farmworkers (like *Arkie, Okie* enjoyed generic application to migrants from other states in 1930s' California) was to be replaced by a connection with two mottoes of state boosterism: "*O*klahoma, *K*ey to *I*ntelligence and *E*nterprise" and "*O*klahoma, *K*ey to *I*ndustrial *E*xpansion." The program involved books, rings, badges, bumper stickers, a USDA-approved "Okie Steak"—and over 30,000 pins and honorary Okie certificates were given out to such figures as Richard Nixon, Hubert Humphrey, and Andy Griffith.

Governor Bartlett included a certificate with his 1968 letter to Henry Bosley Woolf, then general editor of Merriam-Webster dictionaries, in which he offered a "redefinition" of *Okie* for future use: "Okie—n. a resident of Oklahoma; originally used as a nickname for migratory farmworkers, but now used to promote pride in Oklahoma and defined within the state as *O*klahoma, *K*ey to *I*ndustrial *E*xpansion, and *O*klahoma, *K*ey to *I*ntelligence and *E*nterprise." This unsuccessful effort bears comparison with the offensive launched against slang meanings of *Hoosier* (q.v.) by Dan Quayle.

Even on the home front in Oklahoma there was resistance to the *Okie* effort. Colonel C. E. Chouteau's Pioneer Committee sponsored an essay contest on the topic "Why I Am Not an Okie." The colonel reported receipt of 34,000 anti-*Okie* responses, and the winner was O. J. Reynolds, who claimed: "The revival of this dirty, nasty word in the minds of all respectable citizens of Oklahoma was originated by a few to enrich the coffers of the money-mad at the expense of the stable citizenship who are being fried in the deep grease of humiliation throughout their state and the nation" (*Oklahoma Journal*, March 5, 1970).

Reynolds also offered a possible origin of the term *Okie:* "Old timers tell us that an Okie was the product of a Texas cowboy and a Kansas prostitute during the cattle driving days across the state. That is why an Okie steer is described as a crossbreed of uncertain ancestry." In any case, the term predates *The Grapes of Wrath* and indeed goes back to before the Depression and the Dust Bowl. McCarville's book reproduces a postcard that

Myrtle Pence of Newcastle, Indiana, sent to a friend in the Oklahoma Territory in 1907: "Hello Okie: Will see you next Monday night."

Although the *Okie* program ended when David Hall became governor in 1971, the undertaking certainly brought attention to Oklahoma pride. Country singer and native Oklahoman Merle Haggard did the same with his 1969 hit, "Okie from Muskogee," which described the Oklahoma town as a place where patriotism still held sway (amid the nation's turmoil over Vietnam) and "white lightning" was still the stimulant of choice. Haggard distanced himself a bit when the song was adopted as a "redneck" anthem but stood by the speaker's claim that he was "proud to be an Okie from Muskogee": "I'm proud to be an American and proud to be an Okie. That part's fine" (*Washington Post,* September 15, 1971).

Oklahoma. *Oklahoman,* preferred to *Oklahomian.* The nickname *Sooner* (tied to the University of Oklahoma Sooners) is also used. According to a 1930 letter from the state historian to George Earlie Shankle that the latter published in his *State Names, Flags, Seals, Songs, Birds, Flowers, and Other Symbols,* the sobriquet *Sooner State* was given to Oklahoma for the following reason, "when the lands of Oklahoma were opened to settlement at a given hour those who did not await the appointed time, but who slipped in clandestinely ahead of time, were dubbed 'sooners' because they did not wait as required by law, but tried to gain an unfair advantage by entering the forbidden precincts too soon."

Traditional personal nicknames: *Okie* (q.v.) and *Sooner.* State nickname: *Sooner State.*

Oklahoma City, Oklahoma. *Oklahoma Cityan.*

Okracoke Island, North Carolina. *O'Cockers.* The residents of this isolated island speak with a fast-disappearing brogue spoken with a "hoi toider" accent ("high tider" with the ninth letter of the alphabet pronounced "oy"). Outsiders are called *Dingbaters.*

Old Colonial. Traditional nickname for a resident of Massachusetts.

Old Liner. Traditional nickname for a resident of Maryland.

Olean, New York. *Oleander.*

Omaha, Nebraska. *Omahan.* An item in the *New York Times* for November 4, 1986, describes "a determined band of Omahans." *Omahog* is the nickname for the city whose demonym is not always at the tip of the tongue. Edna Ferber, in an article for *Liberty* magazine (May 2, 1925) entitled "Middle-Class, Middle West Me": "To the Chicagoan, New York is the East. But to the Oma— (Omahan?—Omahawan—Omahaan?) well anyway, to the resident of Omaha, Chicago is East."

Oman (Sultanate of Oman); *formerly* **Muscat and Oman.** *Omani,* which is also an adjective.

Onion. Honorific name for those born and bred in Bermuda, from the exported Bermuda onion.

Ontario, Canada. *Ontarian.*

Opelika, Alabama. *Opelikian.*

Orange, New Jersey. *Orangeite.*

Orange County, California. *Orange Countian.* The term "Orange Curtain" is being used to mark those characteristics, real or imagined, that differentiate Orange County from Los Angeles and the rest of California.

Orcadian. Resident of the Orkney Islands, Scotland.

Oregon. *Oregonian,* also an adjective.
    Traditional personal nicknames: *Webfoot, Beaver,* and *Hard*

Case. Beaver derives from Oregon's historic fur trade; *Webfoot* and *Hard Case* are discussed at their respective individual entries.

State nickname: *Beaver State*.

Oriental Republic of Uruguay. See URUGUAY.

Orkney Islands, Scotland. *Orcadian,* although *Orkneyan* is sometimes used, as are *Orkney Islander* and *Orkneyman/Orkneywoman.* The common adjective for the island is also *Orcadian,* as in "one particularly muggy Orcadian day" (*Daily Telegraph,* August 31, 1991).

Orlando, Florida. *Orlandoan,* as in this item from the *Orlando Sentinel* of December 12, 2005: "Several teams are waiting on free-agent center fielder and Orlandoan Johnny Damon, who has been offered a four-year deal for $40 million by Boston."

Orleanian. Resident of New Orleans, Louisiana.

Oshkosh, Wisconsin. This comment appeared in George R. Stewart Jr.'s "Names for Americans" in *American Speech,* February 1934: "Oshkosh is stumped by its own name, the press there sticking to 'Oshkosh man' or 'Oshkosh woman.' The name is of Indian origin, so that 'Oshkosher' might not be kosher."

Oskaloosa, Iowa. *Oskaloosan.*

Oslo, Norway. *Osloer.*

Ossining, New York. *Ossiningite* or *Ossininger.*

Ottawa, Kansas. *Ottawan.*

Ottawa, Ontario. *Ottawan,* but see also BYTOWNER. *Blahttawa* is a derogatory name for Canada's capital, referring, according to the

Wikipedia.com, "to its lack of club scene, lack of culture, and boring postcard-esque perfection."

Ottumwa, Iowa. *Ottumwan.*

out-of-stater. In the United States, a generic term for a tourist or other visitor. It can be, but isn't always, used as a term of derision. "Most of the trout fishermen were Easterners, middle-age men with money. It wasn't considered polite anymore to say 'dudes.' 'Out-of-stater' was the currently accepted epithet" (*Incident at Big Sky,* by Johnny France and Malcolm McConnell, 1986).

Owensboro, Kentucky. *Owensboroan.*

Oxbridgian. A graduate of Oxford or Cambridge University in England; the two are sometimes referred to as a single entity, *Oxbridge.* Oxbridgians are an elite who, among other things, were said to have been the mainstay of the British intelligence service MI-6.

Oxford, England. *Oxonian,* a term that also applies to a graduate of Oxford University. The journal published by the Association of American Rhodes Scholars is *The American Oxonian. Oxfordian* is sometimes used for residents of Oxford as well as for those who ascribe the writings of Shakespeare to Edward de Vere, the 17th earl of Oxford. The *Oxford English Dictionary,* 2nd edition lists a number of other derivatives, including *Oxfordish, Oxfordy,* and *Oxonolatry* (for love of the place).

Ozark Mountains. *Ozarker* or *Ozarkian,* which is also an adjective. Historically, the area seems to have had a number of odd local nicknames designed to puzzle outsiders. A March 3, 1934, Associated Press dispatch in the *San Francisco Call Bulletin* (Tamony Collection) attempted to sort them out: "The 'Hog Rangers' live south of the Osage River and their neighbors, the 'Elm Peelers,' live on the north side of the River. In the hunting country live the

'Rabbit Twisters,' who save ammunition by twisting a stick in the fur of rabbits in hollow logs and dragging them out. The 'Squirrel Knocks' kill their game with rocks. The 'Scissorbills' live in the valleys; the 'Ridge Runners' atop the cedar studded hogbacks. The 'Sprout Splitters' are in the cut over timber country."

Ozzie. A resident of Australia, which is sometimes called *Oz*. For example, on the World Wide Web one finds the *West Oz Web* in western Australia.

Pacific Islands. *Pacific Islander.* Term used especially in the western United States as a term of association as in the Pacific Islanders' Cultural Association of Northern California. The term includes Polynesians, Melanesians, and Micronesians.

Paducah, Kentucky. *Paducahan.*

Paisley, Scotland. *Paisley Buddies* or *Buddies.* According to the town's official Web site "Paisley folk, or 'Buddies,' as they refer to themselves, are very proud of their town and are fiercely loyal to it." A term that is *not* used is *Paisleyite,* which since the 1960s has been used to refer to the followers of the anti-Catholic Reverend Ian Kyle Paisley and his Protestant Unionists in Northern Ireland.

Pakistan (Islamic Republic of Pakistan). *Pakistani,* also an adjective. The shortened *Pak* is also used, but the term *Paki,* as used in jokes, is clearly derogatory.

Palau (Republic of Palau). *Palauan,* also an adjective.

Palestinian. One who lives in the region of Palestine, which includes modern Israel and the West Bank, and especially a member of an Arab people native to the area.

Palm Beach, Florida. *Palm Beacher.*

Palmetto. Traditional nickname for a resident of South Carolina.

Palo Alto, California. *Palo Altan.*

Palois. Resident of Pau, France.

Panama (Republic of Panama). *Panamanian,* also an adjective.

Panama City, Panama. *Panamanian.*

panethnic. Term for a broader identification: Asian and Hispanic are two common examples.

Panhandler *or* **Panhandleite.** Traditional nickname for a resident of West Virginia, which has been called the *Panhandle State.*

Paonia, Colorado. *Paonian.*

Papua New Guinea (Independent State of Papua New Guinea). *Papua New Guinean,* which is also an adjective.

Paraguay (Republic of Paraguay). *Paraguayan,* also an adjective.

Paris, France. *Parisian* or *Parisienne* (for a woman).

Park City, Utah. *Parkites.*

Pasadena, California. *Pasadenan.*

Passaic, New Jersey. *Passaicite.*

Patagonia. *Patagonian,* also an adjective.

Paterson, New Jersey. *Patersonian.*

Patrick's People. Name that the Irish have sometimes applied to themselves, in reference to Saint Patrick, their patron saint.

Pau, France. *Palois.*

Paulista. Resident of São Paulo, Brazil. The term has also denoted a Brazilian born of a Portuguese colonist (as an explorer of the interior) and a native woman.

Pea Souper. Contemptuous term for a French Canadian, derived from the diet of the voyageurs in the days of the fur trade. The term is also used to describe a dense fog.

Pecos, Texas. *Pecosite.*

Peekskill, New York. *Peekskillite.* H. L. Mencken added this footnote to his 1948 article in *American Speech:* "Mr. E. Joe Albertson, of the Peekskill *Evening Star,* tells me that *Peekskiller* was formerly in use, but that his paper now avoids it on the ground that 'it had too murderous a sound.'"

Pegger. Resident of Winnipeg, Manitoba.

Pelham, New York. *Pelhamite.*

Pelican. Traditional nickname for a resident of Louisiana.

Pennsylvania. *Pennsylvanian,* also an adjective. A sports story from the *Baltimore Sun* describes a Maryland college going into a lacrosse tournament with "more Pennsylvanians than Marylanders."

Traditional personal nicknames: *Coal Miner, Cohee, Iron Puddler, Leatherhead, Loggerhead, Pennanite,* and *Quaker. Pennanite* is an old slang name for the followers and admirers of William Penn. *Cohee* (or *Coohee*) is an old slang term for "an inhabitant of western Pennsylvania or western Virginia" (*Webster's Third New International Dictionary*). A *Cohee* was distinguished from a *Tuckahoe,* one from the other side of the Blue Ridge Mountains in eastern Virginia. *Cohee* has often been said to come from a local usage of archaic "quoth he," pronounced "quo' he," but H. L. Mencken reported in *American Speech* (February 1949) that it may come from "an Indian word signifying a bend in the river." No other information is given, however.

State nickname: *Keystone State,* from the time when there were 13 states and a popular woodcut depicted the new nation as an arch with Pennsylvania as the keystone.

Pennsylvania Dutch. The descendants of German immigrants to Pennsylvania who cling to certain Germanic speech patterns and customs are known as the *Pennsylvania Dutch,* with *Dutch* in this case meaning "German." Their dialect goes by the same name and is based on High German. Hence the *New York Times* could carry an item like this: "Pennsylvania State University is offering a course in 'Pennsylvania Dutch'—spoken only by 300,000 Pennsylvanians" (October 2, 1955). Briton Ross Reader writes to point out that *Pennsylvania Dutch* is a very confusing term to strangers coming to the United States. The singular *Pennsylvania Dutchman* is well established in use.

Pensacola, Florida. *Pensacolian.*

People's Republic of Angola. See ANGOLA.

People's Republic of Bangladesh. See BANGLADESH.

People's Republic of Benin. See BENIN.

People's Republic of China. See CHINA.

People's Socialist Republic of Albania. See ALBANIA.

Peoria, Illinois. *Peorian.*

Perth Amboy, New Jersey. *Perth Amboyan.*

Peru (Republic of Peru). *Peruvian,* also an adjective.

Philadelphia, Pennsylvania. *Philadelphian.*

Philippines (Republic of the Philippines). *Filipino.* Adjective: *Philippine.*

Phoenix, Arizona. *Phoenician.* "There are business opportunities here, and the kids were born here. They are Phoenicians" (*Arizona Republic,* November 20, 2005). The demonym is of course a clean play on the name of an ancient people and culture, since *Phoenician* (or *Phenician*) usually refers to a citizen of ancient Phoenicia. Phoenix is said to have been so named in the 1860s because, like the mythical bird who rises from the ashes, it was to spring up from the ruins of an earlier American Indian settlement on the same site. Both *Phoenicia* and *phoenix* (the bird) trace back to Greek *phoinix,* and so the Arizona Phoenicians owe their demonym as well as the name of their city to the development of that word.

Pierre, South Dakota. *Pierrite.*

Piker. Archaic and pejorative term for a Missourian. In his *Dictionary of Americanisms,* Mitford Mathews suggested that it originated in the days of the California gold rush when so many of the Missourians came from Pike County.

Pilltowner. Resident of Hollywood, California, according to the slang of the 1950s, when the film colony there was building its reputation as an enormous consumer of tranquilizers. A typical *Pilltown/Pilltowner* quip of the time was this one from Earl Wilson's syndicated column (October 2, 1956): "Out in Pilltown . . . many of the stars now have pool-shaped kidneys. . . ."

Pine Barrens, New Jersey. *Pineys.*

Pine Bluff, Arkansas. *Pine Bluffian.*

Pine Treeman. Traditional nickname for a resident of Maine, the *Pine Tree State.*

Piqua, Ohio. *Piquard.*

Pitcairn Island. *Pitcairner* or *Pitcairn Islander.* Pitcairners (of which there were 62 in 2005) descend from the mutineers on the H.M.S. *Bounty* who settled on the island in 1790.

Pittsburgh, Pennsylvania. *Pittsburgher* is preferred but *Pittsburger* is acceptable. The regional quirks in vocabulary and speech (rubber bands are "gumbands" in this town, where the sidewalks get "slippy," not slippery) are lumped together under the name *Pittsburghese.* The blend *Pittsylvania* is used to describe an area of southwestern Pennsylvania along with neighboring portions of Maryland and West Virginia that is dominated by the city of Pittsburgh. A book by George Swetnam entitled *Pittsylvania Country* was published in 1951.

Plainfield, New Jersey. *Plainfielder.*

Plains, Georgia. *Plainsman* and *Plainswoman*—terms that received exposure with the election of Jimmy Carter as president in 1976.

Pleasant Island. See NAURU.

Plymouth, Massachusetts. *Plymouthian.* A bumper sticker spotted in that town on May 11, 1988, alluded to its recent development: NATIVE PLYMOUTHIAN—AN ENDANGERED SPECIES.

Plymouth, Pennsylvania. *Plymouthite.*

Poblano. Resident of Puebla, Mexico.

Pocatello, Idaho. *Pocatellan.*

Podunk. Generic term for a hick town inhabited by boors, rubes, and *Podunkers.* Several real Podunks exist, including a sparsely settled section of East Brookfield, Massachusetts, and the town of Podunk Center, Iowa, which was offered for sale in 1969 for $7,000 (at the time it had no population).

Pohnpei *or* **Ponape, Micronesia.** *Pohnpeian* or *Ponapean.*

Poland (Republic of Poland). *Pole.* Adjective: *Polish.*

Polynesia. *Polynesian.* This designation includes the islands dotting the triangle covering the east-central region of the Pacific Ocean. It is bounded by Hawaii in the north, New Zealand in the west, and Easter Island in the east. The rest of Polynesia comprises Samoa (American and Western), the Cook Islands, French Polynesia (Tahiti and the Society Islands, Marquesa Islands, Austral Islands, and the Tuamotu Archipelago), Niue Island, Tokelau and Tuvalu, Tonga, Wallis and Futuna, and Pitcairn Island.

Pomona, California. *Pomonan.*

Pomponian. Resident of Portsmouth, England, also known by its nickname *Pompey.* Philip Chaplin of Ottawa was once stationed there in the navy and reports that the traditional name for him and his

itan. Traditional nickname for a resident of Massachusetts.

htoonistan. One who lived in this short-lived nation on Afghanistan's eastern border that proclaimed its independence in 1949 was a *Pushtoonistani.*

-in-Bay, Ohio. *Mossback,* an allusion to the nontransient nature of the year-round residents. Nicknamed the *Key West of the North,* Put-in-Bay is located in Lake Erie on South Bass Island. A popular bar and restaurant on the island is called Mossback's.

mates was "the Pompey ratings." *Pompey* is also a widely used nickname for the Portsmouth Football Club, the city's soccer team.

Ponape, Micronesia. See POHNPEI.

Pontiac, Michigan. *Pontiacker.*

Porkopolitan. Resident of Cincinnati, from the time when the city processed hogs and was known as *Porkopolis.*

Port Arthur, Texas. *Port Arthuran.*

Porteño. Resident of Buenos Aires, Argentina.

Portland, Maine. *Portlander.*

Portland, Oregon. *Portlander,* although the demonym *Stumptowner* is sometimes used colloquially (*Stumptown* is one of the oldest nicknames for the city dating back to the time in the 19th century when the city was booming and land was cleared so quickly that there was no time to remove the stumps) along with *PDXer,* from the three-letter airport baggage code for the city.

Portsmouth, New Hampshire. *Portsmouthite.*

Portsmouth, Virginia. *Portsmouthite.*

Portugal (Portuguese Republic); *anciently* **Lusitania.** *Portuguese* (both singular and plural). The demonym and adjective *Lusitanian,* based on the country's ancient name, have sometimes been used as synonyms of *Portuguese,* though this does not appear to be done much. In May 1915 the *American Agriculturist* attempted, through an editorial and a letter to Merriam-Webster, to establish *lusitanian* (rendered *luisitanian* in the editorial by an infelicitous typo) as an adjective to describe the "acme of atrocity," since the Germans had sunk the British liner *Lusitania* on May 7 off the coast of Ireland. The editorial stated hopefully, "The new word, the same in all languages, forever will express the world's repudiation of the act of 7 May 1915!" There is no evidence that the adjective caught on.

Portuguese East Africa. See MOZAMBIQUE.

Portuguese Guinea. See GUINEA-BISSAU.

Portuguese Republic. See PORTUGAL.

Port Vue, Pennsylvania. *Port Vueite.*

Poughkeepsie, New York. *Poughkeepsian.*

Prague, Czech Republic. *Praguer.*

Prince Edward Island, Canada. *Prince Edward Islander* or *Spud Islander* (slang but common), which comes from the fact that the tiny province exports potatoes. *Islander* is also used.

Princeton, New Jersey. *Princetonian,* which is also used to describe the students and graduates of Princeton University.

Principality of Andorra. See ANDORRA.

Principality of Liechtenstein. See LIECHTENSTEIN.

Principality of Monaco. See MONACO.

Proper Bostonian. Another name for a *Boston Brahmin.* See BOSTON.

Providence, Rhode Island. *Providentian,* although many residents of the city seem content to be called *Rhode Islanders* instead.

Provo, Utah. *Provoan.*

Prune Picker. Traditional nickname for a resident

Puebla, Mexico. *Poblano.*

Pueblo, Colorado. *Puebloan.*

Puerto Rico. *Puerto Rican* is the common term *Puertorriqueño* is appearing in more and more publications. A much less common term is *Bor* ter the name of the Indian tribe on the island at rival of Columbus. See also NEORICAN, NUYORICAN

Puke. Derogatory nickname for a Missourian that w World War I at a time when Illinoisans were and the term *Hoosier* had a rougher edge to toyed with two possible origins for the term: pronunciation of the *Pike* of *Pike County* an about when a lead-mine boom in Illinois in Suckers to say that Missouri had "taken a puke ited up its people. Another notion suggests it ett's 1835 *Almanac of Wild Sports of the We Backwoods,* where he gives a long and highl tion of the Missouri *Puke,* emphasizing extren quently, wrote Crockett, "the Pukes never loo face but once a year, an' that's in the spring, vomit off their surplus bile."

Pulaski, Virginia. *Pulaskian.*

Punxsutawney, Pennsylvania. *Punxyite.*

Purdulian. Person associated with Purdue Lafayette, Indiana.

Qatar (State of Qatar). *Qatari,* which is also an adjective.

Quaker. Traditional nickname for a resident of Pennsylvania, in reference to the commonwealth's rich history as a home for religious Quakers.

Quebec *or* **Québec, Canada.** *Quebecker, Quebecer, Quebecois, Québecois,* or *Québécois. Quebecois* can refer specifically to a francophone resident of the province. The *New York Times Manual of Style and Usage* calls for *Quebecer* in news stories but adds that "*Québécois* (sing. and pl.) may be used in references to the distinctive French-Canadian culture of Quebec; a *Québécois novelist,* or, '*Above all,' the separatist leader said, 'I am proud to be Québécois.'*" Use of the term *Parti Québécois* in English is an exception to a general rule followed by the *Times* and other newspapers, which is to translate the names of foreign political parties. (Interestingly, *Times* language columnist William Safire opposed this exception, writing, "If we're going to speak English, let's put it in English.") Likewise, the *Bloc Québécois* is a national party with seats in the Canadian parliament that goes by the same name in English and French. See also HABITANT.

Queens, New York. *Queensite,* according to Theodore Doehner, former Queens librarian.

Queensland, Australia. *Queenslander* or *Banana-Bender* (q.v.).

Queuetopia. See UTOPIA.

Quincy, Illinois. *Quincyan.*

Quito, Ecuador. *Quiteño.*

Racine, Wisconsin. *Racineite.*

Raleigh, North Carolina. *Raleighite.*

Ramona, California. *Ramonaite.*

Ranger. Traditional nickname for a resident of Texas. A *Texas Ranger* is "a member of a formerly mounted police force in Texas" (*Merriam-Webster's Collegiate Dictionary*, 11th edition) or a member of the Texas Rangers baseball team.

Razorback. A nickname for those (as athletes) associated with the University of Arkansas that is sometimes applied to the residents of the state. The razorback is a wild hog. In another incarnation the name *razorback* shows up as slang for a circus or carnival laborer who loads and unloads the equipment.

Reading, Pennsylvania. *Readingite.* H. L. Mencken appended a footnote to his entry for Reading in "What the People of American Towns Call Themselves": "But Mr. J. E. Barry, of Reading, tells me that many residents prefer to use Berks County Dutchman."

Red Bank, New Jersey. *Red Banker.*

Red Horse. Traditional nickname for a resident of Kentucky. This may come from a suckerfish of the same name.

redneck. Term for a rural southern white who is usually poor and has presumably reddened the back of his neck working in the fields. In most contexts it is a term of derogation but can be worn by rednecks themselves as a badge of pride. The term has been around for some time. Peter Tamony found this adjectival citation in the writings of George Ade: "Every time I see him over at the City Hall he's whisperin' to one of them red-necked boys and fixin' it up to give somebody the double-cross" (*Artie,* 1896). By the 1930s the term was used in news accounts of elections to describe the untutored, bigoted segment of the electorate: "It soon became apparent to Theodore Bilbo that his camp-meeting rabble-rousing rant had a definite appeal for rural 'red-necks'" (*Time,* October 1, 1934). Despite this, the term was once used by trade unionists as a synonym for the slang *roughneck*—a tough, hard worker.

Red Wing, Minnesota. *Red Wingite.*

Regina, Saskatchewan. *Reginan.*

Regiomontano. Resident of Monterrey, Mexico.

Reno, Nevada. *Renoite.* Nevadan Robert J. Throckmorton is not the first to point out that this demonym looks clumsy in print: "When I first saw it, I wondered what a 'Ree-noit-ee' was." H. L. Mencken (*American Speech,* 1948) quoted a note he received from John Sanford of the *Reno Evening Gazette,* dated May 3, 1944: "'About twenty years ago there was a more or less feeble effort to substitute *Renoan,* but it never proved popular. The sponsors of *Renoan* were several professors at the State university.'"

resident. Generic term for a person living in a particular place. Since states and cities cannot grant citizenship, the *Associated Press Stylebook and Libel Manual* holds that one can be a *citizen* of the United States but a *resident* of Oklahoma.

Réunion (Department of Réunion). *Réunionese* (both singular and plural), which is also an adjective. However, *Réunionais* is used by those who prefer to keep closer to the French. Réunion is located to the east of Madagascar in the Indian Ocean.

Rhinelander. Resident of the Rhine Valley region of Germany, but the term is sometimes erroneously applied to any German. It has also been used for a Cincinnati resident because of the city's heavy concentration of German-Americans. The term is used less and less today, but as recently as 1959 the report of a baseball game from the city began like this: "It's like old times here in the Rhineland. Willie Mays still is the favorite 'brush-ball' target of the Redleg pitchers" (*San Francisco News,* May 5, 1959; from Peter Tamony).

Rhode Island. *Rhode Islander. Gun Flint* is a nickname that shows up in slang collections but is little used, if at all, today. According to George Earlie Shankle's *State Names, Flags, Seals, Songs, Birds, Flowers, and Other Symbols,* it was "applied through the use of fire arms by its citizens at the time of the Dorr Rebellion of 1842, the arms being mostly of the old gun-flint pattern, the resource being those taken from the garrets where they had laid for years." The adjective *Rhodian* was used as early as 1722, when a poet was called "a Rhodian muse" in the *New England Courant.*
State nicknames: *Little Rhody* and *Ocean State.*

Rhodes, Greece. *Rhodian.*

Rhodesia. See ZIMBABWE.

Ricebird. Traditional nickname for a resident of South Carolina.

Richmond, California. *Richmondite.*

Richmond, Indiana. *Richmondite.*

Richmond, Virginia. *Richmonder.*

Rio de Janeiro, Brazil. *Carioca.*

Rioja, Spain. *Jarrillero* is what the locals call one another because of their jam-making heritage.

Riverside, California. *Riversider.*

Roanoke, Virginia. *Roanoker.*

Rochester, Indiana. *Rochesterite.*

Rochester, New York. *Rochesterian.*

Rockford, Illinois. There is no commonly accepted term in use, but *Rockfordian* could be used in a pinch.

Rocky Mount, North Carolina. *Rocky Mounter.*

Romania *or* **Rumania.** *Romanian* or *Rumanian.* Both are also adjectives.

Rome, Italy. *Roman,* also an adjective.

Rome, New York. *Roman.*

Roswell, New Mexico. *Roswellite.*

Rouen, France. *Rouennais.*

Rover. Traditional nickname for a resident of Colorado.

Royal Oak, Michigan. *Royal Oaker.*

Rumania. See ROMANIA.

Russia (Russian Federation); *formerly* **Russian Soviet Federated Socialist Republic.** *Russian,* also an adjective. *Russian*
can have specific ethnic reference as well as "national" meaning.
It was often used formerly to mean "Soviet" even though the Soviet Union included many other republics besides Russia.

Russki or Russky or Russkie. Cold war–era nickname for a Russian. Clearly it is a term of mild disparagement along the lines of
calling a Communist a *Commie;* however, it is sometimes used
with some affection. A news account of the meeting of American
and Russian troops at the Elbe River in 1945 told of GIs putting
their arms around Soviet troops and calling them "Russkys" (Associated Press dispatch of May 4, 1945).

Rutland, Vermont. *Rutlander.*

Rwanda (Republic of Rwanda). *Rwandan,* also an adjective,
which appeared in countless 1995–96 headlines paired with the
word "refugee." *Rwandese* is also used widely.

Ryukyu Islands. *Ryukyuan,* which is also an adjective.

Saba, Netherlands Antilles. *Saban,* also an adjective.

Sacramento, California. *Sacramentan.*

Sagebrusher. An inhabitant of the rural American West, and a traditional nickname for a resident of Nevada or Wyoming.

Sage Hen. Traditional nickname for a resident of Nevada.

Saginaw, Michigan. *Saginawian.*

Saint Augustine, Florida. *Saint Augustinian.*

Saint Christopher. See SAINT KITTS.

Saint Christopher and Nevis. See SAINT KITTS–NEVIS.

Saint-Cloud, France. *Clodoaldien.* The town and demonym come from Clodoald, or Cloud, who founded an abbey there in the sixth century.

Saint Croix *also* **Santa Cruz, Virgin Islands of the United States.** *Cruzan.*

Saint-Dié, France. *Déodatien.* The town developed around a monastery set up by Saint Deodatus in the seventh century.

Saint-Dizier, France. *Bragard.*

Saint Grottlesexer. Term used to designate students and graduates of a group of elite northeastern prep schools with church affiliations. The schools covered collectively by the term are Groton, Saint Mark's, Saint Paul's, Saint George's, and Middlesex.

Saint Helena. *Saint Helenian.* This British island in the South Atlantic Ocean about two-thirds of the way from South America to Africa was Napoleon Bonaparte's place of exile and burial (his remains were taken to Paris in 1840).

Saint-Hyacinthe, Quebec. *Maskoutains* after the Yamaska River, which runs through it.

Saint Ives, England. Older residents call themselves *Hakes* according to *The Observer,* June 21, 1988.

Saint John, New Brunswick. *Saint Johner,* but pronounced "Sinjohner," according to a Canadian source, who says that the term is useful in distinguishing the Saint Johners from their counterparts in Saint John's, Newfoundland, who are known as *Noofi-johners.*

Saint Joseph, Missouri. *Saint Josephite,* although H. L. Mencken noted in 1948: "I am told that this is rare. The town is usually spoken of as St. Joe."

Saint Kitts *or* **Saint Christopher.** This Caribbean island makes up part of the country of Saint Kitts–Nevis, and an inhabitant is a *Kittitian.* Compare NEVISIAN.

Saint Kitts–Nevis *or* **Saint Christopher–Nevis.** This Caribbean nation is comprised of two islands (Saint Kitts and Nevis), which supply the appropriate demonyms, *Kittitian* or *Nevisian.*

Saint Louis, Missouri. *Saint Louisan.* The city has several nicknames—including *The Lou, Gateway to the West*—but *Saint Louie* is apparently not a favorite among locals and is discouraged in most contexts save for the song "Meet Me in Saint Louie, Louie," which alludes to the 1904 Louisiana Purchase Exposition held here.

Saint Lucia. *Saint Lucian.*

Saint-Malo, France. *Malouin.*

Saint Marys, Pennsylvania. *Saint Marysite.*

Saint Paul, Minnesota. *Saint Paulite,* but also, because Minneapolis and Saint Paul are the *Twin Cities,* a *Twin Citian.*

Saint-Paul-Trois-Châteaux, France. *Tricastin* or *Tricastinois.*

Saint Petersburg, Florida. *Saint Petersburgite* appears correct, but bulky. Locally, a resident seems to be described as a "Saint Pete man" or "Saint Pete woman."

Saint Petersburg, Russia. *Saint Petersburger.* The *Washington Post* reported on June 12, 1991, that a faction in the city preferred the name *Leningrad* and so opposed changing it back to its original *Saint Petersburg.* (It was *Petrograd* for a brief period from 1914 to 1924.) The *Post* headline was "What's in a City's Name? Plenty, Leningraders Say." Nevertheless, Leningraders voted for *Saint Petersburg* and the name was officially restored later in 1991.

Saint Pierre and Miquelon. The residents of these islands in the North Atlantic Ocean (south of Newfoundland) are, according to the Central Intelligence Agency's *World Factbook,* known as *Frenchmen* and *Frenchwomen,* and the proper adjective is prescribed as *French.*

Saint-Valéry-en-Caux, France. *Valéricais.*

Saint-Valéry-sur-Somme, France. *Valéricain.*

Saint Vincent and the Grenadines. *Saint Vincentian* or *Vincentian.*

Saipan. *Saipanese,* also an adjective.

Salem, Massachusetts. *Salemite.*

Salem, Oregon. *Salemite.*

Salida, Colorado. *Salidan.*

Salina, Kansas. *Salinan.*

Salinas, California. *Salinan.*

Salisbury, North Carolina. *Salisburian.*

Salopian. Resident of Shropshire, England (q.v.).

Salt Lake City, Utah. *Salt Laker.*

Salvadoran. Resident of El Salvador. Researcher Charles Poe has found the variant *Salvadorian* in print, but it appears to lack widespread support.

Samoa. See AMERICAN SAMOA, WESTERN SAMOA.

San Antonio, Texas. *San Antonian.*

Sand-groper. Resident of Western Australia (q.v.).

Sandhiller. Traditional nickname for a resident of Georgia; it has been used for poor residents from sandy areas of the South besides Georgia, such as South Carolina.

San Diego, California. *San Diegan.*

Sandlapper. Traditional nickname for a resident of South Carolina, said to derive from a habit of eating dirt on the part of the state's children before the Civil War. *Sandlapper* has also had wider dialect use to signify one from a low-lying area of the South.

San Francisco, California. *San Franciscan.* Because this city is unlike the cities to the south (notably Los Angeles and San Diego), there are those who have parroted horseman Harry McCarty's line: "I am not a Californian, I am a San Franciscan." As H. L. Mencken noted (*American Speech,* 1948), "To reduce [*San Franciscan*] to *Friscan* is regarded as offensive, locally." See also FRISCAN. The term *born and raised* is used among old guard San Franciscans to distinguish themselves from recent arrivals, according to Alice Kahn in the *San Francisco Chronicle,* July 10, 1988.

San Jose, California. *San Josean.* Officially, the name of this city carries a diacritical mark over the the last letter of Jose.

San Juan, Puerto Rico. *San Juanero.*

San Leandro, California. *San Leandroite.*

San Luis Obispo, California. *San Luis Obispan.*

San Marino (Republic of San Marino). *Sammarinese* (both singular and plural); *San Marinese* is also used. *Filatelia Sammarinese* is the name of the agency that sells the nation's postage stamps, which account for almost a third of this small country's income.

San Mateo, California. *San Matean.*

Santa Ana, California. *Santa Anan.*

Santa Barbara, California. *Barbareno, Santa Barbareno,* or *Santa Barbaran.*

Santa Cruz, California. *Santa Cruzan.*

Santa Fe, New Mexico. *Santa Fean,* as in "sophisticated Santa Feans" (Conrad Richter writing in *Holiday,* December 1953).

Santa Monica, California. *Santa Monican.*

Santa Rosa, California. *Santa Rosan.*

Santiago, Chile. *Santiaguino* or *Santiagan.*

São Paulo, Brazil. *Paulista* (q.v.).

São Tomé and Príncipe (Democratic Republic of São Tomé and Príncipe). *São Toméan.*

Sarajevo, Bosnia and Herzegovina. *Sarajevan.*

Saratoga Springs, New York. *Saratogian,* which is also the name of a newspaper there. Known as the *Spa City,* it is also known more familiarly as *Toga.*

Sardinia, Italy. *Sardinian.*

Sarnia, Ontario. *Sarnian.*

Saskatchewan, Canada. *Saskatchewanian,* though *Saskatchewaner* is also used. The province is sometimes called *The Gap* because the shape of the province is basically a rectangle and looks like a "gap" on a map: as in "that *gap* between Manitoba and Alberta."

Saskatoon, Saskatchewan. *Saskatonian,* although *Saskatooner* is sometimes used: "With a frothy pint in one hand and a Staedtler technical pen in the other, I looked at the Winnipeger on the left of me and the Saskatooner on the right, and at the Prince Georgian flirting with the Monctonite by the door" (Toronto *Star,* February 26, 2002). Also, *S'tooners* in current Canadian slang.

Saturn. *Saturnian.*

Saudi Arabia (Kingdom of Saudi Arabia). *Saudi* or *Saudi Arabian;* both are also adjectives.

Saugus, Massachusetts. *Saugonian.*

Sault Sainte Marie, Michigan. *Sooite.* H. L. Mencken reported the term in his 1948 *American Speech* article, and the term is still common, according to Bud Mansfield, director of the Sault Sainte Marie Area Chamber of Commerce in 1997. He said that the demonym is also applied to residents of the sister city, Sault Sainte Marie, Ontario, on the other side of the Saint Marys River.

Savannah, Georgia. *Savannahian.*

Scandinavia. *Scandinavian* or *Norse.* The latter can be confusing since it is also used as an adjective to refer specifically to Norway. *Scandahoovian, Scandinovian,* and *Scoovian* are playful nicknames likely to show up in a humorous context. Evidence in the Tamony Collection suggests that these names may have first appeared in the Minnesota humor magazine *Capt. Billy's Whiz Bang* in the 1920s. *Skijumper* is still another nickname but has not been popular for many years.

Schenectady, New York. *Schenectadian.* Geof Huth of Schenectady reports that the city is often referred to as *Dorp*—making a citizen a *Dorpian*—which he adds is a blessing to headline writers. This term obviously fascinated H. L. Mencken, who wrote about it in his 1936 article on "municipal onomastics" in *The New Yorker*: "A citizen of Schenectady, New York, will answer sheepishly to the name of *Schenectadian*, but he greatly prefers *Dorpian* from the ancient Dutch designation of the town—the *Dorp*, or the *Old Dorp*." *Dorp* is the Dutch word for "village," and a part of Staten Island in New York City is *New Dorp*.

Scotland. *Scot, Scotsman/Scotswoman,* or *Scotchman/Scotchwoman* are all used commonly. Adjectives: *Scots, Scottish,* and *Scotch.* Robert W. Chapman wrote in his *Adjectives from Proper Names*, "These variations should be received as a compliment to the national versatility."

Scouse *or* **Scouser.** Resident of Liverpool, England (q.v.).

Scranton, Pennsylvania. *Scrantonian.*

Seattle, Washington. *Seattleite* (sometimes spelled *Seattlite*). A *Washington Post* headline for November 22, 1973: "Seattleites Try Free Bus Rides." The alternative term *Seattler* has been used from time to time—"Seattlers may have even a better solution to the maritime parking problem" (*Newsweek*, August 3, 1959)—but it is confusing since it may sound like "settlers" when spoken, and perhaps for that reason it is rare.

Informal lifestyle has led to the use of the city in slang constructions such as a *Seattle Tux*, which is defined as "a flannel shirt and clean jeans."

Selma, Alabama. *Selmian.*

Seminole, Oklahoma. *Seminolian.*

Senegal (Republic of Senegal). *Senegalese* (both singular and plural), which is also an adjective.

Serbia. *Serb* is far and away the preferred term, though *Serbian* is sometimes used. Both *Serb* and *Serbian* are common adjectives.

Serbia and Montenegro. *Serb, Serbian and Montenegrin.* This is a nation carved out of the former Yugoslavia—tentatively. Quoting from the 2005 edition of the CIA's *World Factbook:* "In 2002, the Serbian and Montenegrin components of Yugoslavia began negotiations to forge a looser relationship. These talks became a reality in February 2003 when lawmakers restructured the country into a loose federation of two republics called Serbia and Montenegro. The Constitutional Charter of Serbia and Montenegro includes a provision that allows either republic to hold a referendum after three years that would allow for their independence from the state union."

Seychelles (Republic of Seychelles). *Seychellois* (both singular and plural). The term is an adjective in English as well as French: "Bird Island Hotel is . . . a remote coral island hotel owned and staffed by resident Seychellois and home to more than a million sooty terns" (*The Times* [London], November 19, 2005).

Shamokin, Pennsylvania. *Shamokinite.*

Shanghai, China. *Shanghailander.*

Sharm El-Sheik, Egypt. *Sharmer,* a term that came into the news after the terrorist attack that was made on the resort town in July 2005. "Many of the 'Sharmers,' as they call themselves, are still in disbelief over the attacks," said an Associated Press dispatch of July 26, 2005.

Sharon, Pennsylvania. *Sharonite.*

Sheboygan, Wisconsin. *Sheboygander* or *Sheboyganite.*

Sheepherder. Traditional nickname for a resident of Wyoming.

Sheffield, England. *Sheffielder.* Residents are also known as *Deedars* from the traditional local pronunciation of "th" in thee and thou, which are pronounced "dee" and "da." This term is in decline.

Sherbrooke, Quebec. *Sherbrookois.*

Sherman Oaks, California. *Sherman Oakie.*

Shetland Islands, U.K. *Shetlander.*

Shoshone, Idaho. *Shoshonean.*

Shreveport, Louisiana. *Shreveporter.*

Shropshire, England. *Salopian. Salopian* comes from *Salop,* another name for Shropshire that comes from *Sloppesberie,* the Anglo-French rendering of Old English *Scrobbesbyrig* "fortified town in the brush," the early form of *Shrewsbury,* which is in Shropshire. (*Shropshire* itself derives from the same Saxon word.) *Salop* was even the official name of the county from 1974 to 1980. A graduate of the Shrewsbury School is an *Old Salopian,* and the category includes such figures as Charles Darwin and Sir Philip Sidney.

Siberia. *Siberian,* also an adjective. An extremely cold weather system coming out of Siberia into North America has been termed a "Siberian Express."

Sichuan *or* **Szechuan** *or* **Szechwan, China.** *Sichuanese,* which is also an adjective. *Szechuanese* and *Szechwanese* are based on the Wade-Giles forms, which are less preferred than the pinyin form *Sichuan* today.

Sicily, Italy. *Sicilian,* also an adjective.

Sierra Leone. *Sierra Leonean,* also an adjective.

Silverine. Traditional nickname for a resident of Colorado.

Silver Stater. Traditional nickname for a resident of Nevada, the *Silver State. Nevadan,* however, is much more common.

Singapore (Republic of Singapore). *Singaporean,* also an adjective. Washingtonian Tim Gibson recalls a classic demonymic blunder at a racetrack's International Day, during which an entry from Singapore was referred to as that "Singapese" horse.

Sioux City, Iowa. *Sioux Cityan* is the term that has been in use locally for decades. George H. Scheetz, director of the Sioux City Library and a member of both the American Name Society and the North Central Name Society, has worked long and hard to protect the demonym against those outside of Sioux City who would like to use the *Sioux Citian* spelling. The urge in Iowa is to create a parallel with Iowa City, whose residents prefer to be called *Iowa Citians.* In a March 23, 1988, letter to the *Des Moines Register,* Scheetz used Sioux City as an example when he insisted that the issue is not what you call the residents of an area but rather what they call themselves: "A primary law of onomastics (the study of names) is to follow local usage."

Sioux Falls, South Dakota. This is a difficult case that prompted Bill McKean of Sioux Falls to write in 1988: "People from Sioux Falls are called PEOPLE FROM SIOUX FALLS. There are limits." There is at least one alternative, however: *Siouxlander* may be used for a person (as one from Sioux Falls) living along the Big Sioux River. A note from Michael McDonald of Hudson, South Dakota, explains: "A number of residents from Sioux Falls, S.D., have adopted the term author Frederick Manfred gave to the residents who live along the Big Sioux River and call themselves

Siouxlanders. However, a Siouxlander includes Sioux Citians, Cantonites, Hudsonites, etc., who also have ties with the river."

Skaneateles, New York. *Skaneatelesean.*

Slaton, Texas. *Slatonite.*

Slovakia (Slovak Republic). *Slovak,* also an adjective. Prior to the independence of this nation, the demonym described a person of the eastern part of Czechoslovakia (or *Czecho-Slovakia* as it was sometimes written by Slovaks in other parts of the world who favored its independence). Slovaks have a distinct identity (language, culture, history, etc.) that sets them apart from the Czechs. See also CZECH REPUBLIC.

Slovenia (Republic of Slovenia). *Slovene,* which is also an adjective along with *Slovenian.*

Smogvillian. Comic name for a resident of Los Angeles, California, based on its characteristic smog. In the same vein, when the Brooklyn Dodgers became the Los Angeles Dodgers, several newspaper columnists suggested they be called the *Smodgers.*

Snake. Traditional nickname for a resident of West Virginia.

Snohomish, Washington. Because this region (city and county) lacked a commonly accepted demonym—*Snohomian* was too unwieldy—the term *Snoho* and the plural *Snohos* have come into prominence among the younger residents of the area (who chose it over the short-lived *Snohomies*). When SNOHOS started showing up on T-shirts at Snohomish High School in the spring of 2005, administrators saw it as a derogatory term aimed at women, i.e., "Snohomish hos" as in whores. But the use elsewhere in town including a coffeehouse known as the SnoHo Mojo Expresso and the use by local sportscasters in describing the school's team finally overcame resistance to the term's use. According to the

Seattle Times, Snohomish High's principal Diana Plumis conceded that the T-shirt did not use "Snohos" in a negative sense. But she warned that officials would take action if the term "is clearly used to demean or insult."

Socialist People's Libyan Arab Jamahiriya. See LIBYA.

Socialist Republic of Vietnam. See VIETNAM.

Solomon Islands. *Solomon Islander.*

Somalia. *Somali,* also an adjective. *Somalian* is also used commonly as both demonym and adjective: "Somalian refugee families were brought to Massachusetts in recent years sponsored by local charities" (*New York Times,* December 28, 2005).

Sooite. Resident of Sault Sainte Marie, Michigan, or Sault Sainte Marie, Ontario.

Sooner. Nickname for a person associated with the University of Oklahoma as well as for an Oklahoman. The name goes back to the opening of the Oklahoma Territory in 1889. The lands were vacant and were to be opened legally for settlement at noon on April 22, 1889. Some sneaked in before the official time and were immediately dubbed "sooners." (*Sooner* has also seen some slang usage for a child born less than nine months after the parents' wedding.)

Soreback. Traditional nickname for a resident of Virginia (q.v.).

Sourdough. Special name for an Alaskan or northwestern Canadian especially in the Yukon with lots of years and experience in the area. Russell Tabbert says in his *Dictionary of Alaskan English* (1991) that the term comes from the importance of sourdough bread in the diets of the early prospectors and miners. Since at least the 1960s the popular folk explanation is that it describes someone who "is sour on the country but doesn't have enough dough to leave." See also CHEECHAKO.

South Africa, Republic of; *formerly* **Union of South Africa.** *South African.*

South America. *South American.*

South Australia, Australia. *South Australian* or *Crow-eater* (q.v.). See also BANANA-BENDER to understand how the slang nickname can be defamatory.

South Bend, Indiana. "Resident of South Bend" or *Michianan* (see MICHIANA) but almost never *South Bender.* Greg Swiercz, former city editor of the *South Bend Tribune,* says that the last term is exceedingly rare and he suspects that his paper might have used it once or twice in the last ten years. A 1994 article on nicknames for the University of Notre Dame football team in the *South Bend Tribune* said that over time "the Fighting Irish" had also been known as the *Notre Damers,* the *Blue and the Gold,* and the *South Benders.* Some references have appeared in print suggesting *Bender* but this is fanciful since no evidence has been found of its actual use by area residents.

South Carolina. *South Carolinian. Carolinian* is used for residents of both North Carolina and South Carolina.

　　Traditional personal nicknames: *Clay Eater, Palmetto, Ricebird, Sandlapper,* and *Weasel.*

　　State nickname: *Palmetto State,* because its coat of arms features a palmetto tree.

South Dakota. *South Dakotan. Dakotan* is used for residents of both North Dakota and South Dakota. An oddity here was a weekly newspaper established in the 1880s titled *Conklin's South Dakotian.*

State nicknames: *Sunshine State, Coyote State,* and *Blizzard State.*

Southeast Asia. *Southeast Asian.*

Southern Rhodesia. See ZIMBABWE.

South Korea. See KOREA, SOUTH.

South-West Africa. See NAMIBIA.

Soweto, South Africa. *Sowetan.* The name is also that of a newspaper that serves the sprawling black township.

Spain. *Spaniard. Spanish* is an adjective and collective demonym.

Spanish Guinea. See EQUATORIAL GUINEA.

Spanish Sahara. See WESTERN SAHARA.

Sparnacien. Resident of Épernay, France, which in ancient times was known as *Sparnacum.*

Spartanburg, South Carolina. *Spartanburger.*

Spinalien. Resident of Épinal, France, which was originally called *Spinalium.*

Spokane, Washington. *Spokanite.* There are a number of playful nicknames for this city including *Spokanistan, The 'Kane,* and *Spokant.*

Springfield, Illinois. *Springfielder* or *Springfieldman/Springfieldwoman.*

Springfield, Missouri. *Springfieldian.*

Springfield, Ohio. *Springfielder* or *Springfieldman/Springfield-woman.*

Spud Islander. Resident of Prince Edward Island, Canada.

Sri Lanka (Democratic Socialist Republic of Sri Lanka); *formerly* **Ceylon.** *Sri Lankan,* although *Ceylonese* is sometimes used. The *Associated Press Stylebook and Libel Manual* states that "the people [of Sri Lanka] may be referred to as *Ceylonese* (n. or adj.) or *Sri Lankans.*"

Stampeder. Nickname for a resident of Calgary, Alberta.

-stan. Suffix that means in Persian "home of," and appears in the names of many countries and regions. Most *-stan* countries and regions have names for residents that end with the letter *i*—such as *Uzbekistani* and *Pakistani*—but there are exceptions, most notably Afghanistan where natives are *Afghans.* The suffix lends itself to imaginary use:

> *Ethniclashistan*—from an article in the satirical
> newspaper *The Onion* about a country formed by
> the UN for the relocation of clashing ethnicities
> *Kerplakistan*—fictional Soviet Republic from the
> Austin Powers movies
> *Sixpackistan*—land known to viewers of *The
> Simpsons.*

State of Bahrain. See BAHRAIN.

State of Brunei Darussalam. See BRUNEI.

State of Israel. See ISRAEL.

State of Kuwait. See KUWAIT.

State-of-Mainer. One of several names for a resident of Maine. Curiously, it is the lone example of a demonym using the words "state of." Theodore Doehner, a correspondent from New Berlin, New York, adds that he has heard a person from New York State referred to as a "New York State man" or a "New York State woman."

State of Qatar. See QATAR.

Staunton, Virginia. *Stauntonian.*

Sterling, Kansas. *Sterlingite.*

Stockholm, Sweden. *Stockholmer.* Adjective: *Stockholmian.*

Stockton, California. *Stocktonian.*

Storrs, Connecticut. *Storrsian.*

Stratford, Ontario. *Stratfordian.*

Stratford-upon-Avon, England. *Stratfordian.* The term is also used for those who defend William Shakespeare as the author of the plays attributed to him, as opposed to those who argue that the bard was Edward de Vere, the 17th earl of Oxford. See OXFORD.

suburbia. *Suburbanite.* A number of mocking synonyms have been created for this realm between the city and the country, among them the *snuburbs* and the *shruburbs*. Commenting on the drinking observed on commuter trains, the late Walter Winchell called the suburbanites *subourbonites*. Aphorist Arthur Brisbane typified the suburb as a "graveyard with modern plumbing."

Sucker. Traditional nickname for a resident of Illinois. One theory is that the yearly migration of people up the Mississippi River to Illinois to work in the lead mines resembled the spawning habits of the sucker-fish (they would return south in the fall); another is that the term was inspired by the drawing of water from holes in the prairie land made by crawfish; and a third theory is that the early settlers were taken advantage of by land speculators, thus being suckers in the custom-ary sense of "dupe." Mathews's *Dictionary of Americanisms* consid-ers the last explanation the best, and records a rich set of *Sucker* compounds and spin-offs, including *Suckerdom* and *Suckerland* for Illinois, and *Suckerism* as a noun denoting an amalgamation of Illi-noisians (in Eliza Farnham's *Life in Prairie Land,* 1846).

Sudan (Republic of the Sudan). *Sudanese* (both singular and plu-ral). It is also an adjective.

Sudanese Republic. See MALI.

Sudbury, Ontario. *Sudburian.*

Sultanate of Oman. See OMAN.

Sumatra. *Sumatran,* also an adjective.

Summit, New Jersey. *Summitite.*

Sunflower. Traditional nickname for a resident of Kansas.

Superior, Wisconsin. *Superiorite.*

Suriname (Republic of Suriname). *Surinamer* or *Surinamese,* though the latter appears most often as an adjective.

Swampscott, Massachusetts. *Swampscotter.*

Swarthmore, Pennsylvania. *Swarthmorean.* The term is also used for those (as alumni) associated with Swarthmore College there.

Swaziland (Kingdom of Swaziland). *Swazi.* The plural is *Swazi* or *Swazis.*

Sweden (Kingdom of Sweden). *Swede.* Adjective: *Swedish.*

Switzerland (Swiss Confederation). *Swiss* (both singular and plural), also an adjective.

Sydney, Australia. *Sydneysider* or *Sydneyite.* The former term is used for the city as well as the neighboring area of New South Wales, of which Sydney is the capital. *Sydneysider* got a great boost in 2000 when Sydney was the site of the 2000 Olympic Games.

Syracuse, New York. *Syracusan.* It is also applied to residents of ancient Syracuse, although Shakespeare used *Syracusian* in *The Comedy of Errors* to refer to the people of that city. The New York city has a number of nicknames including *The 'Cuse.*

Syria (Syrian Arab Republic). *Syrian,* also an adjective.

Szechuan *or* **Szechwan, China.** See SICHUAN.

Tacoma, Washington. *Tacoman.* An online site devoted to slang of the Seattle area contains an entry for *Tacomatose,* referring to someone (usually in their 20s) who is stuck in Tacoma, not doing much, maybe living with their parents, with no intent to move on or do anything much with their life, submitted by someone who'd apparently spent a fair amount of time stuck in Tacoma.

Tadzhik. A resident of Tajikistan (q.v.).

Tadzhikistan. See TAJIKISTAN.

Tadzhik Soviet Socialist Republic. See TAJIKISTAN.

Tahiti. *Tahitian,* also an adjective.

Taiwan. *Taiwanese.* For reasons that are related to United States government policies with regard to mainland China, the Central Intelligence Agency's *World Factbook* lists the demonym for this nation as *Chinese,* a name that is not used by Taiwanese in speaking of nationality. The United States does not officially recognize Taiwan, which was expelled from the United Nations General Assembly in 1971. See also FORMOSA.

Tajikistan *also* **Tadzhikistan;** *formerly* **Tadzhik Soviet Socialist Republic.** *Tajik* or *Tadzhik.* Both terms are essentially ethnic, denoting "a member of a Persian-speaking ethnic group living in Tajikistan, Afghanistan, and adjacent areas of central Asia" (*Merriam-Webster's Collegiate Dictionary,* 11th edition), and while there is some evidence of a noun *Tajikistani,* the adjective of the same form is clearly more common. A 1994 State Department report on human rights in Afghanistan, for example, referred to demonstrations "against alleged Russian and Tajikistani bombardment of Afghan villages."

Tallahassee, Florida. *Tallahasseean.*

Tampa, Florida. *Tampan.*

Tangier, Morocco. *Tangerine,* also an adjective; what was first the "Tangerine orange" later became known simply as the *tangerine.*

Tanzania (United Republic of Tanzania); *formerly* **United Republic of Tanganyika and Zanzibar.** *Tanzanian,* also an adjective.

Taos, New Mexico. *Taoseno.*

Tarboiler. Traditional nickname for a resident of North Carolina.

Tar Heel. Resident of North Carolina, also known as a *North Carolinian,* and a nickname for one associated with the University of North Carolina. Once a term of derision, it has long since become honorific—for instance, the *Raleigh News and Observer* runs a regular feature on prominent citizens called the "Tar Heel of the Week." William S. Powell wrote in the March 1982 issue of the university's *Tar Heel* magazine, "North Carolina residents have taken an albatross from around their necks and pinned it on their chests like a badge of honor." The late New York–born Harry Golden, editor, publisher, and only contributor to *The Carolina Israelite* once asked his readers if he qualified as a Tar Heel and they responded with a resounding yes. "Being so," wrote Edwin M. Yoder Jr. in the *Washington Post*, a week after Golden's death in 1981, "is a state of spirit not origin."

The term *Tar Heel* derives from the tar and pitch produced by the state's pine forests. As a colony, North Carolina produced tar for the British navy, exporting some 100,000 barrels of tar and pitch to England in the years just before the American Revolution. In *American Folklore and Legend* (1981), the editors of *Reader's Digest* ascribe the label to the Civil War: "The Tarheel State acquired her sobriquet when a North Carolinian regiment stood its ground so stubbornly in battle it seemed the men were glued to the spot." A more detailed explanation credits Confederate general Robert E. Lee with coining *Tar Heel*, and is adapted from R. B. Creecy's *Grandfather Tales of North Carolina History* (1901) and Walter Clark's *Histories of the North Carolina Regiments*, Volume III. It has appeared in state publications such as a card printed by the North Carolina Travel and Tourism Division. The North Carolina soldiers felt "let down" by the regiment of another state after a fierce battle, and were thus in a resentful mood when they met up with other regiments later:

> "Any more tar down in the Old North State, boys?" members of the other regiments taunted the battle-weary North Carolinians.
>
> "Not a bit. Jeff Davis bought it all up," retorted the Carolinians.
>
> "How's that, what's he going to do with it?"
>
> "He's gonna put it on your heels to make you stick better in the next fight," answered the soldiers from the land of tar, pitch and turpentine.
>
> General Lee, hearing of the incident, remarked: "God bless the Tar Heel boys."

Another theory is that poor North Carolinians had no shoes on while boiling turpentine, and so ended up with tar-coated feet.

Tasmania, Australia. *Tasmanian, Taswegian,* the puckish *Tasmaniac,* or *Tassie,* which also means "Tasmania" as a noun and "Tasmanian" in adjectival use.

Taunton, Massachusetts. *Tauntonion.*

Tehran, Iran. *Tehrani.*

Tel Aviv, Israel. *Tel Avivian.*

Telluride, Colorado. *Tellurider.*

Tennessee. *Tennessean* is preferred over *Tennesseean.*

Traditional personal nicknames: *Big Bender, Butternut, Cotton-Mainie, Hardhead, Mudhead,* and *Whelp. Big Bender* derives from the nickname *Big Bend State,* discussed below. *Butternut* was applied to soldiers or partisans of the Confederacy in the Civil War because of the butternut color of uniforms used by the South in that conflict. The origins of the other traditional terms have been obscured by time.

State nickname: *Volunteer State,* from the 30,000 men said to have volunteered for service in the Mexican War. The name *Volunteers* is used by University of Tennessee sports teams and is often shortened to *Vols.* Tennessee has also been called the *Big Bend State,* from the huge arc made by the Tennessee River as it swings down, below, and then back up through the state on its way to the Ohio River.

Terrapin. Traditional nickname for a resident of Maryland. It also finds use in relation to the University of Maryland and its sports teams and in the plural is often shortened to *Terps* in such contexts.

Terre Haute, Indiana. *Terre Hautean.*

Territorial Collectivity of Mayotte. See MAYOTTE.

Territorian. Resident of Northern Territory, Australia.

Territory of French Polynesia. See FRENCH POLYNESIA.

Territory of the Wallis and Futuna Islands. See WALLIS AND FUTUNA ISLANDS.

Teslin, Yukon Territory. *Teslinite.*

Texarkana, Arkansas. *Texarkanian.*

Texarkana, Texas. *Texarkanian.*

Texas. *Texan.* The term *Texian* has a long and distinguished history but is becoming increasingly archaic. One finds a book review (of Frank X. Tolbert's *Informal History of Texas*) in which the word *Texian* appears four times, but *Texan* is never mentioned (*San Francisco Chronicle,* August 4, 1961; from Peter Tamony). Texas-born writer Joseph C. Goulden reports on *Texian:* "My father used this term for the name of his bookstore in Marshall, from the late 1950's until his death in 1972. The printer delivered his first batch of 5,000 envelopes and letterheads with the remark, 'Mr. Joe, I cleaned up yo' spelling.' He did a reprint with a mutter and a protest." Another term that shows up that is clearly a blend of *Texan* and *Mexican* is *Texican,* which, among other things, was the name of a 1966 movie starring Audie Murphy.

A 1988 letter from Ralph D. Copeland of Bellaire, Texas, reports on the traditional distinctions between the various demonyms: "Here in Texas . . . generations of schoolchildren have been led to believe that the name for an inhabitant of the State of Coahuila and Texas—that is, a citizen before the Alamo and the battle of San Jacinto led to Texas' independence—was a Texican. Someone resident in the state between 1836 and 1845, while we were a Republic, was entitled to be known as a Texian. It was only those latecomers who arrived after we became part of the U.S. proper . . . who were to be called Texans."

In their *Dallas Morning News* column on language, "A Few Words," for January 6, 1991, Laurence McNamee and Kent Biffle wrote: "In the case of Texas, some specific names have been used in certain instances. We've seen Texian and Texican used to distinguish Anglo rebels from the Hispanic rebels who fought side by side to win independence for Texas, which was then a subprovince of Mexico."

Much has been written on these terms and their distinctions by the likes of J. Frank Dobie, Edna Ferber, and Alan LeMay. For example, the late distinguished writer Bernard De Voto, writing in *Harper's Magazine* for December 1952, asserted: "The Texan began as the Texian, a character part created by pulp writers in an effort to cash in on the activities of such men as Davy Crockett, Sam Houston and Big-Foot Wallace." An article in the *Saturday Evening Post* for September 11, 1943, titled "Maverick Professor" contains this set of distinctions: "To [Professor J. Frank] Dobie there are only three classes of people in Texas, whether they be college presidents or janitors. They are either *Texians*, *Texans*, or people who just live in Texas. Texians are the old rock; Texans, a term which came into use only after the Civil War, are those out of the rock; the people who live in Texas are those who are wearing the old rock away." In the *Saturday Evening Post* for April 21, 1962, Stanley Walker wrote, "My ancestors were Texans, or *Texians*, when the place was a howling solitude."

Texan C. F. Eckhardt, who also holds that the term *Texan* did not actually emerge until after the Civil War, charts the change from *Texican* to *Texian* to *Texan:* "The original self-name for the Anglo-American settlers was Texican—Americans in Texas who didn't quite consider themselves Mexicans; though they were living in Mexican territory and holding Mexican citizenship. Following the revolution in 1836 the 'c' was dropped and 'Texicans' became 'Texians.' After the war, with the influx of Yankee carpetbaggers and similar vermin, the 'i' was assaulted by what the *Texas Almanac* called 'that harsh and unpleasant name, "Texan."'" Eckhardt adds that there are two special cases: *Tejano* and *Texaner*. "*Tejanos* (pronounce it Tay-HAHN-ohs) are descended from Spanish and Spanish-Mexican families who were here before 1836" (undated letter to the author). As for the latter, *Texaners* are Texas Germans.

Tejano is also a form of music from Texas that fuses Latino dance music with elements of jazz, country, and especially German and Polish music (as the accordion and polka) brought to the state by immigrants in the 19th century. Tejano music has received national recognition since the tragic 1995 murder of Selena Quintanilla Perez, known as Selena. The Texas-born Mexican-American was, in the words of the 1996 *Britannica Book of the Year,* the "queen of Tejano," and her posthumous album *Dreaming of You* entered *Billboard*'s national Top 200 chart at number one.

Texas is used playfully in describing excess or bigness. A Rolex watch is known as a "Texas Timex." That which is characteristic of the state is *Texana,* and the blend of Lone Star and Mexican cooking is *Tex-Mex.*

Traditional personal nicknames: *Beefhead, Boll Weevil, Cowboy, Longhorn,* and *Ranger.* A common nickname for a specific individual from Texas is *Tex.*

State nickname: *Lone Star State.* This term is used with great regularity in Texas. An example: "In the Lone Star State, barbed wire was pitched to wary ranchers as 'light as air, stronger than whiskey and cheap as dirt'" (*Dallas Morning News,* August 18, 1995).

Thailand (Kingdom of Thailand). *Thai,* also an adjective.

Third World. *Third Worlder.* The Third World comprises the world's underdeveloped or emerging nations. Most Third World nations are in Africa and Asia. The term distinguishes these countries from the Old World (Europe, Russia, China, and India) and the New World (the United States, Canada, and the more developed parts of Latin America) and also implies independence from the "free world" and the "communist world." Although still in wide use, it is losing favor to "developing nations" among those who find the term has lost its utility or is demeaning.

Thunder Bay, Ontario. *Thunder Bayite,* as in "Tom Annelin, a Thunder Bayite, living in Oshawa" (the *Times-News* of Thunder Bay, October 20, 1989).

Ticino, Switzerland. Ticenese. Ticino is an Italian-speaking canton in the south of Switzerland.

Tijuana, Baja California, Mexico. *Tijuanenese.* Because of its long-established reputation for prostitution and pornography, the term *Tijuana bible,* since the 1920s, been an American slang expression for small cheap pornographic comic books. In truckers' CB slang a *Tijuana taxi* is any vehicle, especially a police car, with flashing lights and bright markings.

Tirol *or* **Tyrol, Austria.** *Tirolean, Tyrolean, Tirolese,* or *Tyrolese.*

Tobago. *Tobagonian.*

Togo (Republic of Togo). *Togolese,* also an adjective.

Tokelau Islands. *Tokelauan.*

Tokyo, Japan. *Tokyoite.*

Toledo, Ohio. *Toledan* or *Toledoan.*

Toledo, Spain. *Toledan.*

Tonga (Kingdom of Tonga). *Tongan.*

Toothpick. Traditional nickname for a resident of Arkansas, from the *Arkansas toothpick,* or Bowie knife.

Topeka, Kansas. *Topekan.*

Top-ender. Nickname for a resident of Northern Territory, Australia.

Toronto, Ontario. *Torontonian.* Unflattering alternatives are *Hog* and *Hogtowner,* which derive from the uncomplimentary nickname *Hogtown* for Toronto. According to *Colombo's Canadian References,* "Its origin and meaning—whether it refers to hogs or 'hogging' the wealth of Canada—are not known."

The city is often referred to as *T.O.* (for Toronto, Ontario—pronounced "Tee-Oh") or *T-dot* (short for "T-dot O-dot").

Torrance, California. *Torrancite.*

Toulouse, France. *Toulousain.*

Townie. (1) Resident of Charlestown, Massachusetts (part of Boston). (2) Name often employed by college or university students to describe local nonmatriculants.

Trashcanistan. *Trashcanistani. Trashcanistan* is used, as a term of derogation or marginalization, to indicate any poor Middle Eastern country or central Asian republic. "You don't have to buy shares in the Trashcanistan Fund to be a global investor," advises *Money* magazine in its January 2000 issue. The term is also used by U.S./U.N. troops assigned to these countries.

Trenton, New Jersey. *Trentonian,* which is also the name of the city's newspaper.

Tricastin or ***Tricastinois.*** Resident of Saint-Paul-Trois-Châteaux, France.

Trinidad. *Trinidadian;* with Tobago, the island makes up Trinidad and Tobago.

Trinidad, Colorado. *Trinidadan.*

Trinidad and Tobago (Republic of Trinidad and Tobago). *Trinidadian, Tobagonian,* or, increasingly, *Trinbagonian.*

Tripoli, Libya. *Tripolitan,* also an adjective.

Trobriand Islands. *Trobriand Islander* or *Trobriander.*

Trois-Rivières, Quebec. *Trifluvien.*

Trolls. Residents of Michigan's Lower Peninsula, so called because they live under the Mackinac Bridge.

Troy, New York. *Trojan.* (Applies to all Troys.)

Truk, Micronesia. See CHUUK.

Tuckahoe. Traditional nickname for a resident of Virginia (q.v.), especially east of the Blue Ridge Mountains.

Tucko. Traditional nickname for a resident of North Carolina.

Tucson, Arizona. *Tucsonan.* One Tucsonan, R. M. Gagliano, writes to say, "Fellow residents of Tucson may be officially known as Tucsonans, but we *true* desert rats prefer *Puebloids.*"

Tulsa, Oklahoma. *Tulsan.*

Tunisia (Republic of Tunisia). *Tunisian,* also an adjective.

Tupelo, Mississippi. *Tupeloan.*

Turkey (Republic of Turkey). *Turk.* Adjective: *Turkish.*

Turkmenistan; *formerly* **Turkmen Soviet Socialist Republic.**
Turkmen, pluralized *Turkmens. Turkmen* comes from Persian, and is also an adjective. *Turkoman* (or *Turcoman*) denotes the same ethnic group, as a noun (pluralized *Turkomans* or *Turcomans*) or adjective, and comes from medieval Latin *Turcomannus,* from the same Persian term that led to English *Turkmen.* There is some evidence of *Turkmenistani* as a national adjective, but whether it will emerge as a useful demonym remains to be seen. Because Turkmens live in several different countries besides Turkmenistan, the ethnic significance of the word should be kept in mind.

Turks and Calcos Islands. Native-born individuals are called *Belongers.*

Turpentiner. Traditional nickname for a resident of North Carolina.

Tuscaloosa, Alabama. *Tuscaloosan.*

Tuscany. *Tuscan.* Because of its popularity with the British middle class, it has been nicknamed *Chiantishire,* after the dry red wine.

Tuscumbia, Alabama. *Tuscumbian.*

Tuvalu; *formerly* **Ellice Islands.** *Tuvaluan,* in place of the former *Ellice Islander.*

Twin Citian. A resident of the Twin Cities, Minneapolis and Saint Paul, Minnesota, or a resident of Winston-Salem, North Carolina.

Tynesider. Resident of Newcastle upon Tyne, England, or the surrounding area; also known as a *Geordie* (q.v.).

Tyrol. See TIROL.

Uganda (Republic of Uganda). *Ugandan,* also an adjective.

Ukiah, California. *Ukiahan.*

Ukraine; *formerly* **Ukrainian Soviet Socialist Republic.** *Ukrainian,* also an adjective. "But please take note," says an article in the *Washington Times* of December 11, 1991, "that the politically correct name is 'Ukraine.' Most of the world says 'the Ukraine' which Ukrainians see as a demeaning relic from when they were a Soviet territory."

Ulster, Ireland. *Ulsterman/Ulsterwoman* or *Ulsterite.*

Union of South Africa. See SOUTH AFRICA.

United Arab Emirates. *Emirian.*

United Arab Republic. See EGYPT.

United Kingdom (United Kingdom of Great Britain and

Northern Ireland). See ENGLAND, NORTHERN IRELAND, SCOTLAND, WALES.

United Mexican States. See MEXICO.

United Republic of Tanganyika and Zanzibar. See TANZANIA.

United Republic of Tanzania. See TANZANIA.

United States of America. *American,* a name that has historically rankled Latin Americans and Canadians. In *The American Language,* H. L. Mencken pointed out that many other alternatives have been proposed—*Unisian, Unitedstatesian, Columbard,* etc.—but none has stuck. Other attempts have included *Uessian, United Statesard, United Stateser, Unitedstatesman, Usanian, U.S.-ian,* and *Saxoamericano,* the creation of a Colombian essayist who hoped to distinguish North Americans from Latin Americans. When William Safire used his popular "On Language" column in the *New York Times Magazine* to solicit a new crop of suggestions, his readers came up with terms like *Usatian, Usonan, Usofan, Us'n, USAmerican, Ussie, Usan, Statesider,* and *United.* An interesting coinage using the *Usa-* prefix is *Usaphobia,* created by the *Economist* of London in 1951, which means "inordinate fear or suspicion of the United States of America," according to Funk and Wagnalls's *New Words and Words in the News* (Fall 1951). See also AMERICAN, COLUMBIAN, YANKEE.

Up-Islander. See ISLANDER.

Upper Peninsula, Michigan. *Yoopers* from the initials U.P.

Upper Volta. See BURKINA FASO.

Urbana, Illinois. *Urbanan.*

Uruguay (Oriental Republic of Uruguay). *Uruguayan,* which is also an adjective.

Usonia. Name for a future Utopian America populated by *Usonians.* The name was borrowed from Samuel Butler by architect Frank Lloyd Wright, who used it to describe his perfect house, "The Usonia."

Utah. *Utahn,* not *Utaan* or *Utahan.* This is one of those terms that is guarded with some fervor by residents of the state. When the U.S. Government Printing Office Style Board ruled in favor of *Utahan,* it was forced to reverse itself in favor of *Utahn* after getting angry letters from Senator Jake Garn (R-Utah) and dozens of other Utahns. Then there is *Utahian,* which shows up in historic citations such as this one from Mitford M. Mathews's *Dictionary of Americanisms:* "We Utahians have become robust in health and strong in the cunning and power of brawny arms" (*Sacramento Union,* January 11, 1864). Despite the clear preference of the people of the state for *Utahn,* others persist in using the *-han* demonym. For instance, the *Sports Illustrated* for July 25, 2005, identified a member of Lance Armstrong's bike racing team as a *Utahan.*

    State nicknames: *Beehive State* and *Mormon State. Beehive State* derives from the beehive depicted in the state seal, which symbolizes the industry of Utahns; the state motto is "Industry." *Mormon State* refers to the state's famed role as the center of the Mormon faith; Mormons were Utah's first permanent white settlers.

Utica, New York. *Utican.*

Utopia. Generic term for an ideal nation or society, from Sir Thomas More's *Utopia* of 1516. Those who believe in or would inhabit such a state are known as *Utopians.* There have been a number of plays on the term, including Winston Churchill's *Queuetopia* to describe the "Utopia of Socialists," a salient characteristic of which will be long lines (queues), and *utopiate* (from *utopia* and *opiate*) for a drug that brings on thoughts of a Utopian existence.

Uzbekistan (Republic of Uzbekistan); *formerly* **Uzbek Soviet Socialist Republic.** *Uzbek.* There is evidence of both adjective and noun use of *Uzbekistani,* though it is not a well-established word yet.

Vail, Colorado. *Vailite.*

Valdosta, Georgia. *Valdostan.*

Valéricain. Resident of Saint-Valéry-sur-Somme, France.

Valéricais. Resident of Saint-Valéry-en-Caux, France.

Vallejo, California. *Vallejoan.*

Vancouver, British Columbia. *Vancouverite.* "Vancouverites fare
well," declared an article on the city in *Gourmet* (July 1982).
　　Lotus-landers is sometimes employed as a mild term of derision by those east of the city as a disdainful reference to the
laid-back West Coast lifestyle in the same sense that residents of
Los Angeles are termed *Lalalanders.*

Vanuatu (Republic of Vanuatu); *formerly* **New Hebrides.** *Ni-
Vanuatu* (both singular and plural), which is also an adjective.

Varsovian. Resident of Warsaw, Poland.

Vectian. Name for a resident of the Isle of Wight in the south of England. It derives from the Roman name for the island, which was *Vectis.*

Venezuela (Republic of Venezuela). *Venezuelan,* also an adjective. *Venezuela* is interesting in that it is a derivative of *Venice.* When the explorers Alonso de Ojeda and Amerigo Vespucci arrived at Lake Maracaibo in 1499 they found an Indian village built over the lake on pilings. They likened it to the famed Italian lagoon city and called it *Venezuela,* or "little Venice."

Venice, Italy. *Venetian,* a term that gets much adjectival application, as in the terms *Venetian glass* and *Venetian blind.*

Venus. *Cytherean,* which came into prominence when the first probes were made of Venus in the late 1960s and astronomers shied away from the logical choice of *venereal,* which was too closely associated with human sexual activity. The next logical choice was the Greek *aphrodisian,* which had similar sexual overtones. The final choice of *Cytherean* derives from the island of Cythera, from which Aphrodite, the Greek Venus, emerged. (*Merriam-Webster's Collegiate Dictionary,* 11th edition, dates the adjective from 1885.) Similarly, the late Carl Sagan related in an article in the *New York Times* that it was once suggested that a Martian volcano be named *Mons Veneris* until he pointed out that it "had been pre-empted by quite a different field of human activity." Despite the preference for *Cytherean,* the *Associated Press Stylebook and Libel Manual* lists *venusian.*

Veracruz, Mexico. *Jarocho.*

Vermont. *Vermonter.* As with other New England demonyms this one is not bestowed on a person when he or she arrives in the state. Michael A. Stackpole, who grew up in Vermont and now lives in Phoenix, Arizona, points out with some exaggeration that "there's a rather strict set of rules as to who has earned that title.

A Vermonter is someone born in Vermont whose parents and grandparents were also born in the state. As some of us were told when we protested (I was born in Wisconsin), 'If you were baking cookies and a puppy crawled into the oven, you wouldn't call it a 'cookie' would you?' Delivered with the proper Vermont accent it makes sense. The rest of us are 'Summer Folk' or, if we stick around for years, 'Year-round Summer Folk.'" Along with *New Yorker, Vermonter* is one of the oldest American demonyms dating back to the early 19th century.

Traditional personal nickname: *Green Mountain Boy.* George Earlie Shankle claimed that this comes from "the fact that many of the inhabitants of the state live among the Green Mountains" (*State Names, Flags, Seals, Songs, Birds, Flowers, and Other Symbols*), but *Webster's Third New International Dictionary* is more accurate when it attributes this nickname for a "male Vermonter" (there is no evidence of *Green Mountain Girl* or *Woman*) to the *Green Mountain Boys.* This was a militia formed in the early 1770s under Ethan Allen to defend Vermont, then known as the New Hampshire Grants, against the encroachments of New York. While their rough methods paid off and culminated in statehood in 1791, the Boys are perhaps best known for their capture of Fort Ticonderoga in New York from the British in 1775, with the help of Benedict Arnold and his troops.

Mathews's *Dictionary of Americanisms* has two citations for *Green Mountaineer* for a Vermonter, both from the 19th century.

State nickname: *Green Mountain State.*

Verona, Italy. *Veronese,* also an adjective.

Verplank. New York. *Pointer* because the town points into the Hudson River near Peekskill.

Victoria, Australia. *Victorian* or *Cabbage-patcher.* The relatively small state of Victoria has often been called the *Cabbage Garden, Cabbage Patch,* or *Cabbage State* by virtue of its size and vegetable crops, hence the nickname *Cabbage-patcher* (*Cabbage Gardener* and *Cabbage-Stater* have also been used). Another historic slang nickname is *Gumsucker,* perhaps from a reported fondness of early colonists for the gum of the wattle (acacia) tree. This nickname is said to have been first applied to Victorians and eventually to any non-Aboriginal native of Australia. According to Australian W. N. Scott, *Yabbie* is synonymous with *Cabbage-patcher* (see his comments at BANANA-BENDER), though the term is better known as an Australian slang term for a kind of crayfish.

Victorians, living south of the border with New South Wales, have been called *Mexicans* by residents of that state, but the people of New South Wales have in turn been called *Mexicans* by the residents of Queensland to *their* north. Similarly, *T'othersider* has been used for a resident of one of Australia's eastern states by people in Western Australia, but those *T'othersiders* in turn might apply the nickname to Tasmanians, on the other side of the water separating Tasmania from the mainland. The Tasmanians themselves, according to the *Australian National Dictionary,* have used *T'othersider* for one who lives on the mainland.

Victoria, British Columbia. *Victorian.*

Vienna, Austria. *Viennese,* which is also an adjective.

Vietnam (Socialist Republic of Vietnam). *Vietnamese* (both singular and plural), which is also an adjective.

Vincentian. Resident of Saint Vincent and the Grenadines.

Vineyarder. Resident of Martha's Vineyard, Massachusetts. See also ISLANDER.

Virginia. *Virginian,* also an adjective. Since Virginia is known as the Old Dominion, its residents are sometimes referred to as *Dominionites.*

Traditional personal nicknames: *Cavalier, Buckskin, Sore-back,* and *Tuckahoe. Cavalier* comes from the adherents of Charles I of England who came to Virginia in the 17th century. *Buckskin* was originally applied to one in buckskin garments, often to "a backwoodsman or countrified person of the earlier periods of American settlement" (*Webster's Third New International Dictionary*), and especially to a "Virginian or Southerner" (Mathews's *Dictionary of Americanisms*). In George Earlie Shankle's *State Names, Flags, Seals, Songs, Birds, Flowers, and Other Symbols,* two explanations are given for the name *Soreback* as applied to Virginians: "One is that the Virginians are so hospitable that they slap one another on the backs until their backs become sore; the other is that people in the southern part of the state raise so much cotton that it makes their backs sore to pick it. The North Carolinians seem to be the originator of this account." *Tuckahoe* has traditionally and specifically referred to a Virginian who lives east of the Blue Ridge Mountains, in contrast with a *Cohee* or *Coohee* on the other side (see PENNSYLVANIA). The only evident explanation for the nickname is that poor rural settlers of the area were forced by necessity to eat *tuckahoe,* a name given to both an edible rootstock and a fungus.

State nicknames: The *Old Dominion,* the *Mother of Presidents,* and the *Mother of States.* The name *Old Dominion* (or *Ancient Dominion*) derives from Virginia's status as a dominion of England in its early days. According to George Earlie Shankle, King Charles II of England (who reigned from 1660 to 1685) "quartered the Arms of Virginia on his royal shield," with his other "dominions" of England, Scotland, Ireland, and perhaps France. The *Mother of Presidents* comes from Virginia's impressive history as the home of seven American presidents, and the *Mother of States* is either from Virginia's status as the first of the states to be settled or from the fact that several states were once part of it.

Virgin Islands of the United States. *Virgin Islander.*

Waco, Texas. *Wacoite.* However, Texan C. F. Eckhardt of Seguin adds, "Anyone from Waco is usually called a Baptist, regardless of his/her actual religious affiliation, since Waco is home to Baylor University, which is sometimes called the 'World's Largest Baptist Preacher Factory.'"

Wales. *Welshman* or *Welshwoman.* Adjective: *Welsh,* as in *Welsh rarebit.* There has always been some uncertainty about the slang verb *welsh* or *welch:* "to avoid payment" or "to break one's word," according to *Merriam-Webster's Collegiate Dictionary,* 11th edition, which states that the verb is probably from the adjective *Welsh.* Another theory is that it came from an old nursery rhyme with the lines "Taffy was a Welshman, Taffy was a thief." For that reason *Taffy* by itself is a derogatory term for a Welshman, even though by modification of *Dafydd,* the Welsh version of the name *David.*

Walla Walla, Washington. *Walla Wallan.* The city has a number of apt nicknames including *Walla.*

Wallis and Futuna Islands (Territory of the Wallis and Futuna Islands). *Wallisian, Futunan,* or *Wallis and Futuna Islander* are the demonyms for residents of this French territory in the South Pacific.

Wallis Islands. *Wallisian,* also an adjective.

Waltham, Massachusetts. *Walthamite.*

Warsaw, Poland. *Varsovian.*

Wash-ashore. Traditional name given by native Cape Codders to "someone who came over the bridge." (Cape Cod is separated from the rest of Massachusetts by the Cape Cod Canal, which is spanned by two bridges.)

Washington. *Washingtonian.*

Traditional personal nicknames: *Washingtoniac* and *Evergreener,* presumably from the nickname *Evergreen State.* At the turn of the century and well into this century, the name *Clam Grabber* was used because of the fact that Washingtonians gather vast quantities of clams annually from the shallow waters of Puget Sound.

State nickname: *Evergreen State.* Washington was also once called the *Chinook State* from the Indian people of that region known as *Chinook.*

Washington, District of Columbia. *Washingtonian.*

Waterbury, Connecticut. *Waterburian.*

Waterloo, Iowa. *Waterlooan.*

Watson Lake, Yukon Territory. *Watson Laker.*

Weasel. Traditional nickname for a resident of South Carolina.

Webfoot. Traditional nickname for an Oregonian, inspired by the volume of rain that falls in the state (as if one would need the webbed feet of a duck to get around).

Welshman/Welshwoman. A resident of Wales.

West Bank. *West Banker.*

Western Australia, Australia. *West Australian, Western Australian,* or the potentially derogatory *Sand-groper. Westralian,* from *Westralia* for "Western Australia," has also been used. There is a Westralia Square in Perth, the capital of Western Australia.

Western Sahara; *formerly* **Spanish Sahara.** *Western Saharan,* as in an electronic publication ("The World") of the staff of the United Nations High Commissioner for Refugees that refers to "80,000 Western Saharans, who have been living in western Algeria since 1975." *Western Saharan* is also an adjective. The *Sahrawi* are a nomadic people of northern Africa, including Western Sahara; the singular is *Sahrawi,* and the plural form *Sahrawis* is sometimes used. *Sahrawi* is also an adjective, as in "Sahrawi independence." The French form is *Sahraoui.*

Western Samoa (Independent State of Western Samoa). *Western Samoan.*

West Indies. *West Indian.*

West Sider. Resident of Manhattan's West Side, especially the Upper West Side between Central Park and the Hudson River. The *Westsider* is a community newspaper.

West Virginia. *West Virginian.*
    Traditional personal nicknames: *Panhandler, Panhandleite,* and *Snake.*

State nicknames: *Mountain State* and *Panhandle State* (after its particular configuration between the Ohio River and Pennsylvania).

Wewoka, Oklahoma. *Wewokan.*

Wheeling, West Virginia. *Wheelingite.*

Whelp. Traditional nickname for a resident of Tennessee; the term is of uncertain origin.

Whistler, British Columbia. *Whistlerite.*

Whitehorse, Yukon Territory. *Whitehorsian* has been used in the area, according to Doug Bell, publisher of the *Yukon News* there and former commissioner of the Yukon. However, he reports that it is not a very common term.

Whittier, Alaska. Residents of this remote and perpetually cloud-covered place, which has been compared to an American Gulag, call themselves *Whittiots* or *POWs* for "Prisioners of Whittier" as per an article in the *Globe and Mail*, November 16, 1992.

Wichita, Kansas. *Wichitan.*

Wichita Falls, Texas. *Wichitan,* which is also the name of the student newspaper at Midwestern State University there, though Texan C. F. Eckhardt points out that "folks from Wichita Falls are usually called 'folks from Wichita Falls' since Wichita Fallers sounds like they've had a mite too much and nobody likes Wichita Fallites or Wichita Fallians."

Wight, Isle of. *Vectian,* from the Roman word for the place, *Vectis.*

Wilkes-Barre, Pennsylvania. *Wilkes-Barrean.*

Williamsport, Pennsylvania. *Williamsporter.*

Wilmington, Delaware. *Wilmingtonian.*

Wilmington, North Carolina. *Wilmingtonian.*

Wiltshire, England. *Moonraker* (q.v.).

Winnipeg, Manitoba. *Winnipegger,* sometimes shortened to *Pegger.*

Winona, Minnesota. *Winonan.*

Winslow, Arizona. *Winslowite.*

Winston-Salem, North Carolina. *Twin Citian,* also used for residents of Minneapolis and Saint Paul, Minnesota.

Wisconsin. *Wisconsinite.*

Traditional personal nickname: *Badger,* also used for athletes at the University of Wisconsin. See the explanation of *Badger State* below.

State nickname: *Badger State.* This explanation appears in George Earlie Shankle's 1941 *State Names, Flags, Seals, Songs, Birds, Flowers, and Other Symbols:* "The origin of Wisconsin's sobriquet, the Badger State is as follows: This term was first applied to the early lead miners, who on first coming to a new location dug in the side of a hill and lived under ground much as the badger digs in his burrow."

Wolverine. Nickname for a person from Michigan, the *Wolverine State.* It is not as commonly used today as it was in earlier times, if one discounts its application to athletes at the University of Michigan. It was among the names defined in *Davy Crockett's Almanac of Wild Sports of the West, and Life in the Backwoods,* published in 1835, the year before he died. He wrote that the Wolverines were "the all-greediest, ugliest, and sourest characters on all Uncle Sam's twenty-six farms, they are, in that natur, like their wolfish namesakes, always so eternal hungry that they bite at the air, and hang their underlips, and show the harrow teeth of their mouths, as if they'd jump right into you, and swaller you hull without salt. They are, in fact, half wolf, half man, and 'tother half saw mill."

According to *Americanisms: The English of the New World,* by M. Schele De Vere (1872), the *Wolverine* nickname was given to the state "from the number of wolverines (literally, little wolves) which used to abound in the peninsula."

Wooden Nutmeg. Traditional nickname for a resident of Connecticut (q.v.).

Wool-hat. A poor, rural person, or in the words of *Webster's Third New International Dictionary,* "a small farmer in the South (as in Georgia)." The term took on a cast of bigotry when Herman Talmadge claimed the governorship of Georgia after the confused and disputed events of 1946 and 1947 with the support of his *woolhatters.* (His father, Eugene Talmadge, had won the 1946 election but died in December; Herman was elected by the state legislature in January 1947 but the court ruled in favor of Lieutenant Governor M. E. Thompson in March.) The press called it the "wool-hat revolt" after Talmadge started making the claim that he could have 25,000 of his supporters on the State House lawn "any time I give the word." Talmadge fought for all-white primaries and supported the poll tax. Huey Long of Louisiana was described by *Life* magazine as an advocate of "wool-hat radicalism."

The term apparently comes from the wool felt hat of the southern rural native, and while the "redneck" connotations of the term came to the forefront in the events of 1947 (it was used often in the late 1940s in such forums as *Time, Newsweek,* and the *New Republic*), it had been in use for a long time before. Mitford Mathews's *Dictionary of Americanisms* has a citation for *wool hat* dating from 1830, and, interestingly, it is also in reference to political supporters, this time those behind Andrew Jackson. It was used in *The Nation* in 1922 in reference to supporters of the South Carolina populist politician "Pitchfork Ben" Tillman: "More than thirty years have passed since Ben Tillman led the revolt of the agrarians, the 'poor white trash,' the 'wool-hats' of the 'upper country' against the old Charlestonian aristocracy."

Woonsocket, Rhode Island. *Woonsocketer.*

Wooster, Ohio. *Woosterite.*

Worcester, Massachusetts. *Worcesterite.*

Wymore, Nebraska. *Wymorean.*

Wyoming. *Wyomingite.*

Traditional personal nicknames: *Sagebrusher* and *Sheep-herder.*

State nicknames: *Equality State,* because it was a pioneer in women's suffrage (Wyoming women were the first to have the right to vote in the United States, in 1868), *Sagebrush State,* and *The Wonderland of America.*

Y, France. *Ypsilonien.* Y is one of the few towns in the world with a one-letter name. The residents also refer to themselves collectively as *Les Yaciens.*

Yakima, Washington. *Yakiman.* The citation used by H. L. Mencken in "What the People of American Towns Call Themselves" is from the *Seattle Times* of April 11, 1935: "Yakima is for the Yakimans."

Yank. An American. This term tends to show up in Canadian and British newspapers. *Yank* is also the preferred term for Americans in Australia.

Yankee. (1) Label used for residents of the New England states. (2) Label used for the residents of the Northern states at the time of the Civil War. In this context the term still has derogatory overtones when used in the South to describe the people of the North. (3) Label used outside the United States to describe Americans. Its applications range from affectionate British use of the shortened *Yank* to the anti-imperialist slogan of the post–World War II era, "Yankee Go Home."

The exact origin of this term defies detection. The file on *Yankee* in the Tamony Collection contains no less than eight etymologies. One of them, for instance, states that it came from the name *Jan Kaas,* which the British used to describe the Dutch freebooters in early New York. The Dutch in turn applied it to English traders in Connecticut and eventually *Jan Kaas* became *Yankee. Jan Kaas,* which means *John Cheese.* (The original family name of Python John Cleese was *Cheese,* so his name actually would have been *John Cheese,* notes Bill Young.)

Some years ago *Reader's Digest* carried an item from the *Woolery Digest* that demonstrated how elusive this term really is: "*The Chicago Tribune* made a study and came up with these facts: Foreigners call all Americans Yankees. Southerners say that Yankees are northerners. Northerners say that Yankees are from the New England states. People in New England say it is the Vermonters who are Yankees. Vermonters reply that a Yankee is just someone who eats pie for breakfast."

The British have long been infatuated with the term and it is used commonly as early as the late 18th century. *The Times* published an "American Ballad" on December 28, 1786, that begins with the line "Boston is a Yankee town, so is Philadelphia."

Yanqui. *Yankee* in Spanish, which is pronounced more or less as it is in English. It is used in English to indicate a Latin American context; for instance, the title of an article in *The Economist* for December 5, 1987, was "Latin America's New Democrats Gang Softly Up on the Yanquis."

Yap, Micronesia. *Yapese.*

Yarmouth, Nova Scotia. *Yarmouthian.*

Yellowknife, Northwest Territories. *Yellowknifer.*

Yemen (Republic of Yemen). *Yemeni* (also an adjective), but *Yemenite* is also used on occasion. Charles Poe finds the term in use in Jean-Jacques Servan Schriber's *The World Challenge*. The Republic of Yemen was formed on May 22, 1990, when the Yemen Arab Republic (or North Yemen) merged with the People's Democratic Republic of Yemen (or South Yemen).

Yoknapatawpha County, Mississippi. A resident of this 2,400-square-mile fictional county created by novelist William Faulkner is a *Yoknapatawphan*. The county, populated most notably by Compsons, McCaslins, and Snopeses, bears strong resemblance to Faulkner's lifelong home of Lafayette County, Mississippi.

Yonkers, New York. *Yonkersite.* In his 1936 *New Yorker* article on demonyms, H. L. Mencken reported that three factions had recently tussled over the preferred term for Yonkers. *Yonkersite* bested "Yonkers man" and the tonier *Yonkersonian.* In "What the People of American Towns Call Themselves," Mencken quoted Kenneth A. Fowler from the *Yonkers Herald Statesman* for April 25, 1935: "The more tony term of *Yonkersonian* is seldom if ever heard."

Yooper. A resident of Michigan's Upper Peninsula from the initials U.P.

York, Pennsylvania. *Yorker.*

Yorkshire, England. *Yorkshireman* or *Yorkshirewoman.* The slang term is *Yorkie.* A *Yorkist* is one who belonged to or supported the English royal House of York against the *Lancastrians* in the "War of the Roses." See LANCASTER.

Youngstown, Ohio. *Youngstowner.*

Ypsilanti, Michigan. *Ypsilantian.*

Ypsilonien. Resident of Y, France. The people of Y also refer to themselves as *Les Yaciens.*

Yucatán, Mexico. *Yucatecan.*

Yugoslavia *or* **Jugoslavia.** *Yugoslav* or *Yugoslavian,* as in "Bird Leads Celtics Past Yugoslavians" (sports page headline, *Washington Post,* October 22, 1988). The forms *Jugoslav* and *Jugoslavian* are less common. Serbia and Montenegro are all that is left of Yugoslavia, since Slovenia, Croatia, and Bosnia and Herzegovina have successfully broken away. See also JUG for a nickname that may be derogatory. In February 2003 lawmakers restructured what remained of the former nation into a loose federation of two republics called Serbia and Montenegro. The Constitutional Charter of Serbia and Montenegro includes a provision that allows either republic to hold a referendum in 2006 that would allow for their independence from the state union.

Yukon Territory, Canada. *Yukoner.* The terms *Cheechako* and *Sourdough* (qq.v.), for newcomers and old-timers respectively, are used here as well as across the border in Alaska.

Yuma, Arizona. *Yuman.*

Yunnan, China. *Yunnanese,* which is also an adjective.

Zaire (Republic of Zaire). *Zairian* or *Zairean,* both of which are also adjectives. The name Zaire only existed as an official designation from 1971 until May 20, 1997, when it became the Democratic Republic of Congo.

Zambia (Republic of Zambia); *formerly* **Northern Rhodesia.** *Zambian,* also an adjective.

Zimbabwe (Republic of Zimbabwe); *formerly* **Southern Rhodesia** *or* **Rhodesia.** *Zimbabwean* is the demonym and adjective. This country was known as *Southern Rhodesia* and then *Rhodesia* during nine decades of rule by the white minority. In April 1979, the country became *Zimbabwe Rhodesia* after general elections. Later in the year, on August 25, *Rhodesia* was dropped from the country's name. *Zimbabwe* (meaning "dwelling of the chief") was the name used for this area from the 15th into the 19th centuries. A nickname used for white Zimbabweans is *Rhodie,* which derives from *Rhodesia.* The full demonym and adjective for the former state was *Rhodesian.*

Zonian. Resident of the Canal Zone in Panama, and almost always an American who resides there and works on the Panama Canal. *Zoniac* is a much less common alternative.

Zonie. Derogatory name for a resident of Arizona. Arizonan Michael A. Stackpole explains: "During August when it becomes unbearably hot here, many folks vacation in San Diego and there we are known as Zonies. This is not an affectionate term. . . ."

Zürich, Switzerland. *Züricher.*

Bibliography

A large part of the research for this book involved hundreds of newspaper articles found in the Tamony Collection at the University of Missouri in Columbia; various clipping morgues, including the old *Washington Star* files now at the Martin Luther King Library in Washington, D.C.; and material on file at the National Geographic Library. The late Charles D. Poe of Houston provided several hundred citations from novels, newspapers, and nonfiction works.

In addition to the major unabridged and college-level dictionaries, the books and articles that provided the most help in separating, as William Safire once put it, the *Whereveronians* from the *Whereverites, Whereverans,* and *Whereverers* are the following:

Adams, J. Donald. *The Magic and Mystery of Words.* New York: Holt, Rinehart and Winston, 1963.

Allen, Irving Lewis. *The City in Slang: New York Life and Popular Speech.* New York: Oxford University Press, 1993.

Associated Press. *The Associated Press Stylebook and Libel Manual.* Ed. Christopher W. French, Eileen Alt Powell, and Howard Angione. Reading, Mass.: Addison-Wesley, 1980.

———. *The Associated Press Stylebook and Libel Manual.* Ed. Norm Goldstein. Cambridge, Mass: Perseus Publishing, 2002.

Avis, Walter S., et al., eds. *A Dictionary of Canadianisms on Historical Principles.* Toronto: W. J. Gage, 1967.

Bardsley, Charles Wareing. *English Surnames: Their Sources and Significance.* London: Chatto and Windus, 1906.

Bates, Robert L., and Julia A. Jackson, eds. *Glossary of Geology.* 3rd ed. Alexandria, Va.: American Geological Institute, 1987.

Beeching, Cyril Leslie. *A Dictionary of Eponyms.* London: Clive Bingley, 1983.

Berrey, Lester V., and Melvin Van den Bark. *The American Thesaurus of Slang.* 2nd ed. New York: Thomas Y. Crowell, 1953.

Blumberg, Dorothy Rose. *Whose What?* New York: Holt, Rinehart and Winston, 1969.

Borgmann, Dmitri. "A Sociological Note." *Word Ways,* February 1986.

Bradley, Henry, and Robert Bridges. *Briton, British, Britisher.* S.P.E. Tract Number XIV. London: Oxford University Press, 1923.

Brandreth, Gyles. *More Joy of Lex.* New York: Morrow, 1982.

———. *Pears Book of Words.* London: Pelham Books, 1979.

Brooke, Maxey. "Everybody Comes from Somewhere." *Word Ways,* August 1983.

Buckley, William F., Jr. "Disgrace Abounding." *National Review,* 16 September 1988.

Campbell, Hannah. *Why Did They Name It?* New York: Bell, 1964.

Cassidy, F. G., and R. B. Le Page. *Dictionary of Jamaican English.* 2nd ed. Cambridge, U.K.: Cambridge University Press, 1980.

Central Intelligence Agency. *The World Factbook 2005.* Washington, D.C.: Central Intelligence Agency, 2005. (An online edition of the *Factbook* is also available at http://www.cia.gov/cia/publications/factbook/. Unlike the print version, the online version is not dated and is updated as needed.)

Chapman, Robert W. *Adjectives from Proper Names.* S.P.E. Tract Number LII. London: Oxford University Press, 1939.

Ciardi, John. *Good Words to You.* New York: Harper and Row, 1987.

Collocott, T. C., and J. O. Thorne. *The Macmillan World Gazetteer and Geographical Dictionary.* New York: Macmillan, 1955.

Colombo, John Robert. *Colombo's Canadian References.* Toronto: Oxford University Press, 1976.

Craig, Mary Stewart. "Do Mamaroneckers Like to Neck?" *Word Ways,* November 1987.

Davies, C. Stella, and John Levitt. *What's in a Name?* London: Routledge and Kegan Paul, 1970.

Dawson, J. Frank. *Place Names in Colorado.* Denver: Golden Bell Press, 1954.

Delahunty, Andrew. *Goldenballs and the Iron Lady.* Oxford, U.K.: Oxford University Press, 2004.

Demorest, Stephen. "A Lexicon of Countries." *Travel and Leisure,* September 1981.

De Vere, M. Schele. *Americanisms: The English of the New World.* New York: Scribner, 1872.

Dolan, J. R. *English Ancestral Names.* New York: Clarkson Potter, 1972.

Eckler, A. Ross. *Names and Games.* Lanham, Md.: University Press of America, 1986.

———. *Word Recreations.* New York: Dover, 1979.

Eisiminger, Sterling. "A Glossary of Ethnic Slurs in American English." *Maledicta* 3 (1979): 153–74.

———. "A Continuation of a Glossary of Ethnic Slurs in American English." *Maledicta* 9 (1988): 51–61.

Espy, Willard R. *An Almanac of Words at Play.* New York: Clarkson Potter, 1975.

———. *Another Almanac of Words at Play.* New York: Clarkson Potter, 1980.

———. *Thou Improper, Thou Uncommon Noun.* New York: Clarkson Potter, 1978.

Farmer, J. S., and W. E. Henley. *A Dictionary of Slang.* 1890. Reprint. Ware, England: Wordsworth Editions, 1987.

Flexner, Stuart Berg. *I Hear America Talking.* New York: Van Nostrand, 1976.

———. *Listening to America.* New York: Simon and Schuster, 1982.

Franklyn, Julian. *A Dictionary of Nicknames.* New York: British Book Center, 1962.

Funk, Charles Earle. *Heavens to Betsy! And Other Curious Sayings.* New York: Harper, 1955.

———. *Thereby Hangs a Tale*. New York: Harper and Bros., 1950.

Gannett, Henry. *The Origin of Certain Place Names in the United States*. Washington, D.C.: U.S. Geological Survey, 1905.

Gard, Robert E., and L. G. Sorden. *Romance of Wisconsin Place Names*. New York: October House, 1968.

Gardner, Martin. "Psychic Astronomy." *Free Inquiry*, Winter 1987.

Gould, John. *Maine Lingo: Boiled Owls, Billdads and Wazzats*. Camden, Me.: Down East, 1975.

Harder, Kelsie B. *Illustrated Dictionary of Place Names*. New York: Van Nostrand, 1976.

Holm, John A., and Alison Watt Shilling. *Dictionary of Bahamian English*. Cold Spring, N.Y.: Lexik House, 1982.

Holt, Alfred H. *Phrase and Word Origins*. New York: Dover, 1961.

Hook, J. N. *The Book of Names*. New York: Franklin Watts, 1983.

Jacobs, Noah. *Naming Day in Eden*. New York: Macmillan, 1969.

Kane, Joseph Nathan. *The American Counties*. Metuchen, N.J.: Scarecrow Press, 1972.

Keaton, Anna Lucile. "Americanisms in Early American Newspapers." Ph.D. diss., University of Chicago, 1933.

Lambert, Eloise, and Mario Pei. *The Book of Place Names*. New York: Lothrop, Lee and Shepard, 1961.

———. *Our Names: Where They Came From and What They Mean*. New York: Lothrop, Lee and Shepard, 1961.

Laycock, Don. "*D'où Êtes-Vous?*" *Word Ways*, May 1986.

Lederer, Richard M., Jr. *The Place Names of Westchester County*. Harrison, N.Y.: Harbor Hill, 1978.

Loughhead, Flora Haines. *Dictionary of Given Names*. Glendale, Calif.: Arthur H. Clark, 1958.

Maclaren, Vernon. "How to Name the Residents." *Word Ways*, May 1988.

Manguel, Alberto, and Gianni Guadalupi. *The Dictionary of Imaginary Places*. New York: Macmillan, 1980.

Marckwardt, Albert H. "Wolverine and Michigander." *Michigan Alumnus Quarterly Review*, Spring 1952.

Marquis Biographical Library Society. *Liverpudlian*. Chicago: 1970.

Mathews, Mitford M., ed. *A Dictionary of Americanisms on Historical Principles*. 2 vols. Chicago: University of Chicago Press, 1951.

Matthews, C. M. *English Surnames*. New York: Scribners, 1966.

———. *Place Names of the English-Speaking World*. New York: Scribners, 1972.

Mawson, C. O. Sylvester. *International Book of Names*. New York: Crowell, 1934.

McCarville, Mike. *Okie*. Oklahoma City: Colorgraphics, 1970.

McDavid, Raven I., Jr., and Virginia McDavid. "*Cracker* and *Hoosier.*" *Names,* September 1973.

Mencken, H. L. "The Advance of Municipal Onomastics." *The New Yorker,* 8 February 1936.

———. *The American Language*. 1st ed. New York: Knopf, 1919.

———. *The American Language*. 4th ed. New York: Knopf, 1936.

———. *The American Language*. Supplement I. New York: Knopf, 1945.

———. *The American Language*. Supplement II. New York: Knopf, 1948.

———. "Names for Americans." *American Speech,* December 1947.

———. "Some Opprobrious Nicknames." *American Speech,* February 1949.

———. "What the People of American Towns Call Themselves." *American Speech,* October–December 1948.

Michaels, Leonard, and Christopher Ricks, eds. *The State of the Language*. Berkeley: University of California Press, 1980.

Mitchell, Edwin Valentine. *It's an Old New England Custom*. New York: Vanguard, 1946.

Moore, W. G. *A Dictionary of Geography*. New York: Praeger, 1969.

Morgan, Jane, Christopher O'Neill, and Rom Harre. *Nicknames*. London: Routledge and Kegan Paul, 1979.

Morris, William, and Mary Morris. *The Harper Dictionary of Contemporary Usage*. New York: Harper and Row, 1975.

Murray, Thomas E. "You $#^%?*&@ Hoosier." *Names,* March 1987.

National Geographic Society. "National Geographic Delimits Near, Middle and Far East." News bulletin, April 27, 1952.

————. "Rules Look the Other Way When Names Are Coined." News bulletin, May 19, 1948.

Newman, Edwin. *Strictly Speaking*. New York: Warner, 1975.

Noble, Vernon. *Nick Names*. London: Hamish Hamilton, 1976.

Noel, John V., Jr., and Edward L. Beach. *Naval Terms Dictionary*. Annapolis, Md.: Naval Institute Press, 1973.

Partridge, Eric. *Name into Word*. New York: Macmillan, 1950.

Payton, Geoffrey. *Payton's Proper Names*. London: Frederick Warne, 1969.

Pizer, Vernon. *Ink, Ark., and All That: How American Places Got Their Names*. New York: Putnam's, 1976.

Ramson, W. S., et al., eds. *The Australian National Dictionary: A Dictionary of Australianisms on Historical Principles*. Melbourne: Oxford University Press, 1988.

Randolph, Vance, and George P. Wilson. *Down in the Holler: A Gallery of Ozark Folk Speech*. Norman: University of Oklahoma Press, 1953.

Rayburn, Alan. "Of Hatters and Capers, Townies and Trifluviens and Other Monikers People Call Themselves." *Canadian Geographic*, August/September 1989.

Read, Allen Walker. "The Terminology of Derivatives from Place Names, with a Synopsis of New York State Derivations." Paper presented at the 13th Annual Names Institute, sponsored by the American Name Society, at Baruch College, New York, N.Y., May 4, 1991.

————. "The Treatment of Nonce Words by Lexicographers." Paper presented at the biennial meeting of the Dictionary Society of North America, at the University of Missouri, Columbia, August 9–11, 1991.

Reader's Digest Association. *American Folklore and Legend*, Pleasantville, N.Y.: Reader's Digest Books, 1978.

Roback, Abraham. *A Dictionary of International Slurs*, Waukesha, Wis.: Maledicta Press, 1979.

Safire, William. *I Stand Corrected*. New York: Times Books, 1984.

————. "My Fellow Americanians." *New York Times Magazine*, 6 June 1982.

———. *On Language.* New York: Times Books, 1980.

———. *Take My Word for It.* New York: Times Books, 1986.

Scheetz, George H. "The Names Iowans Call Themselves." Letter to *Des Moines Register,* 23 March 1988.

Severn, Bill. *Place Words.* New York: Ives Washburn, 1969.

Shankle, George Earlie. *State Names, Flags, Seals, Songs, Birds, Flowers, and Other Symbols.* New York: H. W. Wilson, 1941.

Shaw, Philip. "Factors Affecting the Formation of Citizen-Names in the United States." *American Speech,* Fall 1986.

Shipley, Joseph T. *Playing with Words.* Englewood Cliffs, N.J.: Prentice-Hall, 1960.

Smith, Benjamin E. *The Century Cyclopedia of Names.* 4 vols. New York: Century, 1895.

Spaull, Herb. *New Place Names of the World.* London: Ward Lock, 1970.

Stacey, Michelle. "Names People Say." *Chicago Reader,* 21 October 1983.

Stewart, George R. *American Given Names.* New York: Oxford University Press, 1979.

———. "Names for Citizens." *American Speech,* February 1934.

———. *Names on the Globe.* New York: Oxford University Press, 1975.

———. *Names on the Land.* New York: Random House, 1945.

Tabbert, Russell. *Dictionary of Alaskan English.* Juneau: Denali Press, 1991.

Tarpley, Fred. *Ethnic Names.* Commerce, Tex.: Names Institute Press, 1978.

Tarpley, Fred, and Ann Moseley. *Of Edsels and Marauders.* Commerce, Tex.: Names Institute Press, 1971.

Thompson, Gary L. "What Do You Call Residents of Iowa Towns?" *Des Moines Register,* 13 March 1988.

Treble, H. A., and G. H. Vallins. *An A.B.C. of English Usage.* Oxford, U.K.: Oxford University Press, 1954.

Weekley, Ernest. *Jack and Jill: A Study of Our Christian Names.* Ann Arbor, Mich.: Gryphon, 1971.

———. *The Romance of Words.* London: John Murray, 1913.

Wells, Evelyn. *Treasury of Names.* New York: Duell, Sloan and Pearce, 1946.

Wells, Helen T., Susan H. Whiteley, and Carrie E. Karegeannes. *Origins of NASA Names.* Washington, D.C.: Government Printing Office, 1976.

Wilkes, G. A. *A Dictionary of Australian Colloquialisms.* 2nd ed. Sydney: Sydney University Press, 1985.

Wolk, Allen. *Everyday Words from Names of People and Places.* New York: Elsevier/Nelson, 1980.

————. *The Naming of America.* Nashville, Tenn.: Thomas Nelson, 1977.

"The Word Wurcher" [Harry Partridge]. *"D'où Êtes-Vous* Revisited." *Word Ways,* August 1986.

Yates, Norris. "The Vocabulary of *Time* Magazine Revisited." *American Speech,* Spring 1981.

Youmans, Charles L. *What's in a Name?* Lancaster, N.H.: Brisbee Press, 1955.

Special Thanks

A full list of helpers appears as the final section of this book, but several individuals contributed so much to this effort that it would be impolite not to acknowledge their contributions here and now. The first is the late researcher and *Houstonian* Charles D. Poe, who located and annotated hundreds of written examples. The second is Senior Manuscript Specialist Randy Roberts of the University of Missouri, who dug up additional hundreds of examples from the aforementioned Tamony Collection. The third is *Londoner* Denys Parsons, who scouted terms throughout the rest of the English-speaking world. *Queenslander* Bill Scott helped with the Australian examples, *Ontarian* Jay Ames with Canadian names and nicknames, and *Texan* C. F. Eckhardt guided the author through the complexity of Lone Star labels.

These individuals along with many other helpers put the flesh on the bones of this project. Two outside experts, Dr. Reinhold Aman, editor of *Maledicta,* and Ross Eckler, editor of *Word Ways,* were kind enough to read through an early manuscript finding major and minor errors. I cannot thank them enough for this help.

Last but not least is Thomas F. Pitoniak of Merriam-Webster, who has contributed many thoughtful hours in checking, editing, and giving vitality to the work.

Naming Names:
An Acknowledgment

A far-flung network of kindly, generous, and knowledgeable people helped me with this book and its predecessor. The help has been spread out over a number of years since I first began collecting demonyms in the early 1980s. I have taken the liberty of applying some appropriate demonyms in offering thanks and deep appreciation to:

Bethesdan Thomas B. Allen
Bavarian-Waukeshan Reinhold
    Aman
Canadian Jay Ames
Briton Roger B. Appleton
Homerite Michael Armstrong
Kansas Citian Joe Arther
Londoner Russell Ash
Hoosier (and former resident of
    Santa Claus) Joseph
    Badger
Philip W. Bateman
New South Welchman Sean
    Bonner

Oregonian Merritt Borden
Larry W. Bryant
Virginian Monique M. Byer
Ottawan Phillip Chaplin
Missourian Gerald Cohen
Golden Stater David Conrad
Texan Ralph D. Copeland
Canterburian David S. Cousins
Berkeleyite Tom Dalzell
Gordon B. Dean
Floridian S. Percy Dean
Virginian Al deQuoy
San Franciscan Charles F. Dery
Garrett Parker Nancy Dickson

New Berliner Theodore
    Doehner
John Duffie
Buckeye Russ Dunn Sr.
Marylander Frederick C. Dyer
Texan C. F. Eckhardt
Missourian G. R. Edwards
Michael A. Emge
The late Oystervillian Willard
    Espy
Hoosier James E. Farmer
Washingtonian Mike
    Feinsilber
New Yorker Wayne H. Finke
Akronite C. H. Fleming
The late Barbara Rainbow
    Fletcher
Puebloid R. M. Gagliano
Walt Gianchini
The late Washingtonian Tim
    Gibson
Thomas E. Gill
Washingtonian Joseph C.
    Goulden
Brooklynite Robert Greenman
The late Irving Hale of Dallas
Gothamite Ralph E. Hamil
Kelsie Harder
N. Sally Hass
Bender John M. Hazlitt
Restonite Bill Hickman
Archie Edward Hinson
Littletonian Margaret Hoekstra
Columbian Lane E. Jennings
The late State of Mainer Warren
    R. Johnston

Venturan Leilani A. Kimmel-
    Dagostino
San Franciscan George Kirby
W. L. Klawe
Martin S. Kottmeyer
Washingtonian Bobby Kraft
Marionite Chris Kuppig
Sarasotan Charles R. Lancaster
New Hampshirite Richard
    Lederer
Washingtonian Ray Leedy
New Yorker Ed Lucaire
Washingtonian Tom Mann
Marylander Jack Mantel
Saint Paulite John Vogt
    Masengarb
Columbian-Marylander Skip
    McAfee
Missourian Sue McCulkin
Siouxlander Michael McDonald
"Person from Sioux Falls" Bill
    McKean
Chicagoan Erin McKean
Bay Stater John M. Morse
Oklahoman Susan Elizabeth
    Musick
Babylonian J. Baxter Newgate
The late Madisonian John
    Ohlinger
Londoner Denys Parsons
M. K. Paskus
Milwaukeean Cate Pfeifer
Gothamite Louis Phillips
Tom Pitoniak
Shreveporter Robert Joseph
    Powers

Allan D. Pratt

Washingtonian Dan Rapoport

The late great Allen Walker
Read

Englishwoman Ross Reader

Barbareno Ron Riopelle

Missourian Randy Roberts

Springfieldian Charles R.
Rosenbaum

Birminghamian Samuel A.
Rumore Jr.

Sioux Cityan George H. Scheetz

Queenslander W. N. Scott

New Yorker David Shulman

Yorkshireman Alan Simpson

Pittsfielder/Bostonian Bob Skole

The late Bob Snider

Tampan/Washingtonian James
Srodes

Phoenician Michael A.
Stackpole

Washingtonian Linda Starke

Nutmegger Norman D. Stevens

Bethesdan J. O. Stevenson

Huntingdonian Rudolf J. Storz

Houstonian Rusti Stover

Kansas Citian Bill Tammeus

Nutmegger James Thorpe III

Las Vegan Robert J.
Throckmorton

OBtian Ellen Todd

Washingtonian Jonathan
Tourtellot

Brooklynite Lillian Tudiver

Saint Louisan turned Floridian
Elaine Viets

Nick Webb

Minneapolitans Bob and Mary
West

Northamptonian Emily Harrison
Wier

Neal Wilgus

Virginian Ben Willis

Bay Stater James Withgott of
Ware (Where?)

Baltimorean Melvin H. Wunsch

Washingtonian Abby Yochelson

Arlingtonian Bill Young

Thanks once again. Also, for future editions of this book, the author will be keeping an active file of demonyms and would like to hear from readers with comments, additions and corrections to this collection. He can be reached at P.O. Box 280, Garrett Park, MD 20896-0280, or through his Web site: http://pauldicksonbooks.com.